Jennie Hansey

The Century Cook Book and Home Physician

Jennie Hansey

The Century Cook Book and Home Physician

ISBN/EAN: 9783744785266

Printed in Europe, USA, Canada, Australia, Japan

Cover: Foto ©Lupo / pixelio.de

More available books at **www.hansebooks.com**

SPECIAL EDITION

The Century Cook[book]

AND

Home Physici[an]

BY

Jennie A. Hansey

AND

Dr. N. T. Oliver

With 301 Illustrations
Including Fine Engravings of Artistic C[...]

Copyrighted, 1894, by Laird & Le[e]
Copyrighted, 1897, by Wm. H. Le[e]

" Feed me with food convenient for me."—*Prover[bs]*

CHICAGO

LAIRD & LEE, P[ublishers]

A Few Press Endorsements.

"Better and more fully illustrated than any other book of the kind."—*Boston Globe.*

"The handsomest book for the purpose we have ever seen."—*St. Paul Dispatch.*

"There has never been a superior book of its kind issued."—*Minneapolis Com. Bulletin.*

"In comparison with books of a similar nature, it is simplicity and directness itself; evidently the work of a practical and experienced housekeeper."—*The American Grocer.*

"Just what its name implies—a Family Book."—*Detroit Evening News.*

"Entirely original and thoroughly practical."—*Baltimore American.*

"Refreshingly English, with names readily understood by American cooks."—*Minneapolis Sunday Tribune.*

"A very useful and valuable book."—*Cincinnati Enquirer.*

"Many explanations omitted in other cook books will be found here."—*San Francisco Chronicle.*

"Will commend itself to womankind if only for its 'Golden Rules for the Kitchen.'"—*Chicago Tribune.*

"Will meet every reasonable requirement."—*Chicago Herald.*

"It tells all about how to take care of the house, the person and the clothes. Treats of the common accidents of life, and what to do in emergencies."—*Chicago Inter Ocean.*

"Contains many practical remedies for common complaints."—*Philadelphia Evening Bulletin.*

"Indexed in such a way that what is wanted may be turned to without difficulty."—*Indianapolis Tribune.*

ALPHABETICAL AND CLASSIFIED INDEX

	PAGE
Appropriate Sauces for Fishes and Meats	28
Artistic Cookery	201-232
Apricots à la Condé	228
Artichokes with Dutch Sauce	219
Asparagus, Boiled	217
Asparagus Heads à la Duchesse	221
Basket of Fruit	226
Beef à la Jardinière	209
Black Fish	203
Blanc Manger Rubané	232
Blue Fish	202
Bombe à la Napolitaine	225
Cardoons with Marrow	223
Cauliflower with Dutch Sauce	221
Charlotte Russe with Pistachios	230
Cod	203
Crust with Cherries	224
Farced Mushrooms	219
Filet of Beef à la Godard	211
Filets of Snipes in Cases	208
Fried Salsify or Oyster Plant	218
Green Peas with Croutons	220
Ham à la Printanière	214
Ham Historié	206
Ices in Fruit Moulds	227
King's Meringues	229
Lamb's Brains à la Italienne	211
Larded and Roasted Turkey with Truffles	216
Lobster Cutlets à la Victoria	205
Loin of Veal à la Montglas	208
Mayonnaise of Chicken with Jelly	207
Muscovite Jelly	230
Noix of Veal	213
Pattles à la Financière	207
Pineapple à la Créole	227
Plum Pudding with Punch	225
Roasted Capons with Water Cresses	215
Roasted Partridges	217
Saddle of Venison	212
Salmis of Woodcocks	206
Shad	203
Sheep's Tongues à la Dominicaine	205
Sirloin of Beef	214
Spinach with Soft Boiled Eggs	220
Suédoise of Fruits, with Jelly	231
Sultan Cake	228
Sweet Breads à la Colbert	210
Trout	204
Truffles in Napkins	222
Beef	29-35
Beef à la Mode	31
Beef Cake	34
Beef, creamed	35
Beef Kidney	32
Beef Kidney No. 2	33
Beefsteak Pie	33
Beef, potted	35

	PAGE
Beef, spiced	35
Beefsteak Toast	32
Beef Stew	30
Boiled Tongue	34
Braised Beef	30
Broiled Beefsteak	32
Corned Beef	32
Filet of Beef, Larded	32
Fried Beefsteak	31
Hamburger Steak	32
How to Select Beef	29
Roast Beef	29
Scotch Roll	31
Stewed Ox Tails	34
Beverages	174-180
Almond Milk	177
Baked Milk	180
Blackberry Cordial	180
Broma and Cocoa	175
Ching Ching	177
Chocolate	175
Coffee	174
Coffee, Essence of	178
Currant Water	178
Egg Wine	177
Elderberry Syrup	180
Iced Tea	175
Koumiss	179
Lemon Syrup	178
Mulled Buttermilk	180
Orangeade	177
Pineapple Water	178
Russian Tea	175
Strawberry Water	178
Strawberry Syrup	180
Tea	175
Bread and Cakes	109-116
Albany Breakfast Cakes	113
Baking Powder Biscuits	113
Boston Brown Bread	110
Bread Griddle Cakes	115
Breakfast Rolls	111
Buckwheat Cakes	115
Chicago Muffins	116
Corn Bread, Steamed	112
Corn Gems	112
Cream Toast	115
Delicate Rolls	110
Flannel Cakes	114
Fried Cakes	113
Fritters	113
Graham Bread	110
Graham Gems	111
Graham Griddle Cakes	114
Green Corn Griddle Cakes	114
Home Made Bread	110
Jolly Boys	116
Parker House Rolls	111
Pop Overs	114
Quick Muffins	112

vii

Index.

	PAGE
Railroad Yeast	109
Rusks	113
Sally Lunn	112
Salt Rising	109
Salt Rising Bread	109
Spanish Toast	115
Spider Corn Bread	113
Toast	115
Vienna Rolls	115
Waffles	114
White Muffins	112
Cake	117-127
Andalusian Cake	120
Angel Food	124
Apple Cake	121
Black Cake	121
Bread Cake	119
Bride Cake, rich	117
Chocolate Cake	124
Christening Cake, rich	117
Clove Cake	119
Cold Water Pound Cake	126
Cream Cake	124
Delicate Cake	126
Dolly Varden Cake	127
Dried Apple Cake	122
Dried Cherry Cake	120
French Cake	121
Fruit Cake	118
Golden Cake	125
Imperial Cake	123
Loaf Cake	126
Marble Cake	126
Measured Pound Cake	120
Molasses Cake	125
Neufchatel Cheese Cake	127
Pork Cake	119
Pound Cake	122
Raised Cake	126
Raisin Cake	120
Silver Cake	125
Snow Flake Cake	124
Soft Ginger Cake	125
Spice Cake	122
Sponge Cake	123
Tip Top Cake	124
Watermelon Cake	119
Water Sponge Cake	123
White Cream Cake	126
White Sponge Cake	123
Wine Cake	123
Candy	172-173
Chocolate Caramels	173
Cream Candy	172
Crystalized Pop Corn	173
French Creams	172
Kisses	173
Molasses Candy	173
Nougat	173
Sugar Candy	172
Creams and Custards	138-144
Berry Ice Cream	139
Blanc Mange	140
Charlotte Russe	141
Chocolate Blanc Mange	140
Chocolate Ice Cream	138
Coffee Ice Cream	139
Custard, boiled	140
Floating Island	140
Ice Cream	138
Jelly with Oranges	143
Lemon Ice	139
Lemon Jelly	139
Orange Custards	144
Orange Jelly	139
Pineapple Jelly	139
Preserved Quinces	143
Rice Snowballs	144
Russian Cream	141
Spanish Cream	141
Stewed Apples and Custard	142
Stewed Pears	143
Whipped Cream	142
Dishes for Invalids	181-187
Appetizers	182
Arrowroot	187
Baked Beef Tea	184
Beef Broth	181
Beef Tea	181
Calf's foot Blanc Mange	186
Corn Coffee	182
Cornmeal Gruel	181
Cream of Tartar Drink	184
Eel Broth	186
Flaxseed Lemonade	182
Gruel, How to make it	182
Herb Teas	187
Iceland Moss	184
Invalid's Cutlet	186
Invalid's Mutton Chop	183
Irish Moss or Carrageen	183
Jellied Chicken	187
Jelly Water	182
Panada	184
Restorative Jelly	185
Rice for Invalids	191
Sago, Cream and Extract of Beef	185
Slippery Elm Bark	187
Toast Water	182
Whey	183
Drop Cakes, Cookies, and Fried Cakes	132-137
Almond Cookies	134
Card Cakes	134
Chocolate Eclairs	136
Cocoanut Cookies	134
Cream for Filling	136
Cream Puffs	135
Cup Cakes	132
Doughnuts	136
Doughnuts, Raised	136
Eclairs	136
Frosting	137
Frosting, boiled	137
Ginger Drop Cakes	132
Ginger Cookies	132
Ginger Drops	132
Ginger Snaps	135
Hermits	135
Jumbles	133
Lady's Fingers	132
Lemon Cakes	134
Lemon Icing	137
Little Currant Cakes	135
Savoy Biscuits	133
Sugar Cookies	133
Transparent Puffs	136
Eggs	86-92
Boiled Eggs	86
Cheese Omelet	89

Index.

	PAGE
Creamed Eggs	92
Curried Eggs	92
Deviled Eggs	86
Dutch Omelet	91
Eggs à la Suisse	92
Egg Baskets	87
Eggs on a Plate	87
Eggs with Creamed Beef or Codfish	88
French Pancakes	90
Fried Eggs	86
Ham or Beef Omelet	89
Hard Boiled Eggs	86
Jam Omelet	90
Mushroom Omelet	89
Omelet, Plain	88
Omelet Soufflée	89
Oyster Omelet	88
Poached Eggs	87
Rum Omelet	89
Scotch Eggs	91
Scrambled Eggs	88
Scrambled Eggs No. 2	88
Snow Eggs	90
Fish, and How to Cook It	14-22
Baked Fish	19
Boiled Cod	15
Boiled Flounders	17
Boiled Salt Cod	17
Boiled Salt White Fish	17
Broiled Fish	17
Eel with Tartare Sauce	21
Escalloped Fish	20
Filets of Mackerel	21
Fish Balls	16
Fish Chowder	20
Fried Fish	18
Fried Herring	19
Fried Smelts	18
General Instructions	14
Salmon with Caper Sauce	21
Salt Cod with Eggs	16
Salt Cod with Eggs No. 2	16
Stewed Fish	16
To Cook Eels	19
Fish and Meat Sauces	69-78
Allemande, or White Sauce	71
Anchovy Sauce	72
Apple Sauce	76
Asparagus Sauce	75
Bread Sauce	76
Caper Sauce	71
Cardinal Sauce	71
Celery Sauce	73
Cheap Gravy for Hashes, etc.	77
Chili Sauce	69
Cream Sauce	70
Curry Sauce	69
Drawn Butter Sauce	70
Egg Sauce	71
Epicurean Sauce	75
French White Sauce	74
Good Sauce for Steaks	74
Good Gravy for Poultry, Game, etc.	77
Hollandaise Sauce	74
Horseradish Sauce	73
Jelly Sauce, for Game	72
Kidney Sauce	75
Maitre d' Hôtel Sauce	70

	PAGE
Mint Sauce	69
Mushroom Sauce	74
Mustard Sauce	70
Normandy Sauce	72
Old Zealand Sauce	72
Olive Sauce	75
Oyster Sauce	73
Parsley Sauce	71
Poivrade Sauce	78
Robert Sauce	78
Tartare Sauce	77
Tomato Sauce	70
Truffle Sauce	72
Golden Rules for the Kitchen	xv
Garnishing	xv
How to Keep Persons and Things Neat and Fresh	233-266
The Care of the Person	235-247
Alcohol Sweat Bath	237
Almond Paste	242
Baths	236
Baths for Children	238
Baths for Person Suffering from Debility	237
Black Spots on the Face	239
Calamine Lotion	240
Care of the Face	238
Care of the Hair	244
Care of the Hands	240
Care of the Nails	242
Care of the Teeth	243
Chapped Lips Cured	240
Cleaning Combs	246
Cleaning Sponges	246
Cold Cream	242
Crimping the Hair	245
Curling the Hair	245
Freckles	239
Hair Restorative	246
Hair Wash	245
Lip Salve	240
Pearl Water for the Complexion	239
Preventing the Skin from Cracking	239
Removing Sunburn	239
Sweetening the Breath	244
Softening the Hands	241
Tooth Powder	243
Violet Mouth Wash	244
Walnut Hair-Dye	245
Wash for the Face	240
Washing Brushes	246
Whitening the Hands	241
Home Made Perfumery	247-248
Almond Paste	248
Essence from Flowers	247
Otto of Roses	247
Perfume for Handkerchief	247
Scent Powder	248
Shampooing Liquid	248
Toilet Soap	248
Violet Powder	248
The Care of the Clothes	249-256
Boot Cleaning	256
Brushing Clothes	255
Cleaning Cloth	254
Cleaning Corsets	256
Cleaning Cream	253
Cleaning Feathers	254
Cleaning Lace	255

Index.

	PAGE
Cleaning Ribbons	253
Glazing Linen	250
Good Blueing	250
Hard Soap	249
Hints for the Laundry	249
Holes in Stockings	251
Making Old Crape Look Nearly as New	254
Patent Leather Boot Cleaning	256
Removing Grease from Cloth	250
Renewing Velvet	254
Renovating Silk	254
Taking Out Spots and Stains from Dresses	251
Washing Flannels	255
Washing Fluid	249
Washing Silk	252
Wax Stains on Cloth	251
The Care of the House, Furniture and Bric-a-Brac	**257-264**
Brightening Gilt Frames	262
Cleaning Brass	258
Cleaning Floor Cloth	257
Cleaning Ivory	262
Cleaning of Lamp Chimneys	263
Cleaning Looking Glasses	258
Cleaning Marble	257
Cleaning and Polishing Old Furniture	259
Cleaning Wall Paper	260
Destroying Carpet Bugs	260
Destroying Cockroaches	261
Dusting a Room	263
Furniture Polish	261
Glue Paint for Kitchen Floor	259
Papering Whitewashed Rooms	260
Polishing Black Grates	263
Polishing Tortoise Shell	263
Preserving Cut Flowers	262
Removing Stains from Boards	257
Reviving Cut Flowers	262
Routine of General Servant's Duties	264
Scouring Boards	258
Stains on Leather	263
Spots on Furniture	261
Sweeping a Carpet	261
Taking out Spots from Mahogany	261
Treasury Dept. Whitewash	259
Wash for Carpets	260
Whitening Stones	258
The Care of the Pantry	**265-66**
Cleaning of Plate	266
Cleaning of Bottles	266
Plate Rags for Daily Use	266
Washing of Glass	265
Washing of Knives	266
Layer Cakes	**128-131**
Caramel Cake	131
Chocolate Cake	131
Cocoanut Cake	129
Cream Cake	130
Cream for Cake	130
Fig Cake	130
Fruit Layer Cake	128
Gaelic Fruit Cake	128
Ice Cream Cake	131
Jelly Cakes	129
Jelly Roll	129
Lemon Cake	131

	PAGE
Pine Apple Cake	131
Meat and How to Cook it	**29-51**
Miscellaneous Dishes	**63**
Almond Paste	68
Apples and Rice	67
Apple Fritters	67
Bananas, Fried	66
Boiled New England Dinner	63
Calf's Liver	64
Crust for Pot Pie	65
Crust for Raised Pie	65
Ham Sandwiches	65
Hash	66
Larding	65
Mock Duck	64
Nudeln	66
Oyster Sandwiches	65
Pot Pie	64
Potted Meats	63
Rissoles	68
Sweetbreads, Broiled	64
Tripe	63
Trout in Jelly	68
Mutton and Lamb	**47-51**
Boiled Leg of Mutton	51
Braised Leg of Mutton	47
Breast of Mutton, Fried	49
Breast of Lamb and Green Peas	50
Broiled Mutton Chops	50
Harricot of Mutton	48
Irish Stew	47
Kidneys on Toast	50
Lamb Chops Sauté with Peas	51
Roast Mutton	47
Roast Saddle of Mutton	48
Roast Saddle of Lamb	49
Scotch Haggis	49
Our Medical Adviser	**267-353**
What to do in Case of Accident or Sudden Illness	269-280
Apoplexy	269
Bleeding	273
Bruises	269
Choking	269
Concussion of the Brain	269
Dislocations	269
Drowning	270
Epilepsy	271
Fainting	271
Foreign Bodies; in the Nose	272
" " in the Ear	272
" " in the Eye	272
Fractures	272
Hemorrhage, from Artery	273
" from Varicose Veins	273
" from the Nose	273
" from Leech Bites	273
" Tooth Extraction	273
" after Confinement	274
" from Umbilical Cord	274
Internal Bleeding	274
Hysteria	274
Intoxication	275
Poisons, General Rule	275
Poisons; *Separate Treatment*	275-277
Aconite	275
Alkalies	275
Arsenic	276
Barytas	276
Belladonna	**276**

Index.

	PAGE
Carbolic Acid	276
Copper	276
Corrosive Sublimate	276
Foxglove	276
Fungi [Mushrooms]	276
Hemlock	276
Henbane	276
Hydrochloric Acid	276
Laburnum	276
Laudanum	276
Lead	277
Nitric Acid	277
Oxalic Acid	277
Phosphorus	277
Prussic Acid	277
Shell Fish	277
Sulphuric Acid	277
Vitriol	277
Scalds or Burns	277
Sprains	278
Suffocation	278
Sunstroke	278
Wounds	278-280
Contused or Lacerated	278
Dog Bites	279
Gun Shot	279
Perforating	279
Poisons	279
Snake Bites	279
Stings	280
Bandaging Taught by Pictures	281-282
Beginning to Bandage the Ankle and Leg	282
Comfortable Arm Sling	281
Fracture of the Arm	282
Hand Bandage	281
Head Bandage	281
Small Sling for Arm	281
Splint for a Fracture of Bones in the Leg	282
Thumb Bandage	281
In the Sick Room	283-290
Administering Medicine	287
Cleanliness	285
Convalescence	285
Doctor's Orders	287
First Stage of Sickness	288
Fomentations	289
Food	284
Furnishing of the Room	283
Influence of Mind on Body	285
Light	284
Poultices	289-290
Linseed Meal	290
Mustard	290
Professional Nurses	288
Sick Nursing	286
Temperature	284
Tranquility	285
Ventilation	283
The Family Doctor	291-353
Asthma	291
Biliousness	292
Bronchitis	292
Bruises	293
Burns and Scalds	294
Catarrh	294
Chilblains	314
Cholera, Asiatic	295-299
Cholera, Asiatic, (Sir Edwin Arnold's Advice)	298
Cholera Morbus	300
Cholera Infantum	300
Chronic Rheumatism	301
Chronic Ulcers	302
Cold in the Head	302
Colic	302
Constipation	303-304
Consumption	305-310
Diarrhœa	310
Digestion of Food	311
Dropsy	311
Dysentery	311
Dyspepsia	312
Epilepsy	313
Facial Neuralgia	314
Frost Bite	314
Frost Bitten Fingers and Toes	314
Gout	314-316
Grippe	318
Healing Ointment	316
Heartburn	316
Heat Stroke	316
Hydrophobia	317-319
Influenza	318
Ingrowing Nail	319
Lumbricoid or Round Worms	319
Mastitis	320
Nasal Catarrh	321-323
Nervous Prostration	322
Nausea in Pregnancy	322
Night Terrors	322
Piles	323
Rheumatism	324
Dr. Agnew's Prescription	325
Sciatica Liniment	325
Seat Worms	325
Sprains	325
Sore Nipples	326
Stomach ache	326
Sweating of the Feet	326
Tape Worm	326
To Abort a Felon	327
Tonsillitis	327
Toothache	328
Water Brash	329
Diseases of Infancy and Childhood	329-341
Chicken Pox	329
Convulsions	330
Croup	331
Diarrhœa	332
Infant's Colic	333
Measles	333-335
Prickly Heat	335
Ring Worm	335
Scarlet Fever or Scarlatina	336-338
Teething	338
Thrush	338
Whooping Cough	339-341
Liniments, Syrups and Troches	341-342
"Best Liniment"	341
Cough Syrup	342
Cough Troches	342
Remedy for Burns	341
Stillingia Liniment	341
Stimulating Balsam	341
Homeopathic Medicines and Their Use in the Family	343-349

	PAGE		PAGE
Advantages of Homœopathy	348	Pickled Apples	169
Diet	348	Pickled Gherkins	166
Homœopathy Defined	343	Pickled Lily	165
Medicines Used in Homœopathy	349	Pickled Nasturtiums	165
Practice of Homœopathy	346	Pineapple Preserves	167
Practice Supported	346	Preserved Fruit	168
Preparation of Homœopathic Medicines	347	Ripe Cucumber Pickles	162
		Ripe Tomato Pickles	164
Principle of Homœopathy	344	Sliced Green Tomato Pickles	164
Principle Supported	345	Spiced Tomatoes	165
Homœopathic Treatment of Diseases	350-353	Sweet Chow Chow	163
		Tomato Catsup	165
Appetite, Failure of	350	Tomato Chutney	165
Biliousness	350	Tomato Preserves	164
Bruises	350	Walnut Ketchup	167
Catarrh	351	**Pork**	41-46
Cold in the Head	351	Baked Pork Tenderloin	43
Colic	351	Boiled Bacon	44
Constipation	352	Boiled Ham	43
Cough	352	Breakfast Bacon	44
Diarrhœa	352	Broiled Sausages	42
Fever	353	Collared Pig's Face	44
Headache	353	Fried Pig's Feet	43
Indigestion	353	Fried Sausages	43
Pastry	154-161	Ham and Eggs	44
Pies	156-161	Pig's Feet, Broiled	43
Apple Cream Pie	159	Pork and Beans	42
Chocolate Cream Pie	159	Pork Chops	45
Cocoanut Pie	159	Pork Tenderloin, Broiled	41
Cream Pie	160	Roast Leg of Pork	46
Custard Pie	159	Roast Pig	42
Fruit Pies	156	Roast Pork	41
Lemon Cream Pie	158	Salt Pork	41
Mince Meat	157	To Bake a Ham	46
Mock Mince Pie	157	**Poultry and Game**	52-62
Neapolitaines	161	Boiled Fowl and Rice	55
Orange Pie	159	Brine for Beef, Bacon, Ham and Venison	62
Orange Tarts	160		
Pie Crust	156	Broiled Chicken	54
Potato Cream Pie	158	Broiled Venison	60
Puff Paste	156	Chicken Fricassee	53
Pumpkin Pie	158	Chicken Patties	55
Rhubarb Pie	161	Chicken Pie	54
Sand Tarts	160	Chicken Pot Pie	55
Sour Milk Pie	160	Curried Chicken	58
Squash Pie	158	Fowl à la Marengo	58
Sweet Potato Pie	160	Fried Rabbit	59
Tart Paste	156	Grand Pacific Game Pie	61
Transparent Pie	159	Grouse, Larded	61
Short Cake	155-156	Jugged Hare	60
Crust	155	Pigeon Pie	62
Fruit for Short Cake	155	Pressed Chicken	55
General Instructions	154	Quail on Toast	56
Roll Puddings	155	Roast Chicken	54
Pickles and Preserves	162-171	Roast Goose	57
Blackberry Pickle	167	Roast Partridge	59
Brandied Peaches	168	Roast Pigeons	56
Canned Fruit	169	Roast Rabbit	59
Chili Sauce	165	Roast Venison	60
Chow Chow	162	Smothered Chicken	54
Citron Preserves	166	Stewed Duck and Peas	57
Cucumber Pickles	162	Stewed Rabbit	59
Fruit Jellies	170	Turkey Stuffed, Giblet Sauce	52
Grape Catsup	169	Turkey Stuffed with Chestnuts	53
Green Tomato Pickles	163	Turkey Stuffed with Oysters	52
Jams	170	**Preface**	V
Melon Preserves	166	**Puddings**	145-150
Mustard Pickles	163	Apple Dumpling	150
Orange Marmalade	170	Black Pudding	148
Plum Catsup	169	Cabinet Pudding	149

GOLDEN RULES FOR THE KITCHEN

Without *cleanliness* and *punctuality* good Cooking is impossible.

Leave nothing *dirty; clean and clear as you go.*

A time for everything, and *everything in time.*

A good Cook *wastes nothing.*

An hour *lost in the morning* has to be run after *all day.*

Haste *without hurry* saves worry, fuss and flurry.

Stew *boiled* is Stew *spoiled.*

Strong fire for *Roasting; clear* fire for *Broiling.*

Wash Vegetables in *three* waters.

Boil fish *quickly,* meat *slowly.*

: : GARNISHING : :

There is a congruity in the serving and garnishing of dishes that is often lost sight of. To be very neat, very simple, and good of the kind, is generally all that is wanted in a moderate household. There never can be any excuse for untidy serving, or food set awry, and grease in the wrong place, sauce spilt over the edges of the dish, or dirt. Such things look worse on an elaborate dinner than a plain one, just as a soiled collar and dirty hands look worst of all with a smart dress and gold bracelets.

One word more: Never attempt to serve a dinner beyond your powers.

THE TIME IT TAKES TO COOK FOOD

NOTE:—The figures found here may vary slightly according to the degree of heat, the nature of the water, the material of the cooking utensils; but they may be relied upon to be, on the average, correct.

NATURE OF THE FOOD.	QUANTITIES IN LBS.	H'RS.	MINUTES	NATURE OF THE FOOD.	QUANTITIES IN LBS.	H'RS.	MINUTES
Asparagus....	....	...	25	Onions, young.	....	1	....
Beef, rib or sirloin; rare....	8	...	45	" winter.	....	2	....
				Peas, green...	....	...	30
				Pigeon.......	....	...	20 to 25
Beef, rib or sirlion; well done	8	1	5	Pork, spare rib.	....	2	30
Ten minutes for each additional pound,				" chine...	....	...	30
				Potatoes, boiled	....	...	30
				" baked	....	...	45
Beef, rump, rare	....	...	55	Shell beans...	....	1	....
" " well done.......	....	1	15	Squash, boiled.	....	...	25
				" baked.	....	...	45
Beets, young..	....	1	....	Spinach.......	....	1	15
" winter..	....	2	....	Sweet potatoes, boiled.......	....	...	45
Cabbage, young	....	1	....				
" winter	....	2	....	Sweet potatoes, baked......	....	1	....
Capon........	full size	1	....				
Chicken......	"	...	20 to 30	Tomatoes	....	...	45
Corn, green...	....	...	30	" canned	....	...	25
Duck........	full size	...	50 to 60	Turkey, stuffed under 10 lbs,		2	....
Duckling.....	....	...	25 to 35	" " 10		3	....
Fowl, large....	large	2	45	" " over 10		4	....
" small...	small	1	....	Turnips, young	....	1	....
Goose	full size	1	....	" winter.	....	2	....
Lamb........	9	1	30	Veal.........	....	2	45

WEIGHTS AND THEIR EQUIVALENTS.

1 lb. of flour..1 quart.
1 pound of granulated sugar......................................2 cups.
1 pound of pulverized sugar... ....2 heaping cups.
1 pound butter ....2 cups.
1 pound of chopped meat .. ..1 pint.
10 medium sized eggs.... ....1 pound.
1 flowing over pint of milk....................................1 pound.
1 teaspoonful of soda and 2 of cream tartar, equal three teaspoonfuls of baking powder.
A cupful of sour milk requires a level teaspoonful of soda.
2 ordinary sized cupfuls equal one pint.

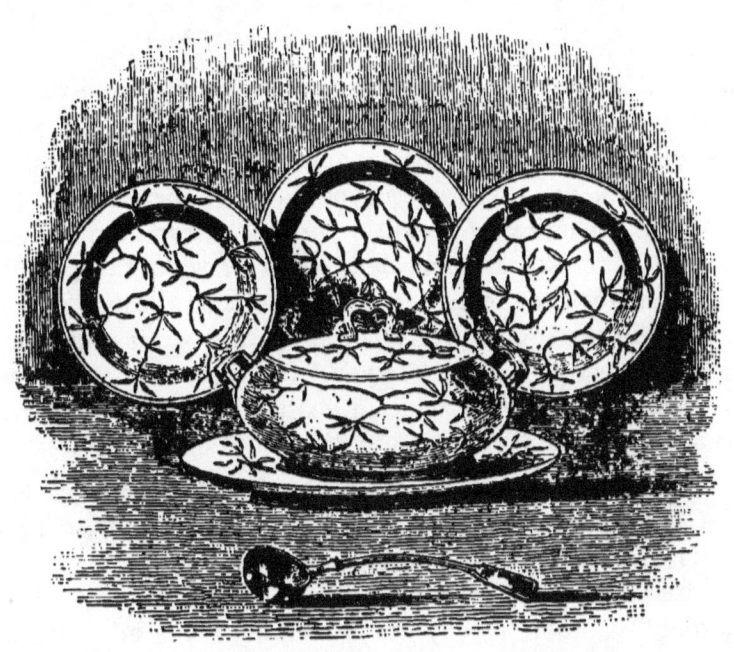

SOUPS AND HOW TO MAKE THEM

Stock. In preparing stock, which is the basis of most soups and meat sauces, it is not necessary to go through the tedious processes prescribed by some. It is simply to extract the juices of meats and bones by long and gentle simmering. A shank or other meat bones, the carcass of a roast turkey or chicken, the trimmings of roasts or steaks are all excellent to prepare stock from. Put in a pot and cover with cold water, add a handful of salt and boil gently for several hours. Do not add any vegetables or spices, as all vegetables lose their freshness and flavor by long continued cooking and the flavor of the spice might conflict with the other ingredients of the soup for which the stock is intended.

Skim off all scum that may rise and add water from time to time as the stock boils away. When you are ready to make the soup, take out all the meat and bones and strain the stock through a sieve, a hair one if you have it; the stock is now ready for use unless you want a perfectly clear soup. In that case, after the stock is strained, put it back in the pot and stir in one or two beaten eggs; put back on the fire and as it boils up the egg will rise; skim off and strain again and your stock will be clear. If you have more than you need for immediate use, put aside in a stone or earthen jar, it will keep for several days in a cold place.

Consomme Soup. Chop one and a half pound of lean beef, one onion and a carrot together; stir in four eggs, shells and all, then add three quarts of cold stock, put in a granite or porcelain kettle and let it come to a boil. Skim thoroughly. Boil slowly for fifteen or twenty minutes then strain through a cloth, and your consommé is ready to serve. If due attention has been given to this soup, it will be as clear as amber.

Consomme with Egg. Poach as many eggs soft as there are people to serve; place an egg in each plate and pour over it a ladle full of the hot consommé and serve at once.

Consomme with Egg No. 2. Make a custard of three eggs and half a cup of sweet milk. Bake but do not brown. When done, cut in half inch cubes, put in the soup; let come to a boil and serve.

Consomme with Tapioca. Boil your tapioca in salted water until clear, (for soups, pearled tapioca is preferable), put in the soup and boil ten minutes before serving.

Consomme with Vermicelli. Boil the vermicelli in salted water until done, add to the soup and boil five minutes before serving. A nice seasoning is made by adding a small handful of chopped parsley or celery leaves.

Consomme with Macaroni. Parboil the macaroni in salted water, when done, drain and add to the soup; boil ten or fifteen minutes and serve.

Tomato.

Tomato Soup. Take three quarts of stock and let it come to a boil; add to it one can of tomatoes, or its equivalent in fresh tomatoes, a half cupful of rice and boil from one and a half to two hours. When the rice is thoroughly done, add a lump of butter the size of an egg, season with pepper and salt and a tablespoonful of sugar.

Cream Tomato (Mock Bisque Soup.) Put two quarts of milk in a double boiler; let it come to a boil. Put in a stew-pan a can of tomatoes, boil until soft, rub through a fine sieve, stir in a teaspoonful of soda to neuttralize the acid. Rub a small tablespoonful of flour in a lump of butter the size of an egg and stir in the boiling water, add the tomato, season with pepper and salt; boil three minutes and serve.

Potato Soup. Shred a large onion in three pints of milk, add two stalks of celery, cut fine, put in a double boiler and let it come to a boil. In the meantime pare and boil six or seven medium sized potatoes; when done, mash thoroughly, beat light and add to the boiling milk, put in a lump of butter equal to two tablespoonsfuls; when melted, season with pepper and salt, put through a seive and serve at once.

Mutton Broth. Take three pounds of lean mutton and cut into small pieces. It is a good plan to get your butcher to cut the meat and break the bones for you. Put the meat in a granite or porcelain kettle, add two quarts of water and an even tablespoonful of salt; cover closely and boil slowly for two hours. Put through a strainer and skim off the fat. Return to the kettle and stir in a well beaten egg; as it comes to a boil skim and continue to do so until clear. It is now ready for use if only a broth is required. If you wish to make it into a soup you can add rice, barley, chopped vegetables or anything that your judgment or taste may suggest.

Barley Soup. Take two quarts of stock, and add to it one pound of lean beef, chopped fine, one teacupful of pearl barley; boil slowly to avoid scorching, cook until the barley is thoroughly done, season with pepper and salt. A little choped parsley is a nice addition.

Barley.

Rice Soup. Take either a shin of veal, a medium sized chicken or the remains of two or three roast chickens, boil in three quarts of water until the meat is tender. Separate the meat from the bones and chop in pieces the size of a kernel of corn, strain the liquor through a sieve, put back in the kettle, add a teacupful of rice and a head of celery, cut fine, boil until the rice is well done, add the chopped meat, season with pepper and salt, boil five minutes longer, and serve.

Rice.

Gumbo Soup. Take a chicken (not too young) and one half pound of bacon. Chip the bacon in small slices and put in a smooth bottom iron kettle. Cut up the chicken, put in with the bacon and fry to a nice brown. Be careful not to scorch. When brown add three quarts of water, one onion cut fine and any sweet herb you like (if the latter is used put it in a small bag), boil slowly for three or four hours. Strain off the liquor, skim off the fat, cut the chicken and bacon in small pieces, put all back in the kettle together with a teacupful of boiled rice and a half teacupful of okra, boil half an hour longer and just before serving add a dozen oysters, cut in halves, with their juice.

Celery Cream. Take three or four heads of nice white celery, cut in small pieces, cover with water and boil until tender, which will take from one-half to a whole hour. When tender, drain off the water and mash fine. Have ready three pints of milk boiling hot and add to it the washed celery, and the water in which it was boiled. Stir a tablespoonful of flour in a lump of butter the size of an egg, add to the cream, season with pepper and salt, boil three minutes and serve.

Celery.

Ox Tail Soup. Cut from a ham bone the small bits that cannot be saved in slices, put in a pan with an onion and a carrot sliced fine and a lump of butter the size of an egg and let brown. Put in the pan four tablespoonsfuls of flour and let brown again; add two quarts of good stock and boil forty minutes. Cut an ox tail in short lengths, put in a frying pan with a lump of butter and a very little water, cover close and let it boil until the water is all gone, let the ox tail fry to a nice even brown all around, strain the stock and pour over the ox tail, add a cupful of boiled barley or rice, season with pepper and salt, let come to a boil and serve.

Vegetable Soup. Three quarts of stock, quarter of a head of cabbage, half a turnip, one carrot, two onions, three potatoes; chop all the vegetables together, add to the stock and boil one hour, season to taste and serve.

Noodle Soup. Two quarts of stock, put in a kettle and let come to a boil. To make the noodles, break an egg in a bowl, put in a pinch of salt and work in as much flour as it will take, put on the pastry-board and mould smooth, roll out as thin as possible, rub a little flour over the surface, begin at one end and make into a compact roll; cut this into very thin slices, sprinkle a little more flour over them and shake them loose. Chop fine a handful of green celery leaves. put noodles and leaves in the stock and boil fifteen minutes, add pepper and salt to taste.

Mulligatawny. Brown an onion and a turnip with half a pound of lean chipped ham in a sauce pan; stir in one cupful of flour and pour over all three quarts of hot stock, add a three-pound can of tomatoes and boil two hours, put through a sieve. Have ready the meat of a chicken cut in dices and a cupful of boiled rice. Season with a tablespoonful of curry powder, salt and pepper.

Pea Soup. Take a can of peas or a quart of fresh peas, boil until tender and rub through a sieve, add a quart of milk, two tablespoonfuls of butter, salt and pepper to taste and boil five minutes. Just before serving roll two soda crackers into the soup. Serve at once.

Sweet Pea.

Split Pea Soup. Wash two pounds of split peas, put in saucepan with two quarts of water and boil for one hour. Drain off the water and add four quarts of good strong stock, a ham bone, and an onion and a carrot chopped together. Let all boil together slowly for three or four hours, put through a sieve, season to taste and serve with sippets of bread.

Asparagus Soup. Take a bunch of asparagus and cut in quarter inch lengths, boil until tender but not soft enough to mash, and drain off the water. Chop an onion very fine, put in a stew-pan with a lump of butter, the size of an egg and fry to a light brown, then add the asparagus and mix carefully; when slightly browned add one quart of boiling milk, let it boil up once, season with pepper and salt and serve.

Okra Soup. Cut the okra in half inch pieces, boil tender in one quart of stock, add the meat of a chicken or some roast veal, cut fine. Season to taste.

Creamed Oyster. Let two quarts of milk come to a boil. Take three pints of oysters, drain off the liquor, put in a chopping bowl and chop fine. Stir two small tablespoonfuls of flour in four of melted butter. Put the oysters in the boiling milk, stir in the butter and flour, season with pepper and salt, let boil up once and serve.

Bean Soup, Extra. Take one cupful of nice white beans, parboil and drain; put in fresh water and boil until tender but not soft enough to mash. When done, add two quarts of milk and let come to a boil, put a lump of butter the size of an egg and season with pepper and salt. A few minutes before serving, break up four or five soda crackers, add to the soup, stir up well and serve.

Lobster Soup. Take a can of lobsters and chop or pound it fine, put it in a sauce-pan and pour over it three pints of white stock and let it boil slowly for ten or fifteen minutes. Cook two tablepoonsfuis of flour with two of butter but do not brown, add to the soup, season to taste and serve.

Lobster.

Egg Soup. To one pint of water add a tablespoonful of butter, salt and pepper to taste; break two fresh eggs in a cup, hold the cup in the left hand and a fork in the right, pour the egg in slowly, beating briskly with the fork until the egg looks like white and yellow shreds. Take from the stove and serve. You can make this soup in a minute after the rest of your dinner is ready to serve. The water must boil when you stir in your eggs which should not be beaten until you beat them in the water. The amount given is enough for two persons.

Cream of Chicken Soup. Get two large fat fowls and boil them until they are very tender, take only the white meat, cut it up and press through a sieve, strain the stock and add to it the sieved chicken; season with a little salt and pepper and let it boil a few minutes; now take the yolks of a dozen raw eggs and whip up with a pint of sweet cream, stir this into the stock and keep stirring until it all begins to thicken; now add two-thirds of a cup of butter, let it boil up once more, strain and serve in cups.

Milk Soup. Take four large potatoes, and two onions, cut fine and boil in two quarts of water until thoroughly done; strain through a colander, put back in the kettle, add a pint of milk, three tablespoonfuls of pearl tapioca, a lump of butter the size of an egg, season with salt and pepper. Boil slowly and stir often for fifteen or twenty minutes and serve hot.

Mock Turtle Soup. Procure a knuckle of veal weighing 3 or 4 lbs., 1 cow-heel, 1 large onion stuck with cloves, 1 bunch of sweet herbs, 2 blades of mace, salt to taste, 8 peppercorns, 1 glass of sherry, 12 balls of stuffing, a little lemon juice, 2 quarts of water. Put all the ingredients, except the balls of stuffing and the lemon juice,

Turtle.

in an earthen jar and stew for 6 hours. Do not open it till cold. When wanted for use, skim off all the fat, and strain carefully; place it on the fire, cut up the meat into inch and a half squares, put it, with the forcemeat balls and lemon juice, into the soup and serve. It can be flavored with a tablespoonful of anchovy, or Harvey's sauce.

Clear Mock Turtle Soup. Take a calf's head, ½ lb. of gravy beef, 1 carrot, 1 turnip, ½ head of celery, 1 onion stuck with 3 cloves, bunch of herbs, 10 peppercorns, blade of mace, salt, 3 oz. of bacon or ham, 1 glass of sherry, 2 quarts of water, the juice of ½ a lemon. Wash and bone the head. Tie the meat in a cloth and chop the bones, put the meat, bones and half the vegetables and seasoning in a stewpan with the water, allow it to boil up and skim well. Simmer about 3 hours. Take the head up and strain the stock into a basin. When the stock is cold carefully remove the fat. Put the stock into a stewpan with the remainder of the vegetables, and the meat finely shredded. Whisk over the fire until the soup is just on the boil. Draw it on one side, and allow it to simmer gently for 10 minutes; when clarified, strain through a clean cloth, add the stock, some force-meat balls, and pieces of the head served in the soup.

Julienne Soup. Procure ¼ pint of carrots, ¼ pint of turnips, ¼ pint of onions, 2 leeks, ½ head of celery, ½ lettuce, a little sorrel, if liked, 1 oz. of butter, 2 quarts of stock. Cut the vegetables into strips of 1¼ inches long, and be particular they are all the same size, or some will be hard whilst the others will be done to a pulp. Cut the lettuce and sorrel into larger pieces; fry the

Strips of Vegetables. carrots in the butter, and pour the stock, boiling, to them. When this is done, add all the other vegetables and herbs, and stew gently for at least an hour. Skim off all the fat, pour the soup over thin slices of bread, cut round, about the size of a shilling, and serve. The soup has a better appearance if each vegetable is boiled separately in water and then added to the clear stock, at the moment of serving.

Carrot and Lentil Soup. Procure 4 carrots, 2 sliced onions, 1 cut lettuce and chervil; 2 oz. butter, 2 pints of lentils, the crumbs of 2 French rolls, half a teacupful of rice, 4 quarts of stock. Put the vegetables with the butter in the stewpan, and let them simmer 5 minutes; then add the lentils, which should have been soaked all night, and 1 pint of the stock, and stew gently for half an hour. Now fill it up with the remainder of the stock, let it boil another hour, and put in the crumbs of the rolls. When well soaked, rub all through a tammy. Have ready the rice boiled; pour the soup over this and serve.

The Lentil.

Cucumber Soup. Procure 1 large cucumber, a piece of butter the size of a walnut, a little sorrel, cut in large pieces, salt and pepper to taste, the yolks of two eggs, 1 gill of cream, 1 quart of stock. Pare the cucumber, quarter it, and take out the seeds; cut it in thin slices, put these on a plate with a little salt, to draw the water from them; drain, and put them in your stewpan with the butter. When they are warmed through, without being browned, pour the stock on them. Add the sorrel, chervil and seasoning, and boil for forty minutes. Mix the well-beaten yolks of the eggs with the cream, which add at the moment of serving.

The Sorrel.

Hodge-Podge. Procure 1 lb. of shin of beef, 2 quarts of water, ½ pint of table-beer, 1 onion, 1 carrot, 1 turnip, 1 head of celery, pepper and salt to taste, thickening of butter and flour. Put the meat, beer and water in a stewpan; simmer for a few minutes, and skim carefully. Add the vegetables and seasoning; stew gently till the meat is tender. Thicken with butter and flour, and serve with turnips and carrots or spinach and celery.

Shrimp Soup. You need two quarts of fish stock, two pints of shrimp, the crumbs of a French roll, anchovy sauce or mushroom ketchup to taste, one blade of mace, ¼ pint of vinegar, a little lemon juice. Pick out the tails of the shrimps, put the bodies in a stewpan, with 1 blade of mace, ¼ pint of vinegar, and the same quantity of water; stew them for quarter of an hour, and strain off the liquor. Put the fish stock into a stewpan, add the strained liquor, pound the shrimps with crumb of a roll, moistened with a little of the soup; rub them through a tammy, and mix them by degrees with the soup; add ketchup or anchovy sauce to taste, with a little lemon juice. When it is well cooked, put in a few pickled shrimps; let them get thoroughly hot, and serve. If not thick enough put in a little butter and flour.

The Shrimp.

NOTE.—This can be thickened with tomatoes and vermicelli served in it, which makes it a very tasteful cup. The soup can be made of shrimps and garnished with prawns, where economy is an object.

Onion Soup. Eight middling-sized onions, 3 oz. of butter, a tablespoonful of rice flour, salt and pepper to taste, 1 teaspoonful of powdered sugar, thickening of butter and flour, 2 quarts of water. Cut the onions small, put them in the stewpan with the butter, and fry them well; mix the rice flour smoothly with the water, add the onions, seasoning and sugar, and simmer till tender. Thicken with butter and flour and serve. It is better to rub the soup through a sieve. Spanish onions make the best soup.

Spinach Soup. Take as much spinach as, when boiled, will half fill a vegetable dish, 2 quarts of very clear stock.

Make the cooked spinach into balls the size of an egg, and slip them into the soup-tureen. This is a very elegant soup, the green of the spinach forming a pretty contrast to the brown gravy.

White Soup. Procure ¼ lb. of sweet almonds, ¼ lb. of cold veal or poultry, a thick slice of stale bread, a piece of fresh lemon peel, 1 blade of mace, pounded; ¾ pint of cream, the yolks of 2 eggs, 2 quarts of white stock. Reduce the almonds in a mortar to a paste, with a spoonful of water, and add to them the meat, which should be previously pounded with the bread. Beat all together and add the lemon peel, very finely chopped, and the mace. Pour the boiling stock on the whole, and simmer for an hour. Rub the eggs in the cream, put in the soup, bring it to a boil and serve immediately.

Semolina Soup. You need 5 oz. of semolina, 2 quarts of boiling stock. Drop the semolina into the boiling stock, and keep stirring, to prevent its burning or going into lumps. Simmer gently for half an hour and serve.

Vegetable Stock. Two quarts of water, 2 oz. of haricot beans, 2 oz. of split peas, 1 onion, 1 carrot, ½ stick of celery, parsley and herbs, pepper, salt, 5 cloves and a blade of mace. Boil in 2 quarts of water for 3 or 4 hours all the above vegetables, spice and herbs. Strain it off. It will keep for some time if it is let to stand and poured off from the sediment.

NOTE.—This may serve as the basis of a good many soups and sauces, just as stock made of meat and bones serves many purposes. All cooks may be assured that if gravy has to be made, and no meat is at hand to make it of, water in which any vegetables have been boiled (except potatoes) will be better than water from the tap or kettle.

White Stock. Four lbs. of knuckle of veal, any poultry trimmings or a rabbit, 4 slices of lean ham, 3 carrots, 2 onions, 1 head of celery, 12 white peppercorns, 2 oz. of salt,

1 blade of mace, a bunch of herbs, 1 oz. butter, 4 quarts of water. Cut up the veal, and put it, with the bones and trimmings of poultry and the ham, into the stewpan, which has been rubbed with the butter. Moisten with ½ a pint of water, and simmer till the gravy begins to flow. Then add the 4 quarts of water and the remainder of the ingredients; simmer for 5 hours. After skimming and straining it carefully through a fine hair sieve, it will be ready for use.

NOTE.—When stronger stock is desired, double the quantity of veal, or put in an old fowl. The liquor in which a young turkey or a fowl has been boiled is an excellent addition to all white stock of soups, and the bird is better boiled in the stock-pot than in water. Bones that have been boiled once for brown stock can be boiled again with fresh vegetables for white.

Fish Stock. Take two pounds of any kind of fish that is cheap, such as shad, flounders or small eels, or the trimming and heads of uncooked fish, a head of celery, a root of parsley, a blade or two of mace, a bay leaf, a few cloves and white pepper, and salt to taste; three quarts of water. Put the whole into a pan, and let it simmer gently for a couple of hours; then strain off the liquor.

The Fennel.

FISH AND HOW TO COOK IT

General Instructions.

Fish cannot be too fresh. The sooner it is eaten after coming out of the water the better. In selecting fish for the table see that the flesh is firm, the eyes bright, the gills red, and the fins stiff. Nothing deteriorates more quickly than fish; as soon as it has lost its first freshness it has also lost its delicate flavor, and moreover becomes decidedly unwholesome. The principal ways of cooking fish are Frying, Boiling, Broiling, Baking and Stewing, and with but few exceptions all varieties can be rendered palatable by any of the above processes. In preparing fish for cooking, cleanse and wash thoroughly in cold water, be careful not to bruise or break, and do not leave it in the water longer than is absolutely necessary, as it destroys the flavor. An exception can be made in case of some varieties of fresh water fish which have a muddy flavor. These can be dressed, washed, and left in salt and water for two or three hours. Be sure and have the water cold. In boiling fish a fish kettle with a perforated bottom is a great convenience, but is not absolutely indispensable. Fish can be boiled very nicely in a deep dripping pan by wrapping it up in thin cloth and if the pan is not deep enough to cover the fish it can be turned over once or twice. The time required to boil a medium sized fish is from twenty to thirty minutes if the water is kept bubbling all the time. But the surest test is to insert the blade of a knife between the fish and the bone; if it flakes readily and separates easily it is ready to take from the fire. Fish that is to be broiled whole should be split down the back.

With regard to sauces for fish it is difficult to give advice. There are many who would consider fish served without sauce as utterly flat, stale and unprofitable. And again there are others, and they are by no means in the minority, who assume that the delicate flavors are disguised if not utterly destroyed by the addition of highly flavored sauces. As a rule people who live near the seashore, and who can obtain fish in the highest state of excellence, seldom use anything besides pepper and salt as seasoning. It is therefore a nice plan for the cook to study the tastes of those to whom she caters.

Boiled Cod. Take a small cod or as many pounds as you need of a large one, cleanse and rub with salt, roll tightly in a thin cloth, pin and put in the kettle or pan, cover with cold water, add a tablespoonful of salt and boil until done. When done lift out of the water, unroll carefully, leaving the cloth under the fish; take the skin off the upper side, turn the fish over by slightly raising the cloth and skin the other side, transfer to a platter, pour over it hot melted butter, garnish with parsley and serve.

The Cod.

These directions will answer for all kinds of boiled fresh fish except salmon, which is rich enough without the melted butter. An egg dressing or Old Zealand sauce is more suitable for fish that are rich in oils.

Salt Cod with Eggs. Pick a pint bowlful of the cod, put in a stew pan, cover with water, set on the back of the stove and as the water becomes salt, change; two or three times will be sufficient. When fresh enough drain off the water and add a lump of butter size of an egg and let it melt, then stir in a tablespoonful of flour and let cook, but do not brown; add three cups of milk and let come to a boil then break in carefully as many fresh eggs as there are persons to serve. Take the eggs out when the whites are done, place on a shallow dish, pour the fish over the eggs and serve.

Salt Cod with Eggs No. 2. Prepare the fish as above and instead of dropping in the eggs whole, put in two and stir in with a fork; cook three minutes and serve.

Fish Balls. Take one part fish and two parts raw potato, about three pints in all. Pare and cut the potatoes in halves, pick the fish, freeing it from bones and put in a kettle with the potatoes, the fish on top; cover with water and boil thirty minutes, drain and mash potatoes and fish together, season with salt and pepper and a lump of butter size of an egg, then add two well beaten eggs and mix all thoroughly together. Have a kettle half full of hot fat, shape the mixture with a spoon and drop into the hot fat and fry to a light brown; serve hot.

Stewed Fish. Any kind of fish are good for stewing but catfish and bullhead are particularly suited to this style of cooking. Skin and cleanse the fish, and if small leave whole but if large cut into pieces suitable for serving. Shred an onion into a flat bottomed pan or kettle, add a lump of butter size of an egg, let brown slightly, then lay the fish side by side in the pan, season with salt and pepper, cover with water, put a close cover over the whole and stew thirty minutes. Take the fish out of the kettle with a tin shovel, put on a hot platter, thicken the liquor with a spoonful of flour, pour over the fish and serve.

Fish and How to Cook It

Boiled Salt Cod. Soak the fish over night; when fresh enough place in a kettle and simmer from twenty to thirty minutes, place the pieces carefully on a platter, pour over it a cream sauce and serve.

Boiled Salt White Fish. Salt white fish can be treated the same as salt cod, except that it must be pinned in a cloth to prevent its breaking while boiling.

Boiled Flounders. Cleanse, wrap in a cloth and boil for twenty-five minutes and serve with melted butter or Old Zealand sauce.

Flounders.

Broiled Fish. All small fish, that is those weighing from one-half to three pounds, are suitable for broiling. Blue fish, cod, mackerel, trout, whitefish, perch, bass, pike, and pickerel are all excellent when broiled. 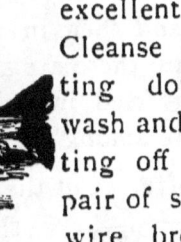 Cleanse the fish, splitting down the back, wash and wipe dry, cutting off the fins with a pair of shears. Have a wire broiler, rub the wires with a piece of bacon or a little fat, to prevent sticking, put the fish in the broiler, and turn the inside to the fire first. As the cooking progresses sprinkle with a little salt and if the fish is of a dry variety put on a little melted butter from time to time. If the fish is very thick and there is danger of scorching before it is cooked through, place the broiler over a dripping pan and put in the oven; the even heat of the oven will soon finish cooking the fish, and will not destroy that peculiar flavor produced by broiling. Broiled fish should be served the instant it is done. Most people prefer broiled fish without sauce, but tomato, capers,

The Pike

anchovy, Old Zealand or Tartare sauce are considered desirable accessories by some.

Fried Fish. Frying is one of the simplest methods of cooking fish, and therefore easily acquired. All small fish should be fried whole, while larger fish can be split down the back and then cut in suitable pieces. Pork fat, lard or drippings are all used, but the first is preferable. After the fish is cleaned and washed, sprinkle with salt and let it stand for some time, but be sure and keep it in a cold place. Fill the spider or kettle half full of fat, roll the fish in flour and put in the hot fat and fry to a nice brown. Serve with or without sauce, as desired, but tomato sauce forms a particularly fine addition to fried fish.

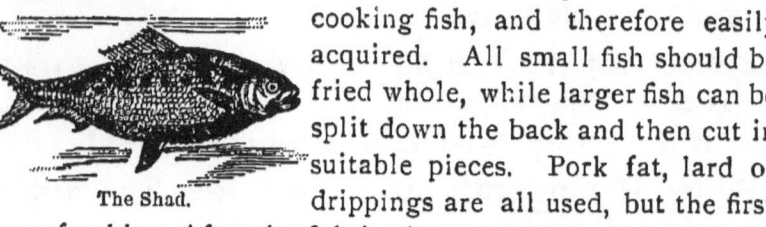
The Shad.

All fish steaks, such as cod, halibut, haddock and salmon, can be cooked and served in the above manner but you can vary the form of cooking by sometimes dipping the steaks in beaten egg and then in cracker crumbs and frying to a brown, and again there are some kinds of fish that are much better by being fried in butter. Brook trout, smelts and salmon steak are among the number.

Fried Smelts. Cut the fish open and cleanse but leave the head on. Lay on a plate and sprinkle with salt. Have enough hot fat in a frying pan to float the fish, dip the smelts in flour and fry from two to three minutes.

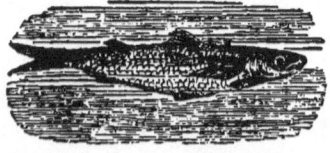
The Smelt.

Fried Smelts No. 2. Make a thin batter of one beaten egg, half a cup of milk and an even tablespoonful of flour, add a pinch of salt. Cleanse the fish removing the heads. and sprinkle with salt as above. Put two tablespoonfuls of butter in a frying pan and when hot pour in half the batter and into this lay the smelts side by side as close as they can be laid and covering the whole bottom of the pan then over the whole pour the rest of the batter and fry to a nice brown, turn over as you would a pancake. When both sides are a nice brown cut in squares and serve at once.

Fried Herring. Fried herring is much nicer when boned before frying. Scale and wash the fish, cutting off the head. Hold the fish in the left hand and insert the thumb of the right hand at the shoulder next the backbone and work the thumb slowly the whole length of the spine, then turn over and do the other side in like manner. If this process is gone through carefully the whole skeleton can be taken out without losing a bone and also without breaking the fish. When loose cut the bone close to the tail and trim off the fins with a pair of shears, sprinkle the fish with salt, roll in flour, fry in hot fat until brown and serve.

The Herring.

To Cook Eels. Skin and cleanse the eels and cut in two inch lengths. Slice half a pound of fat pork and fry to a crisp; take out the pork and put the eel in the pan; if small set the lengths up on end, but if large you can put them in the pan lengthwise; sprinkle with salt and a very little pepper, add half a cup of water, cover lightly so that part of the steam can escape, put on the fire and cook until the water has all boiled away and one side of the eel is fried to a nice brown, then turn over carefully and fry the other side.

The Eel.

Baked Fish. Only large fish are suitable for baking and all varieties are treated in much the same manner. Scale and clean the fish, leaving on the head and rub with salt.

Make a dressing of a bowl of bread or cracker crumbs a quarter of a pound of salt pork chopped fine, a small onion or a tablespoonful of chopped parsley; salt and pepper to taste; mix thoroughly together and put in the body of the fish. Cut gashes along the back of the fish about an inch apart, into each gash place a small strip of fat pork securing them in place with small skewers; tooth picks will answer nicely, put the fish in the pan and dredge with salt, pepper and flour, put a cupful of water in the bottom of the pan and bake for about an hour, basting frequently. If the water in the pan evaporates, add more.

Fish Chowder. Haddock, cod and striped bass are best for chowder but any kind of fresh fish can be used.

The Haddock.

Cut a pound of salt pork in slices put in an iron kettle and fry till crisp; remove the pork leaving the fat and put in the kettle a layer of fish cut in pieces one inch thick and two inches square; sprinkle the fish with salt, pepper and a dash of red pepper, put in a layer of broken crackers, some of the fried pork chopped fine and a finely sliced onion, then another layer of fish, another of cracker, seasoning and so on. Cover with water, and stew until done. Remove the fish, thicken the liquor with rolled cracker or flour, pour over the fish and serve. Sauce or wine can be added if desired.

Escalloped Fish. Take any cold fresh fish, as trout or whitefish; that left from a previous meal will do nicely; pick into flakes and be careful to free from all bones, put in the bottom of an earthen pudding dish a layer of cracker crumbs then a layer of fish, put in a little pepper, salt if necessary, add a tablespoonful of melted butter, then another layer of crumbs, then of fish, seasoning and so on until the dish is nearly full. Have a layer of cracker on top and over the whole pour enough milk to nearly cover, put a small plate on top and bake for thirty or forty minutes in a brisk oven. Ten minutes before serving, take off the plate to let it brown. If possible serve out of the dish in which it was prepared by placing the dish inside another and putting a garnish of parsley around the edge.

Eel with Tartare Sauce. Take 2 lbs. of eels, 1 carrot, 1 onion, a little flour, 1 glass of sherry; salt, pepper and nutmeg to taste; bread crumbs, 1 egg, 2 tablespoonfuls of vinegar. Rub the butter on the bottom of the stewpan; cut up the carrot and onion, and stir them over the fire for five minutes; dredge in a little flour, add the wine and seasoning, and boil for half an hour. Skin and wash the eels, cut them into pieces, put them to the other ingredients, and simmer till tender. When they are done take them out, let them get cold, cover them with egg and bread crumbs, and fry them a nice brown. Put them on a dish, pour sauce piquante over, and serve them hot.

Fillets of Mackerel. Procure 2 large mackerel, 1 oz. butter, 1 small bunch of chopped herbs, 3 tablespoonfuls of good fish stock, 3 tablespoonfuls of French white sauce, salt, cayenne and lemon juice to taste. Clean the fish, and fillet it; scald the herbs, chop them fine, and put them with the butter and stock into a stewpan. Lay in the mackerel, and simmer very gently for 10 minutes; take them out, and put them on a hot dish. Dredge in a little flour, add the other ingredients, give one boil, and pour it over the mackerel.

The Mackerel.

Salmon with Caper Sauce. Take 2 slices of salmon, ¼ lb. butter, ½ teaspoonful of chopped parsley, 1 shalot, salt, pepper, and grated nutmeg to taste. Lay the salmon in a baking dish, place pieces of butter over it, and add the other ingredients, rubbing a little of the seasoning into the fish; baste it frequently; when done take it out and drain for a minute or two; lay it in a dish, pour caper sauce over it, and serve. Salmon dressed in a similar way, and with tomato sauce, is very delicious.

Stewed Trout. You need 2 good-sized trout, ½ onion, cut in thin slices; a little parsley, 2 cloves, 1 blade of mace, 2 bay leaves, a little thyme, salt and pepper to taste, 1 pint of stock, 1 glass of claret or port wine, 1 oz. each of butter and flour. Wash the fish very clean, and wipe it quite dry. Lay it in a stewpan, with all the ingredients but the butter and flour, and simmer gently for half an hour, or rather more, should the fish be not quite done. Take it out, strain the gravy, thicken; pour it over the trout and serve.

The Bay.

SHELL FISH AND HOW TO PREPARE IT

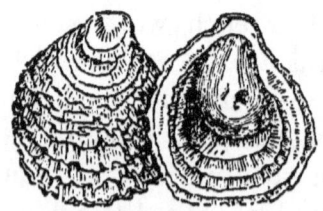

The Oyster.

Oysters on the Half Shell. Oysters to be eaten on the half shell should not be opened until just before serving. If possible get a market man to open your oysters for you or at least show you how it is done. About six are allowed for each person. Put the oysters on the half shell on a dinner plate, put a slice of lemon in the center and serve.

Oysters on the Half Shell, No. 2. Place half a dozen oysters on the half shell on a dinner plate, and an empty shell in the middle to contain the vinegar, etc. If it is not convenient to obtain shell oysters, very nice ones can be obtained in bulk; these are served on small plates with a slice of lemon or on regular oyster plates, which have cavities for half a dozen oysters, also extra ones for the seasoning. Put both oysters and plates on the ice for an hour or two before serving.

Oysters on a Block of Ice. Saw a block of ice to fit a platter, square if you have one. A block twelve or fourteen inches square, by eight or nine deep, is a nice size. Into the middle of the block make a cavity by placing on it a tin basin of hot water; as the ice melts pour off the water and keep renewing the water in the tin until the cavity will hold as many oysters as you wish to serve. You can judge the capacity of the cavity by that of the basin. Drain the oysters in a colander, then put them in the ice; garnish or trim the dish with parsley, celery, cress or flowers. This is not only a nice way to serve oysters, but is also an elegant ornament for a table.

Fried Oysters. Put the oysters in a colander, pour water over them, then take out and wipe dry. Have some crackers rolled fine, season with pepper and salt and put on a platter. Beat an egg and dip the oysters in it, then roll in the cracker crumb and lay them on a plate covered with the cracker dust. Fry crisp and brown in hot lard or butter, or half and half of each. Serve at once.

Broiled Oysters. Dry large selected oysters, place on a fine wire broiler, turning often. Have some toast prepared, butter the oysters, season with salt and pepper, place on the toast, put in the oven for a moment to heat, and serve.

Oysters Roasted in the Shell. Wash the shells and wipe them dry, put in a baking pan and bake for twenty or twenty-five minutes in a brisk oven. Serve on hot plates as soon as taken from the oven.

Escalloped Oysters. Put a quart of oysters in a colander, wash thoroughly by pouring cold water over them. Reduce eight or ten crackers to dust by rolling them. Butter an earthen pudding dish, put a layer of cracker dust in the bottom of the dish, then a layer of oysters, sprinkle with salt and pepper and pour then two tablespoonfuls of melted butter and three of milk, then another of cracker and so on until the dish is nearly full. Have a layer of the cracker dust on top with small lumps of butter through it. Bake about one half hour.

Oyster Stew. Let three pints of water come to a boil, put in one quart of oysters, half a cup of butter and season with salt and pepper, let it boil up once more and serve at once.

Milk Stew. One quart of milk and one pint of water, let them boil together, then add one quart of oysters, a lump of butter the size of an egg, season with salt and pepper and let come to a boil once more, then add a double handful of crushed crackers and serve.

Pickled Oysters. Put in a porcelain kettle a hundred large oysters with the liquor and simmer until the edges curl; take out the oysters and add to the liquor a scant pint of vinegar, ten or a dozen blades of mace, a tablespoonful each of peppercorn and cloves; let it come to a boil and pour over the oysters.

Oyster Pie. Line a pudding dish with a rich biscuit crust and dredge well with flour, put in a quart of washed oysters, season with salt and pepper, add two tablespoonfuls of butter and half a cup of milk, dredge with flour, put on the top crust cutting a small opening for the steam to escape. Bake about half an hour.

Oyster Patties. Boil a quart of oysters with just enough liquor to cover them; as soon as they come to a boil, season with salt and pepper and three tablespoonfuls of butter.

Shell Fish and How to Prepare It

Line some patty pans with puff paste, fill with the oysters and cover then well with rolled cracker. Bake fifteen or twenty minutes.

Fricassed Oysters. Put in a stewpan a pint of drained oysters, add a tablespoonful of hot water, salt and pepper, and a dash of cayenne pepper. Boil for about three minutes, shaking the pan to keep from sticking. Strain out the oysters and add to the liquor a gill of cream. Cook, but do not brown, a tablespoonful each of butter and flour together. Add slowly the oyster liquor and cream; when boiling hot stir in one well beaten egg, add the oysters, pour the whole over buttered toast, and serve.

Boiled Lobster. Put in a kettle of water and add a good sized handful of salt; when the water boils fast plunge in the lobsters alive. Boil for about half an hour; take out the fish and rub the shell with a little oil or lard, split the body the whole length with a sharp knife, crack the claws, cut off the head, and serve.

The Lobster.

Broiled Lobster. Take the meat of the claws and tail; split if too thick, season with salt and pepper, and dust with flour; put in a wire broiler and cook over a clear fire; as it cooks, pour over it a little melted butter; when a nice brown put on a hot dish and serve. Sauce can be added if desired.

Lobster Cutlets. Take two cans of lobster or the meat of a large fresh one and cut into pieces half an inch square.

Put in a stewpan a lump of butter the size of an egg and cook into it a small tablespoonful of flour and two rolled crackers, then add a cupful of milk and a beaten egg; when it boils, add the lobster, stir and take off the fire. Butter a square tin pan and pour the mixture into it. It should be about an inch thick. When cool cut in squares, dip in beaten egg, then in cracker crumbs, put in a wire basket, plunge in hot fat and fry to a nice brown. Arrange on a hot platter, garnish with parsley, and serve.

Lobster Curry. Put in a frying pan a lump of butter size of an egg and shred into it a small onion, and fry brown; when brown add a tablespoonful of flour, two small teaspoonfuls of curry powder, a very little cayenne and a pinch of salt; then add two cupfuls of milk or water; when it boils up add the meat of one large lobster or two cans of lobster, cut into small bits, simmer a few minutes; pour on a hot platter, border with rice croquettes and serve.

Soft Shell Crabs. After lifting off the shell, remove the spongy substance found on the back, pull off the apron, season with salt and pepper, and fry in hot fat for about ten minutes.

The Crab.

Clam Chowder. One-half pound salt pork cut in dice, one-half an onion minced fine, fry them together, strain off the grease and put in one and one-half gallons of stock; let it boil, add six large potatoes, cut in slices or dice, add three dozen clams cut up; when potatoes are quite soft add one quart of boiling milk, one-half pound good butter, season with salt and pepper; if not thick enough dissolve two tablespoonfuls of corn starch, and thicken the soup with it.

Mussels. Take one quart of mussels, one onion, parsley, one oz. of butter, one oz. of flour, one or two eggs, vinegar. Clean the shell and put the mussels in a pan with a little water and vinegar, mix parsley, pepper and salt. Set them over a small fire; as soon as the shells open they are done. Melt the butter in another pan, add the flour and the strained liquor, then the yolks of eggs. Pour over the mussels, and serve at once. Chopped parsley may be added.

Lobster Patties. Take minced lobster, four tablespoonfuls of French white sauce, six drops of anchovy sauce, lemon juice, cayenne to taste. Line the patty pans with puff paste, and fill each with flour; cover with paste, brush over with egg, and bake of a light color. Take as much lobster as is required, mince the meat very fine, and add the above ingredients; stir it over the fire for five minutes; remove the lids of the patty pans, take out the flour, fill with the mixture, and replace the covers.

Patties.

Buttered Prawns. Needed one pint of picked prawns, three-quarters of a pint of stock; thickening of butter and flour; salt, cayenne and nutmeg to taste. Pick the prawns and put them into stewpan with the stock. Add a thickening of butter and flour, season, and simmer gently for three minutes. Serve on a dish garnished with fried bread or toasted sippets. Cream sauce may be substituted for the gravy.

The Prawn.

To Choose Lobsters. These are chosen more by weight than size; the heaviest are best; a good, small-sized one will not infrequently be found to weigh as heavily as one much larger. If fresh, a lobster will be lively and the claws have a strong motion when the eyes are pressed with the fingers.

The male is best for boiling; the flesh is firmer, and the shell a brighter red; it may be readily distinguished from the female; the tail is narrower, and the two uppermost fins within the tail are stiff and hard. Those of the hen lobster are not so, and the tail is broader.

FISHES, MEATS AND THEIR APPROPRIATE SAUCES

Roast Beef.............. { Grated Horseradish. Tomato Catsup. Worcestershire Sauce.

Boiled Mutton............ { Caper Sauce.

Roast Mutton............ { Stewed Gooseberry.

Roast Lamb.............. { Mint Sauce.

Roast Pork.............. { Apple Sauce.

Roast Turkey............ { Cranberry Sauce. Celery Sauce.

Roast Chicken........... { Plum or Grape Catsup. Currant Jelly.

Boiled Turkey........... { Oyster Sauce.

Roasted Venison or Duck.. { Black Currant Jelly.

Pigeon Pie.............. { Mushroom Sauce.

Broiled Steak............ { Mushrooms or Fried Onions.

Roast Goose............. { Stewed Gooseberries. Apple Sauce.

Broiled Mackerel......... { Stewed Gooseberries.

Fried Salmon............ { Egg Sauce. Cream Sauce. Stewed Tomato.

Boiled or Baked Fish..... { White Cream Sauce. Old Zealand Sauce. Drawn Butter Sauce.

Boiled or Baked Cod...... { Egg Sauce. Tomato Sauce.

MEAT AND HOW TO COOK IT

BEEF

How to Select Beef. In selecting beef see that the grain is smooth and open; if the fiber parts or breaks readily on being pressed by the finger, it will be found to be tender. The color should be a deep rose, and the fat a rich cream color; if the fat is white it is an indication that the beef is young and lacking in flavor, and if of a deep yellow, the meat will be apt to be tough and of inferior quality. The choicest cuts for roasting are the sixth, seventh and eighth ribs, the sirloin and porterhouse cuts. In selecting steak, avoid the first three or four cuts, as they are apt to be broken and stringy. Sirloin and short cut porterhouse steaks are best, although the pinbone steak is considered best by some. Round steak is almost invariably tough. Beef tenderloin, cut across the grain, makes most delicious steak.

Sirloin of Beef.

Roast Beef. After selecting the roast at the market if the rib is too long for the roast to present a symmetrical appearance, have the butcher saw off about four inches of the rib and remove the chine, leaving the ribs in the roast. All meats are better flavored and more nutritious by being cooked without removing at least some of the bones. To prepare for roasting, wash the meat and wipe dry with a towel, dredge with salt and pepper, put in the pan on a rack, if you have one, pour a pint of water in the pan, and put in the oven. The oven should be very hot for the first ten or fifteen minutes, to harden the albumen, after that a more moderate heat will answer. The time required to roast beef is from ten to twenty minutes to the pound, according as it is to be rare, medium, or well done. Baste every ten or fifteen minutes. Some cooks dredge the roast with flour to prevent the juices from escaping. A few minutes before serving, remove the meat from the pan, place in the warming closet and into the gravy stir a tablespoonful of flour mixed with half a cup of water; if too thick, add more water. If there is too much fat it should be skimmed off before thickening the gravy. Serve the roast on a hot platter and the gravy in a hot boat.

Braised Beef. Take four or five pounds of beef, that with a little fat on it is best, and have it cut in squares about three inches long by two broad, and one and a half or two inches thick, dredge with salt and pepper and a little flour. Slice half a pound of fat pork into an iron dripper or braising pan, fry until crisp, draw to one side and slice in two onions and half of a small carrot, fry these until brown and then put in the beef, laying the pieces side by side, add two tablespoonfuls of water and cover, cook slowly until the meat is brown on all sides; it will take from two to three hours; when done, take out the meat, add a pint of water, stir a tablespoonful of flour mixed smooth with a little water, pour around the meat and serve.

Beef Stew. Take two or three pounds of clean beef or the remnants of a roast, cut into small pieces, put in a stewpan, cover with water and boil until tender, add a small lump of butter and thicken with a tablespoonful of flour mixed smooth with a little cold water. Some prefer a few vegetables boiled with the meat, or a few dumplings make a nice addition.

Beef a La Mode. You need about 3 lbs. of clod or flank of beef, 2 oz. of clarified dripping, 1 large onion, flour, 2 quarts of water, 12 berries of allspice, 2 bay-leaves, ½ teaspoonful of whole black pepper, salt to taste. Cut the beef into small pieces, and roll them in flour; put the dripping into a stew-pan with the onion, which should be sliced thin. Let it get quite hot; lay in the pieces of beef, and stir them well about. When nicely browned all over, add by *degrees* boiling water in the above proportion, and, as the water is added, keep the whole well stirred. Put in the spice, bay-leaves, and seasoning, cover the stew-pan closely, and set it by the side of the fire to stew *very gently*, till the meat becomes quite tender, which will be in about three hours, when it will be ready to serve. Remove the bay-leaves before it is sent to table.

Pimento. (Allspice.)

Scotch Roll. Take four or five pounds of the flank of a beef, wash and dry with a towel, spread on the board and dredge with salt and pepper. Make a dressing of a quart of bread crumbs, moistened with milk or water, and seasoned with two tablespoonfuls of melted butter, a small onion chopped fine, a tablespoonful of powdered sage, and pepper and salt to taste, mix all well together and spread evenly over the meat. Roll up and tie with twine, put in a pan with a pint of water and bake for two or three hours, rolling over often so as to cook even on all sides.

Fried Beefsteak. In very hot frying pan put a little fat then your steak, season with salt and pepper; fry to a nice brown; cover not while cooking. When done, spread some good butter over it and serve.

Broiled Beefsteak. Have your steak from three-quarters to an inch in thickness. Never pound steak. Butter your steak and broil quickly over a clear fire, season with salt and pepper, put a piece of good butter on a hot plate and the steak on top. Serve at once.

Hamburger Steak. Chop a pound of lean beef very fine, a small piece of suet makes a good addition; shred an onion, mix with the beef, season with salt and pepper, and a little savory; fry in butter and serve.

Corned Beef. It takes a cook to make nice corned beef This meat shou'd be boiled slow and when done take pot and all off the fire, leaving the corned beef in its stock until wanted to send to the table. Any piece left over to be used cold, should be left in the stock until cold and then taken out, put on a plate and placed in the refrigerator.

Filet of Beef Larded. Order the filet from your butcher larded. About five pounds will be enough for a dinner of eight persons. Cut an onion, a carrot and one-fourth of a turnip in slices, and put in the pan intended to roast the filet; salt the meat, pour a little fat over it and put in the oven to roast. Should the top or larding ends get too brown, butter a piece of paper on both sides and place over the meat. Thirty minutes will be required to cook a five pound filet rare. Serve with mushroom sauce.

Beefsteak Toast. Chop pieces of cold steak very fine, put in a stew pan with a small lump of butter and enough water to more than cover. Boil twenty minutes, then stir in a well beaten egg. Season with salt and pepper, pour over toasted bread and serve hot.

Beef Kidney. Take one kidney, one desertspoonful of minced parsley, 1 teaspoonful of minced shalot, salt and pepper to taste, ¼ pint of gravy, 3 tablespoonfuls of sherry. Take off a little of the kidney fat, mince it very fine, and put it in a frying pan; slice the kidney, sprinkle over it parsley and shalots in the above proportion, add a seasoning of pepper and salt, and fry it of a nice brown. When it is done enough, dredge over a little flour, and pour in the gravy and sherry. Let it just simmer, but not boil any more, or the kidney would harden; serve very hot, and garnish with croûtons. Where the flavor of the shalot is disliked, it may be omitted, and a small quantity of savory herbs substituted for it.

Beef Kidney, No. 2. (A more simple method.) Cut the kidney into thin slices, flour them, and fry of a nice brown. When done, make a gravy in the pan by pouring away the fat, putting in a small piece of butter, ¼ pint of boiling water, pepper and salt, and a tablespoonful of mushroom ketchup. Let the gravy just boil up, pour over the kidney and serve.

Beefsteak Pie. Take three pounds of steak, seasoning to taste, of salt, cayenne and black pepper, crust, water and the yolk of an egg. Have the steaks cut from a rump that has hung a few days, that they may be tender, and be

Beefsteak Pie.

particular that every portion is perfectly sweet. Cut the steaks into pieces about three inches long and two wide, allowing a *small* piece of fat to each piece of lean, and arrange the meat in layers in a pie-dish. Between each layer sprinkle a seasoning of salt, pepper and, when liked, a few grains of cayenne. Fill the dish sufficiently with meat to support the crust, and to give it a nice raised appearance when baked, and not to look flat and hollow. Pour in sufficient water to half fill the dish, and border it with paste (*see* PASTRY); brush it over with a little water, and put on the cover; slightly press down the edges with the thumb, and trim off close to the dish. Ornament the pie with leaves or pieces of paste, cut in any shape that fancy may direct, brush it over with the beaten yolk of an egg; make a hole in the top of the crust, and bake in a hot oven for about an hour and a half. The addition of some sheep's kidneys is an improvement; or, if these cannot be had, some bullock's kidney, cut up small, is almost as good, and forms an excellent gravy.

Beef Cake. Take the remains of cold roast beef; to each pound of cold meat allow ¼ lb. of bacon or ham; seasoning to taste, of pepper and salt, 1 small bunch of minced savory herbs, 1 or 2 eggs. Mince the beef very finely (if under done, it will be better), add to it the bacon, which must also be chopped very small, and mix well together. Season, stir in the herbs, and bind with an egg, or 2 should 1 not be sufficient. Make it into small square cakes, about half an inch thick, fry them in hot dripping, and serve in a dish with good gravy poured round them.

Boiled Tongue. You need one tongue, a bunch of savory herbs and water. If the tongue is salted, it must be soaked in fresh water over night if fresh, salt must be added to the water in

which it is boiled; when tender take out of the kettle, put in a pan, pour cold water over it, and peel off the skin, trim off the roots and tip, and serve.

Stewed Ox-Tails. Procure 2 ox-tails, 1 onion, 3 cloves, 1 blade of mace, ¼ teaspoonful of whole black pepper, ¼ teaspoonful of allspice, ½ teaspoonful of salt, a small bunch of savory herbs, thickening of butter and flour, 1 tablespoonful of lemon juice, 1 tablespoonful of mushroom ketchup. Divide the tails at the joints, wash and put them into a stewpan with sufficient water to cover them, and set them on the fire; when the water boils remove the scum, and add the onion cut into rings, the spice, seasoning and herbs. Cover the stewpan closely, and let the tails simmer very gently until tender, which will be in about two and a half hours. Take them out, make a thickening of butter and flour, add it to the gravy, and let it boil for a quarter of an hour. Strain it through a sieve into a saucepan, put back the tails, add the lemon juice and ketchup; let the whole just boil up, and serve. Garnish with croutons or sippets of toasted bread.

Potted Beef.  You need the remains of cold roast or boiled beef, ¼ lb. of butter, cayenne to taste, 2 blades of pounded mace. Cut up the meat into small pieces and pound it well, with a little butter, in a mortar; add a seasoning of cayenne and mace, and be very particular that the latter ingredient is reduced to the finest powder. When all the ingredients are thoroughly mixed, put it into a glass or earthen potting pot, and pour over the top a coating of clarified butter.

Creamed Beef. Put a lump of butter the size of an egg in a frying pan, when it is melted add cold roast beef, cut in thin slices or chipped dried beef, and fry to a nice brown; then add a tablespoonful of flour, and stir well; last of all add enough water or milk to make a nice cream. You can serve on toast or not, as you please.

Filet of Beef. A filet of beef is the tenderloin, but, as tenderloin is very expensive, a very good filet can be made from the "roll," which is simply the thick part of the rib separated from the bone.

Directions for cooking a filet of beef will be found under the head of Roast Beef.

Spiced Beef. Four pounds of round beef chopped fine; take from it all fat; add to it three dozen small crackers rolled fine, four eggs, one cup of milk, one tablespoonful ground mace, two tablespoonfuls of black pepper, one tablespoonful melted butter; mix well and put in any tin pan that it will just fill, packing it well; baste with butter and water, and bake two hours in a slow oven.

VEAL.

Roast Veal.  A loin of veal roasted makes a splendid dinner dish. Roast in a pan with some sliced vegetables, put a piece of bread in the pan, and it will cook to pieces and thicken the gravy; small pared potatoes baked with the meat in the same pan make a good vegetable to serve with veal; both should be basted every few minutes.

Filet of Veal.

Fricassee of Veal. The breast or shoulder of veal cut into pieces are the best for fricassee. Wash the veal and put on in cold water, let it come to a boil, take out the meat, wash again and put in fresh water once more, and let stew until done; mix a cupful of flour with half a cup of butter, dissolve this in the pan of veal, season with salt and pepper, and serve.

Breast of Veal Stuffed.  Obtain a breast of veal, boned and opened; fill your breast loosely with a good bread stuffing, sew up the open end and braise in a pan with vegetables; as for roasting only keep your pan covered; cook well done and make sauce in pan as for roast beef.

Breast of Veal.

Veal Loaf. Take three or four pounds of cold roast or boiled veal, that off the leg or loin is best; chop fine and mix in six rolled crackers, two eggs, a lump of butter the size of an egg, season with salt and pepper; mix all well together, and shape into a loaf covering the outside with cracker dust. Bake forty-five minutes. To be eaten cold.

Veal Cutlet Broiled. Season the cutlet with salt and pepper, put in a double wire broiler and cook over a quick fire; baste several times with a little melted butter, and serve hot.

Veal Cutlet Fried. Season the cutlet with salt and pepper, and let stand a few minutes before frying; then dip in beaten egg and then in cracker dust; fry in hot butter or pork fat; cook slowly until well done. Serve with tomato sauce.

Veal Cutlet.

Veal Curry. Cut two pounds of lean veal in pieces, put in a pan with a piece of butter, size of an egg, and let it fry to a nice brown; then mix in a large tablespoonful of flour, a teaspoonful of curry powder, salt and pepper; when all are well mixed, add a pint of hot water, and let it boil about twenty minutes, skimming off all fat. Rice croquettes are nice served with this dish.

Boiled Calf's Head. Procure one calf's head, without the skin, water, a little salt, 4 tablespoonfuls of melted butter, 1 tablespoonful of minced parsley, pepper and salt to taste, 1 tablespoonful of lemon juice.

Calf's Head.

After the head has been thoroughly cleaned, and the brains removed, soak it in water to blanch it. Lay the brains also in warm water to soak, and let them remain for about an hour. Put the head into a stewpan with sufficient cold water to cover it, and when it boils, add a little salt; take off every particle of scum as it rises, and boil the head until perfectly tender. Boil the brains, chop them, and mix with them melted butter, minced parsley, pepper, salt and lemon juice in the above proportion. Take up the head, skin the tongue, and put it on a small dish with the brains round it. Have ready some parsley and butter, smother the head with it, and the remainder send to table in a tureen. Bacon, ham, pickled pork, or a pig's cheek are indispensable with calf's head. The brains are sometimes chopped with hard-boiled eggs, and mixed with a little French white sauce.

Calf's Liver Sausages. Use ¾ lb. of fat bacon, 1 lb. of calf's liver, ½ lb. of bread crumbs, 3 eggs, 1 bay leaf, ¼ teaspoonful of thyme, ¼ teaspoonful of grated lemon peel, ¼ teaspoonful of nutmeg, 1 teaspoonful of salt, 1 teaspoonful of parsley, ¼ teaspoonful of pepper. Mince the bacon and liver finely, then add the remaining ingredients and incorporate thoroughly. Beat the eggs thoroughly, then moisten the mixture with them and encase it in the skins; fry them with a little butter or lard in the pan, of a nice rich brown, pricking the skins with a fork to prevent their bursting. Serve on toast or with mashed potatoes.

The Lemon Thyme.

Broiled Kidneys. Split veal kidneys lengthwise, removing all fat, and broil over a clear fire for twelve or fifteen minutes; baste with butter while broiling, season with salt, pepper, butter and a little chopped parsley. Serve hot.

Stewed Kidneys. Take beef kidney, remove all fat, and wash clean; put in a stew pan, cover with cold water and boil for one hour. Put half a cupful of butter in a frying pan with a small onion minced fine; when frying put in the kidneys, turning them over until they are a nice brown; then add a tablespoonful of flour, stir in thoroughly, and add enough of the hot stock to make a thick sauce, add half a can of mushrooms, season with salt, pepper, a tablespoonful of Worcestershire sauce and a glass of sherry. Serve on toast.

Veal and Ham Pie. You need 2 lbs. of cutlets, ½ lb. of boiled ham, 2 tablespoonfuls of minced savory herbs, ¼ teaspoonful of grated nutmeg, 2 blades of pounded mace, pepper and salt to taste, a strip of lemon peel finely minced, the yolks of 2 hard boiled eggs, ¼ pint of water, nearly ½ pint of good strong gravy, puff-crust. Cut the veal into nice square pieces, and put a layer of them at the bottom of a pie dish; sprinkle over these a portion of the herbs, spices, seasoning, lemon peel, and the yolks of the eggs cut in slices; cut the ham very thin, and put a layer of this in. Proceed in this manner until the dish is full, so arranging it that the ham comes at the top. Lay a puff-paste on the edge of the dish, and pour in about half a pint of water; cover with crust, ornament it with leaves, brush it over with the yolk of an egg, and bake in a well-heated oven for 1 to 1½ hour, or longer, should the pie be very large. When it is taken out of the oven, pour in at the top through a funnel nearly half a pint of strong gravy; this should be made sufficiently good that, when cold, it may cut in a firm jelly. This pie may be very much enriched by adding a few mushrooms, oysters, or sweet-breads; but it will be found very good without any of the last-named additions.

Fricandeau of Veal. You need a piece of the fat side of a leg of veal (about 3 lbs.), lardoons (strips of bacon cut for larding), 2 carrots, 2 large onions, 1 faggot of savory herbs, 2 blades of pounded mace, 6 whole allspice, 2 bay-leaves, pepper to taste, a few slices of fat bacon, 1 pint of stock. The veal for a fricandeau should be of the best quality, or it will not be good. It may be known by the meat being white and not thready. Take off the skin, flatten the veal on the table, then at one stroke of the knife, cut off as much as is required, for a fricandeau with an uneven

Veal

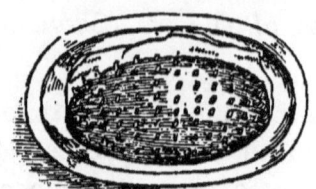

Fricandeau of Veal.

surface never looks well. Trim it, and with a sharp knife make two or three slits in the middle, that it may taste more of the seasoning. Now lard it thickly with fat bacon, as lean gives a red color to the fricandeau. Slice the vegetables and put these, with the herbs and spices, in the *middle* of a stewpan, with a few slices of bacon at the top; these should form a sort of mound in the centre for the veal to rest upon. Lay the fricandeau over the bacon, etc., without touching the veal. Let it gradually come to a boil; then put it over a slow and equal fire, and let it *simmer very* gently for about 2½ hours, or longer should it be very large. Baste it frequently with the liquor, and a short time before serving, put it into a brisk oven, to make the bacon firm, which otherwise would break when it was glazed. Dish the fricandeau, keep it hot, skim off the fat from the liquor, and reduce it quickly to a glaze, with which glaze the fricandeau, and serve with a puree of whatever vegetable happens to be in season—spinach, sorrel, asparagus, cucumbers, peas, etc.

The Basil.

PORK

Roast Pork.

Roast Pork. Take five or six pounds of the loin, wash clean and dredge with salt and pepper, a little flour, and a teaspoonful of powdered sage; put in a pan with a teacupful of water and roast two hours.

Pork Tenderloin Broiled. Have your butcher either split the tenderloin lengthwise or cut crosswise and flatten; put on a wire-broiler and cook over a clear fire; when done put in a pan with a lump of butter and let the juice of the meat and the butter come to a boil. This makes a delicious sauce; season with salt and pepper and serve hot.

Salt Pork. Cut into slices, put in a pan, pour on cold water and let come to a boil. This, unless the pork is very salt, will freshen sufficiently. Take out the pork, throw the water away, roll the pork in flour, and fry to a nice brown. Serve with cream gravy.

Salt Pork No. 2. Freshen as above, make a batter of one beaten egg, 2 tablespoonfuls of milk and one of flour, well beaten together, put a little fat in the frying pan, dip the pork in the batter, fry slowly and serve hot.

Spare Rib of Pork.

Salt Pork No. 3. Cut the pork in slices and soak for twelve hours in equal quantities of milk and water; then fry carefully, as it is liable to scorch. When done, take out the meat, pour off part of the fat, and into the remainder pour a cupful of cream, let it cook two or three minutes, pour over the pork and serve.

Pork and Beans. Soak two pounds of beans in cold water over night, wash thoroughly, put in a pot or jar in which they are to be baked, cover with clear stock, put a piece of freshened salt pork on top and bake in a moderate oven for six hours, add water from time to time as the beans cook dry. Another way to bake beans is to soak over night, put in the pot next morning with a piece of salt pork and boil until done, strain the liquor off the beans, stir in two tablespoonfuls of molasses, a teaspoonful of mustard, pepper, and salt, if necessary, put in a baking pan, with the pork in the middle and bake in the oven for thirty or forty minutes.

Broil Sausages. Take off the skin and flatten the link to half its thickness, put in a wire broiler and broil until done over a clear fire, arrange on a platter, put a small lump of butter on each piece, put in the oven for a few moments, and serve.

Sausages.

Roast Pig. A pig from three to six weeks old is best for roasting. Leave the pig whole and wash inside and out, chop the liver and mix with equal quantities of bread crumbs and mashed potatoes, add two chopped onions, a little parsley, and salt and pepper to taste, mix into a paste with two beaten eggs, a lump of butter and about a teacupful of milk, stuff the pig with dressing, sew it up, put in a pan and roast from one and a half to two hours, basting frequently. Make a dressing with a glass of wine, some of the stuffing, and the drippings. When the pig is done, put on a platter, put

Roast Sucking Pig.

a lemon or apple in its mouth, and serve with the sauce.

Baked Pork Tenderloin. Split the tenderloin through lengthwise; make a stuffing of bread, seasoned with salt, pepper and some kind of sweet herb, stuff the tenderloin and tie a string around it to keep the filling in, add a cupful of water and bake some forty to fifty minutes; baste frequently.

Boiled Ham. If the ham is quite salt and has been cured some time, it will require soaking from ten to twenty-four hours, during which the water should be changed several times. After the ham has been soaked sufficiently, scrape and clean thoroughly, cutting away any part that may be rusty or discolored. Put the ham in any vessel suitable for boiling it and cover plentifully with water, let it come to a boil very slowly and skim off the scum as it rises. When it boils clear, set the pot on the back of the stove and let it simmer slowly but steadily until done, then take out of the liquor, strip off the skin, dust with cracker or bread crumbs and put in the oven and brown.

Ham.

Pig's Feet Broiled. Pig's feet should be boiled for about six hours. When cold, split in two and broil on a wire broiler over a clear fire, baste with butter, seam with salt and pepper and serve.

Fried Pig's Feet. Boil the pig's feet and when cold split open, dip in beaten egg, then in bread crumbs and fry in hot fat and serve with tomato sauce.

Fried Sausages. Prick the sausages with a fork (this prevents them from bursting), and put them into a frying pan with a small piece of butter. Keep moving the pan about, and turn the sausages three or four times. In from 10 to 12 minutes they will be sufficiently cooked, unless they are *very large*, when a little more time should be allowed for them. Dish them with or without a piece of toast under them, and serve very hot. In some countries, sausages are boiled and served on toast. They should be plunged into boiling water, and simmered for about 10 or 12 minutes.

NOTE.—Sometimes, in close, warm weather, sausages very soon turn sour; to prevent this, put them in the oven for a few minutes with a small piece of butter to keep them moist. When wanted for table, they will not require so long frying as uncooked sausages.

Ham and Eggs. Have the ham cut in very thin slices, cut off rind and any imperfections or discolorations that may be in the meat and fry carefully until done, remove to a platter and break the eggs one at a time in a saucer and then slip it into the hot fat, being careful not to break the yolk. Do not turn the eggs over, but baste the hot grease over them, to cook the top; when done, lay around the ham, pour on the gravy, and serve.

Breakfast Bacon. Cut nice bacon in thin slices and fry to a crisp. This is nice to serve with calf's liver.

Boiled Bacon. As bacon is frequently excessively salt,

Boiled Bacon.

let it be soaked in warm water for an hour or two previous to dressing it; then pare off the rusty parts, and scrape under-side and rind as clean as possible. Put it into a saucepan of cold water, let it come gradually to a boil, and as fast as the scum rises to the surface of the water, remove it. Let it simmer very gently until it is *thoroughly* done; then take it up, strip off the skin, and sprinkle over the bacon a few bread-raspings, and garnish with tufts of cauliflower or Brussels sprouts. When served alone, young and tender broad beans or green peas are the usual accompaniments.

Collared Pig's Face. (A breakfast or luncheon dish.) You need one pig's face; salt. For brine, 1 gallon of spring water, 1 lb. of common salt, ½ handful of chopped juniper berries, 6 bruised cloves, 2 bay-leaves, a few sprigs of thyme, basil, sage, ¼ oz. of saltpeter. For forcemeat, ½ lb. of ham, ½ lb. of bacon, 1 teaspoonful of mixed spices, pepper to taste, ¼ lb. of lard, 1 tablespoonful of minced parsley, 6 young onions. Singe the head carefully, bone it without breaking the skin, and rub it well with salt.

Pig's Face.

Make the brine by boiling the above ingredients for a quarter of an hour, and letting it stand to cool. When cold, pour it over the head, and let it steep in this for 10 days, turning and rubbing it often. Then wipe, drain and dry it. For the forcemeat, pound the ham and bacon very finely, and mix with these the remaining ingredients, taking care that the whole is thoroughly incorporated. Spread this equally over the head, roll it tightly in a cloth, and bind it securely with broad tape. Put it into a saucepan with a few meat trimmings, and cover it with stock, let it simmer gently for four hours, and be particular that it does not stop boiling the whole time. When quite tender, take it up, put it between two dishes and a heavy weight on top, and when cold, remove the cloth and tape. It should be sent to table on a napkin, or garnished with a piece of deep white paper, with a ruche at the top.

Pork Chops. You need a loin or fore-loin of pork, egg and bread crumbs, salt and pepper to taste; to every tablespoonful of bread crumbs allow ½ teaspoonful of minced sage: clarified butter. Cut the cutlets from a loin or fore-loin of pork; trim them the same as mutton cutlets, and scrape the top part of the bone. Brush them over with egg, sprinkle with bread crumbs, with which have been mixed minced sage and a seasoning of pepper and salt; drop a little clarified butter on them, and press the crumbs well down. Put the frying pan on the fire, put in some lard; when this is hot, lay in the cutlets, and fry them a light brown on both sides. Take them out, put them before the fire to dry the greasy moisture from them, and dish them on mashed potatoes. Serve with them any sauce that may be preferred, such as tomato sauce, sauce piquante, or pickled gherkins.

Roast Leg of Pork. Take a leg of pork, a little oil, stuffing of sage and onions. Choose a small leg of pork, and score the skin across in narrow strips, about a quarter of an inch apart. Cut a slit in the knuckle, loosen the skin, and fill it with a sage and onion stuffing. Brush the joint over with a little salad oil (this makes the crackling crisper, and a better color), and put it down to a bright, clear fire, not too near, as that would cause the skin to blister. Baste it well, and serve with a little gravy made in the dripping pan, and do not omit to send to the table with it a tureen of well made apple sauce.

To Bake a Ham. You need a ham; a common crust. As a ham for baking should be well soaked, let it remain in the water for at least 12 hours. Wipe it dry, trim away any rusty places underneath, and cover it with a common crust, taking care that this is of sufficient thickness all over to keep the gravy in. Place it in a moderately-heated oven, and bake for nearly 4 hours. Take off the crust, and skin, and cover with raspings, the same as for boiled ham, and garnish the knuckle with a paper frill. This method of cooking ham is, by many persons, considered far superior to boiling it, as it cuts fuller of gravy and has a finer flavor, besides keeping a much longer time good.

MUTTON AND LAMB

Roast Mutton. Wash and wipe dry a nice leg of mutton; with salt, pepper and flour, put in the dripping pan with a little water. Baste frequently with the drippings. Cook from an hour and a quarter to an hour and a half. A few vegetables sliced in the pan always improve the flavor of the roast.

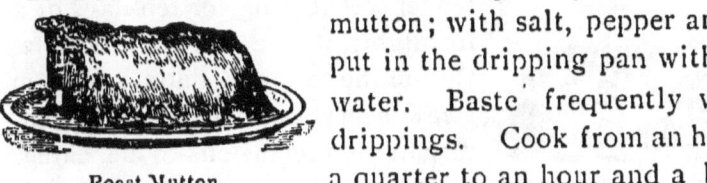

Roast Mutton.

Irish Stew. Blanch three pounds of mutton chops by dipping alternately in hot and cold water, put in a stewpan and barely cover with water; let come to a boil; skim carefully; season with salt, parsley, mace and a few whole pepper corns, boil half an hour; then add a quart of small onions, boil half an hour longer, and add a quart of small potatoes; boil until done; lay the chops around the edge of a platter, skim out the potatoes and onions, and put in the middle; thicken the gravy with a very little flour and pour over the vegetables. Sprinkle over the whole two or three tablespoonfuls of finely chopped parsley.

Braised Leg of Mutton. You need 1 small leg of mutton, 4 carrots, 3 onions, 1 faggot of savory herbs, a bunch of parsley, seasoning to taste of pepper and salt, a few slices of bacon, a few veal trimmings, ½ pint of gravy or water. Line the bottom of a braising pan with a few slices of bacon;

put in the carrots, onions, herbs, parsley, and seasoning, and over these place the mutton. Cover the whole with a few more slices of bacon and the veal trimmings, pour in the gravy or water, and stew very *gently* for 4 hours. Strain the gravy, reduce it to a glaze over a sharp fire, glaze the mutton with it, and send it to table; place on a dish of white haricot beans boiled tender, or garnished with glazed onions.

Roast Saddle of Mutton. To insure this joint being tender, let it hang for ten days or a fortnight, if the weather permits. Cut off the tail and flaps, and trim away every part that has not indisputable pretensions to be eaten, and have the skin taken off and skewered on again. Put it down to a bright, clear fire, and when the joint has been cooking for an hour, remove the skin and dredge it with flour. It should not be placed too near the fire, as the fat should not be in the slightest degree burned, but kept constantly basted, both before and after the skin is removed. Sprinkle some salt over the joint; make a little gravy in the dripping pan; pour it over the meat, which send to table with a tureen of made gravy and red currant jelly.

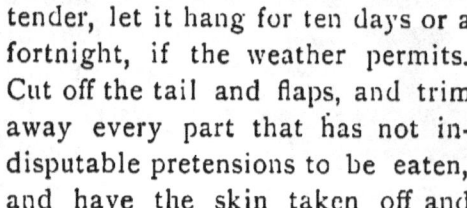
Saddle of Mutton.

Haricot of Mutton. The breast or shoulder of mutton is generally used for a haricot. Put your meat with a lump of butter in a roasting pan and put in the oven and roast to a nice brown; transfer to a saucepan, cover with stock, and let boil; cut a carrot or nice sweet turnip into regular shaped pieces and let them boil with the mutton; also prepare a few small onions and put in the stew whole; pare and cut some potatoes the same shape as the other vegetables, and put in stew; season with salt and pepper, a

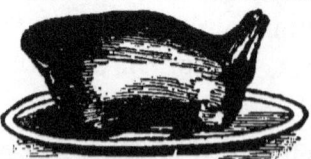
Shoulder of Mutton.

Mutton and Lamb

little Worcestershire sauce, and a glass of sherry. This stew should have a nice brown color. If the sauce is too thin thicken with a little flour.

Roast Saddle of Lamb. This joint is now very much in vogue, and is generally considered a nice one for a small party. Have ready a clear, brisk fire, and put down the joint at a little distance, to prevent the fat from scorching; keep it well basted all the time it is cooking. Serve with mint sauce and a fresh salad, and send to table with it either peas, cauliflowers, or spinach.

Breast of Mutton Fried. Cut a two-inch square out of the breast and boil until very tender; lay the pieces on a platter and draw the bones out very carefully; after boning the pieces lay in a pan, cover with a plate, put a weight on top, and press until cold; cut into squares suitable for serving, dip in beaten egg, then in bread crumbs and fry in hot fat, and serve with tomato sauce and string beans.

Roast Lamb.

Scotch Haggis. You need a sheep's pluck and stomach, ½ lb. of suet, ½ lb. of oatmeal, an onion, pepper and salt. Have the stomach bag properly cleaned by the butcher, wash it well and put it in a saucepan of cold water and bring to the boil, which will make the bag contract. Take it out of the water at once, wash and scrape it well and lay it in salt and water. Wash the pluck thoroughly and boil it gently for one hour and a half with the windpipe hanging out over the edge of the pot that all impurities may escape through it. Take all gristly parts from the lungs and heart, and mince the remainder, grate the best parts of the liver, chop the suet and onion fine, toast the oatmeal in the oven and put all in a basin, with a dessertspoonful of salt and rather less than half the quantity of pepper. Moisten with half a pint of the liquor in which the pluck was boiled. Take the stomach bag from the brine, and keeping the smooth side inside, fill it with the mixture (not quite full) and sew it up. Put the haggis in a pot of boiling water and boil gently for 3 hours, with a plate under to prevent it from sticking, and prick it now and then with a needle to prevent its bursting.

Kidneys on Toast. Procure 2 sheep's kidneys, or 1½ lb. of bullock's kidney, 1 oz. of butter, cayenne, a squeeze of lemon, salt, 2 slices of hot buttered toast. Stew the kidneys with a very little water until tender, remove the skin and gristle, and pound smooth in a mortar, with the butter, lemon juice, salt and cayenne to taste. Spread the mixture on the toast, which should be buttered on both sides, and put in the oven to get hot through.

Kidneys on Toast.

Breast of Lamb and Green Peas. Remove the skin from a breast of lamb, put it into a saucepan of boiling water, and let it simmer for 5 minutes. Take it out and lay it in cold water. Line the bottom of a stewpan with a few thin slices of bacon; lay the lamb on these; peel the lemon, cut it into slices, and put these on the meat, to keep it white and make it tender; cover with 1 or 2 more slices of bacon; add a pint of stock, onion, and herbs, and set it on a slow fire to simmer very gently until tender. Have ready some green peas, put these on a dish, and place the lamb on the top of these. The appearance of this dish may be much improved by glazing the lamb, and spinach may be substituted for the peas when variety is desired.

Broiled Mutton Chops. Cut the chops from a well-hung, tender loin of mutton, remove a portion of the fat, and trim them into a nice shape; slightly beat and level them; place the gridiron over a bright, clear fire, rub the bars with a little fat, and lay on the chops. Whilst broiling frequently turn them, and in about 8 minutes they will be done. Season with pepper and salt, dish them on a very hot

Mutton and Lamb

dish, rub a small piece of butter on each chop, and serve very hot and expeditiously.

Lamb Chops Saute with Peas. Trim the lamb chops neatly and evenly, place in a frying pan with a little butter, season with salt and pepper, and fry to a nice brown; when done arrange on a platter alternating each chop with a nicely browned piece of toast; strain the water off a can of French peas, put in a pan with a piece of butter, season with salt and pepper, stir until hot, and pour in the middle of platter.

Boiled Leg of Mutton. Select a nice leg of mutton, cut off the shank bone, wash and put in a pot with a handful of salt, cover with water and let it come to a boil, skim until clear; then set the pot on the back part of the stove and let boil very slowly until tender; it will take from two to three hours. Serve with caper sauce or drawn butter gravy.

Leg of Mutton.

The Capsicum.

POULTRY AND GAME

Turkey Stuffed with Oysters. Select a nice plump turkey, draw and wash thoroughly. Prepare stuffing in the following manner: Take a pint of oysters, put in a pan and stew in their own liquor, drain off the liquor and cut the oysters into bits, add half a cup of butter, a shredded onion and a spoonful of powdered thyme; let all simmer together; moisten three pints of stale bread crumbs with the oyster liquor, add the oysters and onion, break in three eggs, season with salt and pepper, and mix all thoroughly together; if the stuffing is too dry, add some milk; if otherwise, add more bread crumbs; stuff the turkey, sew up the openings, take some butter in the hand and rub over the outside, dredge with salt, pepper and flour, put in a pan with a pint of water, place in the oven and wash. No time can be given, as so much depends upon the age, size and condition of the fowl. A large turkey a year old will take as much, as three and a half, four, or even five hours of slow roasting; while a younger and smaller one may not require more than half that time. Baste every ten or fifteen minutes.

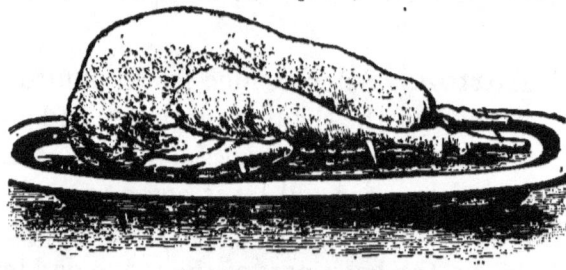

Turkey Ready for Cooking.

Stuffed Turkey, Giblet Sauce. Stuff a turkey with the following dressing: Take stale bread and cut in pieces,

Poultry and Game

rub fine with your hands the soft part; what you cannot rub fine put in a pan and pour boiling water over it, just enough to soften, not soak, cover closely until steamed, put with the crumbs, mix thoroughly with plenty of butter, pepper and salt, and a little sage or chopped onion to suit taste. While the turkey is roasting boil the gizzard of the turkey well done, put the liver and heart in hot water for a few minutes, then fry brown in a little butter; when this is done chop all together very fine, and set aside for use. When the turkey is done, put on a platter and set in a warm place, skim all the fat off the gravy in which the turkey was roasted, add the chopped giblets, thicken with a little chopped parsley just before serving.

Turkey Stuffed with Chestnuts. Put three dozen chestnuts in a pan, and bake in the oven; as the skin begins to crack take them out, skin and chop fine; put in a frying pan with a piece of butter, half an onion cut fine, and fry to a nice brown; put in a glass of port wine; mix enough soaked bread with the chestnuts to make the amount of stiffening wanted; season with salt, add pepper, a little thyme; mix in four eggs and stuff the turkey. Roast as above.

Chestnut.

Chicken Fricassee. Cut nice fat chicken into joints, wash, and put in a pot, cover with cold water and let come to a boil; skim carefully as long as any scum rises; boil until well done, season with salt and pepper; cook two-thirds of a cup of flour in half a cup of butter, stir this into the chicken stock, leaving in the chicken, stir carefully to avoid breaking the chicken, toast slices of bread, cut in squares, put on a platter, pour the chicken, sauce and all, over it and serve.

Roast Chicken. Chicken can be prepared for roasting the same as turkey and any stuffings or dressings that are nice for turkey will also answer for chicken.

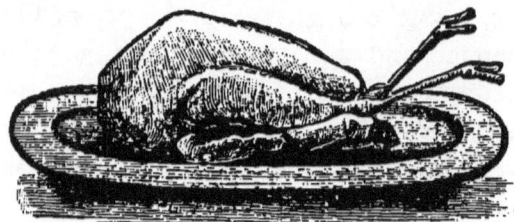
Roast Chicken.

Smothered Chicken. Cut a young chicken into joints, wash, and put in a frying pan, with half a cup of butter and the same measure of water; season with salt and cover closely; let cook until the water boils dry, let the chicken fry brown on both sides, take out and lay on a platter, put a tablespoonful of flour in the frying pan, cook till slightly brown, then add to it a cupful of milk or water, stir smooth. This will make a delicious brown gravy, pour over the chicken, set in the oven for a moment and serve.

Broiled Chicken. Only young chickens are suitable for broiling. Draw the chicken and split it down the back, wash clean, lay it on the board and break down the breast bone by pressing with the rolling pin, put on a double wire broiler, season with salt and broil over a clear fire, presenting the inside to the fire first. Baste with melted butter while broiling, and serve as soon as done.

Chicken Pie. Cut up two chickens and boil, putting on just enough water to cover them, and season with salt and pepper, skim carefully; when tender, rub two tablespoonfuls of flour in half a cup of butter and add this to the stew. Line an earthen pan with a rich crust, put in the chicken, gravy and all, cover with crust, pinching down the sides, cut an opening in the center for the steam to escape, and bake one hour.

Chicken Pot Pie. Prepare chicken as for pie, but have more gravy, put in the crust (see directions for making) and boil twenty minutes; when done place the chicken in the middle of a platter, place the crust around it, pour some of the gravy over all, and serve the rest in a gravy boat.

Pressed Chicken. Boil nice plump chickens until tender; take off the skin, and pick the meat off the bones; pick the meat up fine (do not chop) season with salt and pepper, and add a head of celery, cut fine; mix all well together. Boil the liquor in which the chicken was cooked down to less than a quart, add a lump of butter the size of an egg, half a box of gelatine, salt and pepper to taste; pour over the chicken, mix all together, put in an earthen dish, cover with a plate, put a weight on top and set away. When cold, cut in slices, and garnish with parsley.

Boiled Fowl and Rice. Take 1 fowl, mutton broth, 2 onions, 2 small blades of pounded mace, pepper and salt to taste, ¼ pint of rice, parsley and butter. Truss the fowl as for boiling, and put it into a stewpan with sufficient clear, well-skimmed mutton broth to cover it; add the onion, mace, and a seasoning of pepper and salt; stew very gently for about one hour, should the fowl be large, and about half an hour before it is ready put in the rice, which should be well washed and soaked. When the latter is tender, strain it from the liquor, and put it on a sieve reversed to dry before the fire, and in the meantime, keep the fowl hot. Dish it, put the rice round as a border, pour a little parsley and butter over the fowl, and the remainder send to table in a tureen.

Chicken Patties. Needed: The remains of cold roast chicken or fowl; to every ¼ lb. of meat allow 2 oz. of ham, 3 tablespoonfuls of cream, 2 tablespoonfuls of veal gravy, ½ teaspoonful of minced lemon peel, cayenne, salt and pepper to taste, 1 tablespoonful of lemon juice, 1 oz. of butter rolled in flour; puff paste. Mince very small the white meat from a cold roast fowl, after removing all the skin; weigh it, and to every quarter of a pound of meat allow the above proportion of minced ham. Put these into a stewpan with the remaining ingredients, stir over the fire for 10 minutes or a quarter of an hour, taking care that the mixture does not burn. Roll out some puff paste about a quarter of an inch in thickness; line the patty pans with this, put upon each a small piece of bread, and cover with another layer of paste; brush over with the yolk of an egg, and bake in a brisk oven for about a quarter of an hour. When done, cut a round piece out of the top, and with a small spoon, take out the bread (be particular in not breaking the outside border of the crust), and fill the patties with the mixture.

Roast Pigeons. Clean and stuff the birds, and pack in rows in a dripping pan, dredge with salt and pepper, and a little flour, spread over then with a knife half a teacup of butter, and pour in the pan a teacupful of water, put in a brisk oven and baste often. No definite time can be given for roasting. Young plump birds will roast in from one-half to three-quarters of an hour.

Pigeons on Toast.

NOTE.—Pigeons, to be good, should be eaten fresh (if kept a little, the flavor goes off), and they should be drawn as soon as killed. Cut off the heads and necks, truss the wings over the back, and cut off the toes at the first joint; previous to trussing, they should be carefully cleaned, as no bird requires so much washing.

Quail on Toast. Pick and clean the quail, split down the back, season with salt and pepper and baste with melted butter while broiling over a clear fire; it takes from twelve to eighteen minutes to broil quail. Have ready as many slices of nicely buttered toast as you have birds, place a bird on each slice and serve at once.

Quail on Toast No. 2. Clean, singe, and draw the quail; wash well, and put inside the bird three oysters and a lump of butter the size of a small hickory nut, put in a dripping pan and sprinkle with salt and pepper, and spread a little butter on each one, put in a hot oven, and roast for ten or twelve minutes. Toast as many slices of bread as you have quails, and slip a slice under each one, baste with butter and the gravy formed by the roasting birds, put back in the oven and roast five minutes longer, and serve hot. If the toast is liable to break up, use a tin shovel in removing the quail from the dripping pan to the platter. This is a most delicious way to cook small birds of any kind.

Quail on Toast.

Roast Goose. Parboil the goose in salt and water for half an hour, fill with stuffing, and roast as you would chicken.

Roast Duck. Roast duck as directed for chicken. A nice stuffing for duck is made of mashed potatoes, seasoned with salt, a lump of butter, and a chopped onion.

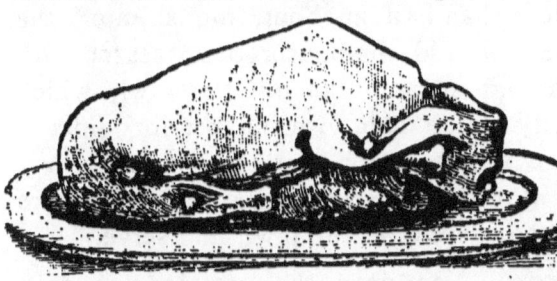
Goose Ready for Cooking.

Stewed Duck and Peas. You need the remains of cold roast duck, 2 oz. of butter, 3 or 4 slices of lean ham or bacon, 1 tablespoonful of flour, 2 pints of thin gravy, a small bunch of green onions, 3 sprigs of parsley, 3 cloves, 1 pint of young green peas, cayenne and salt to taste, 1 teaspoonful of pounded sugar. Put the butter into a stewpan; cut up the duck into joints, lay them in with the slices of lean ham or bacon; make it brown, then dredge in a tablespoonful of flour, and stir this well in before adding the gravy. Put in the onion, parsley, cloves and gravy, and when it has simmered for a quarter of an hour, add a pint of young green peas, and stew gently for about half an hour. Season with cayenne, salt and sugar; take out the duck, place it round the dish, and the peas in the middle.

Fowl a La Marengo. You need 1 large fowl, 4 tablespoonfuls of salad oil, 1 tablespoonful of flour, 1 pint of regular stock, or water, about 20 mushroom-buttons, salt and pepper to taste, 1 teaspoonful of powdered sugar, a very small piece of garlic. Cut the fowl into 8 or 10 pieces; put them with the oil into the stewpan, and brown them over a moderate fire; dredge in the above proportion of flour; when that is browned, pour in the stock or water; let it simmer very slowly for rather more than half an hour, and skim off the fat as it rises to the top; add the mushrooms; season with salt, pepper, garlic and sugar; take out the fowl, which arrange pyramidically on the dish, with the inferior joints at the bottom. Reduce the sauce by boiling it quickly over the fire, keeping it stirred until sufficiently thick to adhere to the back of a spoon; pour over the fowl, and serve.

Garlic.

Curried Chicken. You need the remains of cold roast fowls, 2 large onions, 1 apple, 2 oz. of butter, 1 dessert spoonful of curry powder, 1 teaspoonful of flour, ½ pint of gravy, 1 tablespoonful of lemon juice. Slice the onions, peel, core and chop the apple, and cut the fowl into neat joints; fry these in the butter, of a nice brown; then add the curry powder, flour and gravy, and stew for about 20

Poultry and Game

minutes. Put in the lemon juice and serve with boiled rice, either placed in a ridge round the dish or separately; 2 or 3 shalots, or a little garlic may be added, if approved.

Roast Partridge. When the bird is firmly and plumply trussed, roast it before a nice bright fire; keep it well basted, and a few minutes before serving, flour and froth it well. Dish it, and serve with gravy and bread sauce, and send to table hot and quickly. A little of the gravy should be poured over the bird.

Roast Partridge.

Roast Rabbit. Dress and clean the rabbit thoroughly, and soak in salt and water. Put in a dripping pan and dredge with salt, pepper and a little flour. Cut salt pork in thin strips and fasten on the rabbit with toothpicks, spread some butter over all, put a little water in the pan and roast in the oven until done, basting often. You can make a stuffing as for chicken, fill the rabbit, and then roast as above, if you choose.

Fried Rabbit. Dress and clean the rabbit and cut up in pieces suitable to serve, let it stand in salt and water until white, put in a kettle and boil until tender, take out of the liquor and let it stand until it stops steaming. Have the frying pan half full of hot drippings or lard, dip the rabbit in beaten egg, then in cracker dust and fry in the hot fat; serve at once.

Rabbits.

Stewed Rabbit. Take 1 rabbit, 2 large onions, 6 cloves, 1 small teaspoonful of chopped lemon peel, a few forcemeat balls, thickening of butter and flour, 1 large tablespoonful of mushroom ketchup. Cut the rabbit into small joints; put them into a stewpan, add the onions sliced, the cloves, and minced lemon peel. Pour in sufficient water to cover the meat, and when the rabbit is nearly done, drop in a few forcemeat balls, to which the liver has been added, finely chopped. Thicken the gravy with flour and butter, put in the ketchup, give one boil, and serve.

Roast Venison. Either the saddle or leg are fine for roasting. Have your market man lard the venison for you, then put in the dripping pan with half a pint of water and good sized lump of butter; dredge with salt and pepper and roast in a hot oven from two to three hours, basting every ten or fifteen minutes.

Roast Venison.

Broiled Venison. Put the venison steaks in the double wire broiler and broil over a clear fire. When done place on a hot platter, season with salt and pepper and pour over it some hot butter, turn it over and put on more of the butter, and serve at once.

Jugged Hare. Need 1 hare, 1½ lb. of gravy beef, ½ lb. of butter, 1 onion, 1 lemon, 6 cloves, pepper, cayenne, and salt to taste, ½ pint of port, good turkey stuffing. Skin, paunch and wash the hare, cut it into pieces, dredge them with flour, and fry in boiling butter. Have ready 1½ pint of gravy, made from the above proportion of beef, and thickened with a little flour. Put this into a jar; add the pieces of fried hare, an onion stuck with six cloves, a lemon peeled and cut in half, and a good seasoning of pepper, cayenne and salt; cover the jar down tightly, put it up to the neck in a stewpan of boiling water, and let it stew until the hare is quite tender. When nearly done, pour in the wine, and add a few stuffing balls; these must be fried or baked in the oven for a few minutes before they are put to the gravy. Serve with red currant jelly.

Larded Grouse. Clean and wash the grouse. Lard the breast and legs. Put a small skewer into the legs and through the tail. Tie firmly with twine. Dredge with salt, and rub the breast with soft butter; then dredge thickly with flour. Put into a quick oven. If it be very rare, cook twenty minutes; if wished better done, thirty minutes. The former time, as a general thing, suits gentlemen better, but thirty minutes is preferred by ladies. If the birds are cooked in a tin kitchen, it should be for thirty or thirty-five minutes. When done, place on a hot dish on which has been spread bread sauce. Sprinkle fried crumbs over both grouse and sauce. Garnish with parsley. The grouse, may, instead, be served on a hot dish, with the parsley garnish, and the sauce and crumbs served in separate dishes. The first method is the better, however, as you get in the sauce all the gravy that comes from the birds.

Grand Pacific Game Pie. Take about two dozen of woodcock, quail, snipe, or other small birds. Split each one in half and put them into a saucepan containing about a gallon of cold water, although beef broth or soup stock would be preferable. See that the fire is hot, and when the boiling point has been reached, carefully skim off all the scum from the surface, and put in for seasoning a little pepper and salt with mace, ground cloves and one bay leaf, adding half a pound slice of salt pork cut into squares, two small carrots and one onion. Boil until tender, being careful that there is enough broth to cover the game. Into another saucepan put four ounces of butter and two tablespoonfuls browned flour, mixing well and stirring into it a part of the broth or gravy so as to make a thin sauce. Strain off what broth remains in the first saucepan, removing therefrom the vegetables and spices to go with the sauce. Slice, and cut into dice shape, potatoes equal in quantity to the meat, and put in a deep baking dish; put on the top crust of dough and bake in an oven that is not too hot. If a separate pie is desired for each person the baking may be done in small vegetable dishes.

Pigeon Pie. Clean and truss three or four pigeons, rub the outside with a mixture of pepper and salt; rub the inside with a bit of butter, and fill it with a bread-and-butter stuffing, or mashed potatoes; sew up the slit, butter the sides of a tin basin or pudding-dish, and line (the sides only) with pie paste, rolled to quarter of an inch thickness, lay the birds in; for three large tame pigeons, cut quarter of a pound of sweet butter and put it over them, strew over a large teaspoonful of salt and a small teaspoonful of pepper, with a bunch of finely-cut parsley, if liked; dredge a large teaspoonful of wheat flour; put in water to nearly fill the pie; lay skewers across the top, cover with a puff paste crust; cut a slit in the middle, ornament the edge with leaves, braids, or shells of paste, and put in a moderately hot or quick oven for one hour; when nearly done, brush the top with the yolk of an egg beaten with a little milk, and finish. The pigeons for this pie may be cut in two or more pieces, if preferred.

Any small birds may be done in this manner.

A Brine for Beef, Bacon, Ham and Venison. For each one hundred pounds of meat, use six pounds of salt, six pounds of sugar, and four ounces of saltpeter. Dissolve all in enough water to cover the meat. Sprinkle a little salt over the bottom of the cask before packing the meat. Be sure the brine covers the meat for six weeks. Smoke the ham and bacon, and if kept in hot weather sew in sacks and whitewash.

MISCELLANEOUS DISHES

Boiled New England Dinner. Take a piece of salt pork and another of corned beef, the size must depend on the number of persons to be served; about three pounds of each will be sufficient for a family of six. Wash the meat and put on fire in separate kettles, boiling slowly for an hour; take the meat out and pour the liquor from one kettle into the other; put fresh water into the empty kettle, put in both pieces of meat and boil for two hours longer. Skim nearly all the fat off the liquor in which the meat was first boiled, taste it and if too salt to boil vegetables in, pour off some and add fresh water. Cut in quarters a small cabbage, one large or two small turnips, three or four carrots and peel six or eight potatoes, and boil all together in the liquor. In winter, all the vegetables except the potatoes, will require from one and three-quarters to two hours' boiling; in summer about one hour will do; potatoes will boil done in thirty or forty minutes. If you wish to add beets to the dinner, they must be boiled in a separate vessel. When the dinner is done, put the beef and pork on the same platter; drain the vegetables in a colander and put on the table in covered vegetable dishes. Serve the dinner hot. Prepared mustard and grated horseradish are indispensable to a boiled dinner.

Tripe. Tripe can be cut in squares and boiled over a quick fire, seasoning with butter, salt and pepper; or it can be boiled tender and then fried in butter, seasoning with salt and pepper.

Potted Meats. Take nice lean meat, beef or veal is the best; cut in small squares, put in a kettle, cover with water, add a little salt and boil until tender. When done take out the meat and put in an earthen or stone dish. Season the stock with salt and pepper, a small lump of butter, a stick of cinnamon and a dozen peppercorns; add half a box gelatine dissolved in a little cold water; boil twenty or thirty minutes, strain, and pour over the meat, mix thoroughly, cover with a plate, put on a weight and set away. When cold cut in slices, garnish with parsley or celery, and serve. This is very nice for luncheon or tea.

Broiled Sweet Breads. Trim and wash the sweet breads and broil on a wire broiler over a clear fire; baste with butter and season with salt and pepper; serve hot.

Sweet Breads No. 2. After trimming and washing the sweet breads, put in a stew pan, cover with water, add a pinch of salt and boil until done. Then take up and set aside until they stop steaming, then split, dip in beaten egg, then in cracker crumbs and fry in equal parts of butter and fat. Serve hot. Tomato sauce is a nice addition.

Calf's Liver. Cut the liver in slices, season with salt and pepper, dip in flour and fry in equal parts of butter and drippings. When nicely browned, lay on a platter; put a spoonful of flour in the frying pan and brown in the fat in which the liver was fried; add a teacupful of water, stir smooth and pour over the liver.

Mock Duck. Take a round of beefsteak, season with salt and pepper; prepare a dressing as for turkey, spread over the steak, roll and sew it up; fasten three or four slices of fat pork on the roll with toothpicks; put in the oven and roast. Baste often. This dish is hard to distinguish from duck.

Pot Pie. Take lean veal, beef, chicken, or any meat suitable for pot pie and cut up in pieces of a size suitable to serve. Wash, cover with cold water, and boil until tender. Skim when it first begins to boil. When done season with butter, pepper and salt. About twenty minutes before serving, add the crust.

Crust for Pot Pie. Take four and one-half cupfuls of flour and add to it two even teaspoonsful of cream tartar, and two even teaspoonfuls of soda and one teaspoonful of salt. Sift twice, then rub in a piece of butter the size of a walnut. Mix with two scant cupfuls of buttermilk, work into dough with as little handling as possible, roll out and cut as you would biscuit; put into the kettle and boil for twenty minutes.

Crust for Raised Pies. (For all Pies with Jelly.) Boil lard, good and fine, in water; add as much excellent dripping as there is lard; there must not be much of either. When still hot, mix it with as much flour as you have calculated will do for your purpose. Make the paste stiff and smooth by kneading, and also by beating it with a rolling-pin. When perfectly smooth, put a ball of it by in a cloth till cold, then use.

Ham Sandwiches. Chop cold, lean ham very fine; cut bread in thin slices and spread with butter; put on a layer of the chopped ham, season with prepared mustard, cover with another.

Oyster Sandwiches. Pound the oysters with lemon juice and cayenne, lay them between the slices of bread and butter and cut into small neat sandwiches, which arrange on a silver plate, one over the other in a ring, like cutlets.

Larding. All dry meats such as venison, a leg of veal, fillet of beef, grouse, partridge, etc., are much improved by larding. To some housekeepers this has a formidable sound, but it is nothing more

Larding Needle.

or less than drawing strips of fat salt pork through the surface of the meat. For this a larding needle is a convenience, but very good work can be done with a small, sharp knife. For a fillet of beef, cut fat salt pork in strips half an inch square by three or four inches long, and put a row on each side; take the stitches about half an inch deep and leave about half an inch of pork exposed at each end. A leg of veal can be larded much the same way, or game, sweetbreads, etc. The strips must be only one-quarter the size they are for beef, veal, or venison.

Nudeln. (*German Macaroni.*) Needed 4 eggs, flour, milk, 2 oz. of butter, grated rusk. With 4 eggs and 4 dessert-spoonfuls of milk, mix sufficient finest flour to make a paste; knead on a paste board, constantly shaking flour over it, until it becomes a stiff dough. Cut into four pieces, roll out as thin as paper, and throw over a pole to dry. When dried half an hour, cut each piece again in four, lay the pieces upon each other, roll up and cut into strips the width of a blade of grass, and shake them apart. They are then ready for use, but can be kept for several weeks. When required, boil tender in plenty of boiling water with salt, turn into a drainer, and pour boiling water quickly over them. Serve up either with brown butter, or sauce made with milk, salt and 2 oz. of fresh butter, and cover over with grated rusk, or a portion of the *nudeln* fried in butter until it has become crisp and brown. *Nudeln* are eaten with roast veal, or fowl, or ham, or as a sweet with stewed prunes or apple compôte.

Nudeln.

Fried Bananas. Cut the bananas in slices and flour each, fry a light brown in a frying pan; serve with fried bread, or with poached eggs, as bacon and eggs are served.

Hash. Take any kind of meat, corned beef is considered the best, and chop very fine; measure with a cup, and to every cup of chopped meat add one of chopped potato; mix well together, and season with salt, pepper and a lump of butter; put in a frying pan, pour on enough water to moisten it; cook for ten or fifteen minutes, stirring often, then set in the oven and brown.

Apples and Rice. Needed: Eight good sized apples, 3 oz. of butter, the rind of ½ a lemon minced very fine, 6 oz. of rice, 1½ pint of milk, sugar to taste, ½ teaspoonful of grated nutmeg, 6 tablespoonfuls of apricot jam. Peel the apples, halve them and take out the cores; put them into a stewpan with the butter, and strew sufficient sifted sugar over to sweeten them nicely, and add the minced lemon peel. Stew the apples very gently until tender, taking care they do not break. Boil the rice, with the milk, sugar and nutmeg, until soft, and, when thoroughly done, dish it, piled high in the center; arrange the apples on it, warm the apricot jam, pour it over the whole, and serve hot.

Apple Fritters. Needed for the batter, ½ lb. of flour, ½ oz. of butter, ½ saltspoonful of salt, 2 eggs, milk, apples, hot lard or clarified beef dripping. Break the eggs; separate the whites from the yolks, and beat them separately. Put the flour into a basin, stir in the butter, which should be melted to a cream; add the salt, and moisten with sufficient warm milk to make it of a proper consistency, that is to say, a batter that will drop from the spoon. Stir this well, rub down any lumps that may be seen, and add the whites of the eggs, which should have been previously well whisked; beat up the batter for a few minutes, and it is ready for use. Now peel and cut the apples into rather thick whole slices, without dividing them, and stamp out the middle of each slice, where the core is, with the cutter. Throw the slices into the batter; have ready a pan of boiling lard or clarified dripping; take out the pieces of apple one by one, put them into the hot lard, and fry a nice brown, turning them when required. When done, lay them on a piece of blotting paper before the fire, to absorb the greasy moisture; then dish on a white d'oyley, piled one above the other; strew over them some pounded sugar, and serve very hot. The flavor of the fritters would be very much improved by soaking the pieces of apple in a little wine, mixed with sugar and lemon juice, for 3 or 4 hours before wanted for table; the batter, also, is better for being mixed some hours before the fritters are made.

Rissoles. Make a nice puff paste, and roll out thin; have some meat chopped very fine, and sprinkle on half of the paste; cover with the other half and press together with the rolling pin; cut in squares, or you can use a biscuit cutter, and fry in hot lard to a light brown.

Almond Paste. Needed: One pound of sweet almonds, ¾ lb. of loaf sugar, gelatine flavoring. Blanch the almonds by putting them into boiling water; soak them for four hours in cold water and pound them well in a mortar, adding a few drops of water to take off the oiliness. When beaten to a paste, put in three-quarters of a pound of well-crushed loaf sugar, and mix all together. When quite fine and smooth, put it into a stewpan over a slow fire, and stir with a wooden spoon till it is white and dry. Put it again in the mortar, and mix with it a little melted and strained gelatine. Keep it covered. Flavor with what you like. Cover with a damp towel, or it will dry up.

Trout in Jelly (or Other Fish.) This is a beautiful supper dish, and may be arranged as follows: Turn the fish into rings, with tail in mouth, prepare a seasoned water in which to boil the trout; the water should have a little vinegar and salt in it, and may be flavored with a shalot or clove or garlic. When the water is cold, place the trout in it, and boil them very gently, so as not to mash or break them. When done, lift out and drain. Baste with fish jelly, for which a recipe is given elsewhere, coat after coat, as each coat hardens. Arrange neatly, and serve.

FISH AND MEAT SAUCES

Chili Sauce. Take twelve ripe tomatoes, one large pepper and two onions; chop all very fine, and put in a granite or porcelain kettle; add two cups of vinegar, one of brown sugar, one tablespoonful of salt and one teaspoonful each of nutmeg, allspice, cloves and ginger. Boil for one hour. This sauce can be canned, and kept for months. It is very nice to serve with roast beef or pork or broiled steak.

Mint Sauce. Heat a teacupful of vinegar boiling hot; put four tablespoonfuls of chopped green mint in a bowl, add two tablespoonfuls of sugar, and pour over them the hot vinegar. This sauce is better when made about an hour before using. Serve with roast lamb.

Mint.

Curry Sauce. Take a lump of butter the size of an egg, put in a sauce pan with a small onion minced fine. Cook until the onion is fried to a nice brown; then add a tablespoonful of flour and a teaspoonful of curry powder; mix well, then add a pint of good stock, and stir until smooth; season with salt and pepper, strain, and serve. This sauce is nice with broiled or fried meat or fish.

Drawn Butter Sauce. Put half a teacup of butter in a sauce pan, and when melted, add two tablespoonfuls of flour; cook, but not brown; then add a pint of water, and stir until smooth; season with salt and pepper. This sauce is a nice addition to boiled or baked fish, mashed potato, etc.

Mustard Sauce. Make a drawn butter sauce, and add to it two tablespoonfuls of prepared mustard and a little cayenne pepper. This sauce goes with broiled smoked fish of any kind and boiled salt codfish.

Tomato Sauce. Put in a sauce pan half a cup of butter or meat drippings and slice into it an onion, a carrot, a very small turnip and a small slice of ham; add a bay leaf and a

The Mustard Plant. few whole peppers; let all brown or braise together; then pour over the whole a pint of water and let it boil for ten minutes. Strain and add to the stock a can of tomatoes and a tablespoonful of sugar; let all boil together for thirty or forty minutes; stirring frequently to prevent scorching, then strain and press through a sieve. This sauce is served with almost all kinds of meat and fish.

Cream Sauce. Put a teacupful of butter in a sauce pan and when melted, stir in a small teacupful of flour, cook but do not brown; then add a little less than a quart of boiling milk, and stir until smooth; season with salt and white pepper. If at all lumpy strain before serving.

Maitre D'Hotel Sauce. Take half a teacupful of butter, put in a bowl, and rub to a cream; then add a teaspoonful of salt and a half one of pepper, two tablespoonfuls of chopped parsley and the juice of a lemon; mix all thoroughly together. Heat three cupfuls of white stock; when boiling stir in two well beaten eggs; this will form a thin custard; last of all add the butter and other ingredients, and boil for three minutes, stirring all the time, Serve at once. The butter with its seasoning, but without the stock and eggs, is used on fried meats and fish instead of butter, and is much relished by some.

Allemande, or White Sauce. Put in a sauce pan a cupful of butter, a sliced onion, and a carrot; when the butter is melted, add a cupful of flour and stir smooth, then pour in two quarts of boiling white stock and let it boil slowly for one hour; season with salt and white pepper and strain. Beat the yolks of two eggs with the juice of a lemon, stir into the sauce and keep hot for use. From this sauce the following sauces can be made.

Parsley Sauce. Chop one-half of a bunch of parsley very fine, squeeze dry through a napkin and stir it into a quart of allemande sauce and serve.

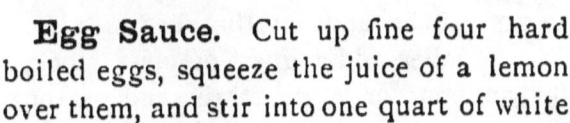

Parsley.

Caper Sauce. Mix in a quart of allemande sauce a cupful of capers. This sauce is nice with boiled mutton.

Caper.

Egg Sauce. Cut up fine four hard boiled eggs, squeeze the juice of a lemon over them, and stir into one quart of white sauce. This sauce is particularly nice with broiled trout.

Cardinal Sauce. Pound the shells of two lobsters very fine, and add some of the coral, also pounded fine, put in a sauce pan with half a cup of butter, let it cook for twenty or twenty-five minutes, then add a quart of allemande sauce, the juice of a lemon, and a glass of sherry; simmer together for two or three minutes, strain and serve. This sauce is nice with broiled or baked fish.

Normandy Sauce. Chop one-half of a can of mushrooms, two shalots, one dozen oysters, and six shrimps; let these articles simmer in a cupful of butter for ten minutes, then add a quart of allemande sauce, season with a glass of sherry and serve.

Anchovy Sauce. To a quart of allemande sauce add one-half of a bottle of anchovy sauce, mix well, and serve.

Shalots.

The Anchovy.

Old Zealand Sauce. Put in a sauce pan a scant half cup of butter, one teacupful of good vinegar, and half a cupful of water, let then come to a boil, and then stir in two well beaten eggs, stir until it creams; if too thick add a little water; season with salt and white pepper. This sauce is excellent with boiled cod fish, either salt or fresh.

Truffle Sauce. Slice an onion, a carrot, half of a small turnip and a medium sized potato and braise in a sauce pan with half a cupful of drippings. When the vegetables are a nice brown, add a tablespoonful of flour and let that brown also, then add a quart of meat stock, and let it simmer for an hour or more, strain and season with the juice of a lemon, a glass of wine, a little Worcestershire sauce, and salt and pepper to taste. Chop your truffles and mix in this prepared sauce.

Truffles.

Jelly Sauce for Game. Put in a sauce pan a glass of Madeira wine and half cupful of jelly, let it dissolve, then add one pint of dark sauce, as per receipt for truffle sauce; let it come to a boil and serve. This is fine for all kinds of game and poultry.

Celery Sauce. Cut up fine two stalks of fine celery, leaves and all, and boil in a sauce pan for ten or fifteen minutes, drain off the water and put in the sauce pan with the celery a lump of butter the size of an egg, and a tablespoonful of flour; cook, but do not brown, then add a pint of milk and season with salt and pepper, stir until smooth and serve hot.

Celery in Glass.

Horseradish Sauce. (*To serve with roast beef.*) You need four tablespoonfuls of grated horseradish, 1 teaspoonful of pounded sugar, 1 teaspoonful of salt, ½ teaspoonful of pepper, 2 teaspoonfuls of made mustard, vinegar. Grate the horseradish, and mix it well with the sugar, salt, pepper and mustard; moisten it with sufficient vinegar to give it the consistency of cream, and serve in a tureen; 3 or 4 tablespoonfuls of cream added to the above, very much improve the appearance and flavor of this sauce. To heat it to serve with hot roast beef, put it in a *bain marie*, or a jar, which place in a saucepan of boiling water; make it hot, but do not allow it to boil, or it will curdle.

The Horseradish.

NOTE.—This sauce is a great improvement on the old fashioned way of serving cold scraped horseradish with hot roast beef. The mixing of the cold vinegar with the warm gravy cools and spoils everything on the plate. Of course, with cold meat, the sauce should be served cold.

Oyster Sauce. Chop a dozen oysters fine and boil in their own liquor, skim and then add a pint of white sauce, season with salt and pepper, and the juice of a lemon.

A Good Sauce for Steaks. Take one oz. of whole black pepper, half oz. of allspice, 1 oz. of salt, ½ oz. of grated horseradish, ½ oz. of pickled shalots, 1 pint of mushroom ketchup or walnut pickle.

Pound all the ingredients finely in a mortar, and put them into the ketchup or walnut liquor. Let them stand for a fortnight, when strain off the liquor and bottle for use. Either pour a little of the sauce over the steaks, or mix it in the gravy.

Mushroom Sauce. Take one can of mushrooms, strain off the liquor, cut the mushrooms in slices, and put in a sauce pan, with a lump of butter and a large tablespoonful of flour, let all cook together, but brown very slightly, if at all. Squeeze in the juice of a lemon, add a tablespoonful of Worcestershire sauce, and a pint of water or stock, stir all smooth, season with salt and a little cayenne pepper and serve hot. This sauce accompanies roast beef and veal, and also steak.

Mushrooms.

"Hollandaise" Sauce. Beat the yolks of three eggs with the juice of a lemon, and a half cupful of soft butter, stir this into a quart of hot allemande sauce, and keep stirring until the egg cooks; this will give the sauce a nice creamy appearance. This sauce can be poured over meat or fish just before it is served.

French White Sauce. Take 1 small bunch of parsley, 2 cloves, ½ a bay leaf, 1 small faggot of savory herbs, salt to taste, 3 or 4 mushrooms, when obtainable; 2 pints of white stock, 1 pint of cream, 1 tablespoonful of arrowroot. Put the stock into a stewpan with the parsley, cloves, bay leaf, herbs and mushrooms; add a seasoning of salt, but no ground pepper, as that would give the sauce a dusky appearance, and should be for use. A small quantity of wine, or any liquor, would very much improve the flavor of this sauce. It is usually served with bread, rice, custard, or any dry pudding that is not very rich.

Olive Sauce. Use ½ lb. of French olives, ½ pint of stock, 1 teaspoonful of lemon juice. Carefully stone the olives by paring them round in ribbons so that they may recover their shape when stoned. Blanch them in boiling water, and throw them into cold water for 5 minutes, and stew slowly for half an hour in the gravy. Add the lemon and serve.

The Olive.

Kidney Sauce. Take 2 kidneys, 1 tablespoonful of flour, pepper and salt, ½ teaspoonful of each, 1 tablespoonful of stock, ½ glassful of claret. Skin and mince the kidneys into fine dice, shake the flour well over them, place all the other ingredients in a stewpan, and let it boil gently for five minutes. Place the stewpan at the side of the fire, add the kidneys, and stew all gently for ten minutes, being careful not to let it boil. Pour over roast fowl, or place in a separate tureen and serve.

Epicurean Sauce. (For Steaks, Chops, Gravies or Fish.) Procure ½ pint of walnut ketchup, ½ pint of mushroom ditto, 2 tablespoonfuls of port, ½ oz. of white pepper, 2 oz. of shalots, ½ oz. of cayenne, ½ oz. of cloves, ¾ pint of vinegar. Put the whole of the ingredients into a bottle, and let it remain for a fortnight in a warm place, occasionally shaking up the contents. Strain, and bottle off for use. This sauce will be found an agreeable addition to gravies, hashes, stews, etc.

Asparagus Sauce. You need 1 bunch of green asparagus, salt, 1 oz. of fresh butter, 1 small bunch of parsley, 3 or 4 green onions, 1 large lump of sugar, 4 tablespoonfuls of white stock Break the asparagus in the tender part, wash well, and put them into boiling salt and water to render them green. When they are tender, take them out, and put them into cold water; drain them on a cloth till all the moisture is absorbed from them. Put the butter in a stewpan with the parsley and onions; lay in the asparagus, and fry the whole over a sharp fire for five minutes. Add salt, the sugar and white stock, and simmer for another 5 minutes. Rub all through a tammy, and if not a very good color, use a little spinach green. This sauce should be rather sweet. This is suitable for garnish.

Apple Sauce. (For Geese, Pork, etc.) Take 6 good sized apples, sifted sugar to taste, a piece of butter the size of a walnut, water. Pare, core and quarter the apples, and throw them into cold water to preserve their whiteness. Put them in a saucepan, with sufficient water to moisten them, and boil till soft enough to pulp. Beat them up, adding sugar to taste, and a small piece of butter. This quantity is sufficient for a good sized tureen.

Bread Sauce. (To Serve with Roast Turkey, Fowl, Game, etc.) Use 1 pint of milk, ¾ lb. of the crumb of a stale loaf, 1 onion, pounded mace, cayenne and salt to taste, 1 oz. of butter. Peel and quarter the onion, and simmer it in the milk till perfectly tender. Break the bread, which should be stale, into small pieces, carefully picking out any hard outside pieces; put it in a very clean saucepan, strain the milk over it, cover it up, and let it remain for an hour to soak.

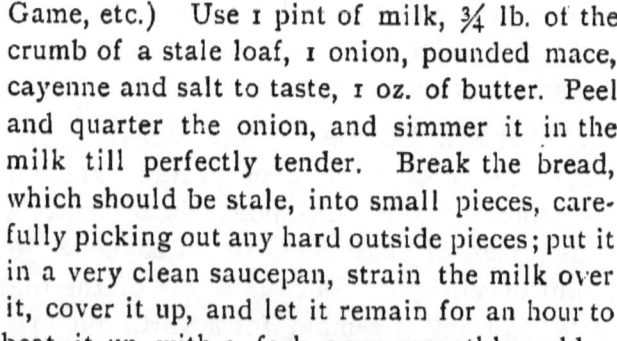
Mace.

Now beat it up with a fork very smoothly, add a seasoning of pounded mace, cayenne and salt, with 1 oz. of butter; give the whole one boil, and serve. To enrich this sauce, a small quantity of cream may be added just before sending it to the table.

Meat and Fish Sauces

Melted Butter. Take 2 oz. of butter, 1 dessertspoonful of flour, salt to taste, ½ pint of water. Mix the flour and water to a smooth batter, which put into a sauce pan. Add the flour and a seasoning of salt, keep stirring *one way* till all the ingredients are melted and perfectly smooth; let the whole boil for a minute or two, and serve.

Tartare Sauce. Use yolks of 4 eggs, 1 teaspoonful of mustard, ½ teaspoonful of salt, olive oil, tarragon vinegar, pepper, cayenne, 2 shalots, or 2 tablespoonfuls of chopped pickled onions and gherkins. Break the yolks into a basin with the salt and mustard, then stir in a tablespoonful of olive oil, and then a teaspoonful of tarragon vinegar alternately until the sauce is of the right consistency. This must be done very gradually. Then add the chopped shalot or pickles.

A Cheap Gravy for Hashes, etc. Take bones and trimmings of the cooked joint intended for hashing, ¼ teaspoonful of salt, ¼ teaspoonful of whole pepper, ¼ teaspoonful of whole allspice, a small faggot of savory herbs, ½ head of celery, 1 onion, 1 oz. of butter, flour, sufficient water to cover the bones. Chop the bones in small pieces, and put them in a stewpan, with the trimmings, salt, pepper, spice, herbs and celery. Cover with boiling water, and let the whole boil for two or three hours. Slice and fry the onion in the butter till it is of a pale brown, and mix in flour in the proportion of 1 dessertspoonful to half a pint of gravy; add the gravy made from the bones; boil for a quarter of an hour and flavor with lemon peel, anchovy sauce, walnut pickle or ketchup, pickled-onion liquor, or any store sauce that may be preferred. Strain, and the gravy will be ready for use. A bacon bone or rind is an improvement.

A Good Beef Gravy for Poultry, Game, etc. Procure ½ lb. of lean beef, pint of cold water, 1 shalot or small onion, ½ a teaspoonful of salt, a little pepper, 1 tablespoonful of store sauce or mushroom ketchup, a teaspoonful of arrowroot. Cut up the beef into small pieces, and put it, with the water, into a stewpan. Add the shalot and seasoning, and simmer gently for 3 hours, taking care that it does not boil fast. A short time before it is required, take the arrowroot, and having mixed it with a little cold water, pour it into the gravy, which keep stirring, adding the sauce, and just letting it boil. Strain off the gravy in a tureen, and serve very hot.

Poivrade Sauce. Needed: Six oz. of ham, 1 oz. of butter, 1 clove of garlic, 1 bay leaf, 1 sprig of sweet basil, 1 of thyme, 2 cloves, 4 young onions, ½ pint of consommè, No. 276; 1 oz. of celery, 1 pinch of pepper and cayenne (where liked); 3 sprays of parsley, wineglassful of tarragon vinegar. Cut the ham into small pieces, and fry it in the butter, with the parsley, onions, garlic, bay leaf, basil, thyme and cloves. When well fried over a quick fire, add the cayenne, sliced celery and pepper, vinegar and consommé; let all simmer gently half an hour. Strain through a tammy and serve.

Robert Sauce. (For Steaks, etc.) Needed: Eight oz. of butter, 3 onions, 1 teaspoonful of flour, 4 tablespoonfuls of gravy, or stock No. 272, salt and pepper to taste, 1 teaspoonful of made mustard, 1 teaspoonful of vinegar, the juice of ½ lemon. Put the butter into a stewpan, set it on the fire, and, when browning, throw in the onions, which must be cut into small slices. Fry them brown, but do not burn them; add the flour, shake the onion in it, and give the whole another fry. Put in the gravy and seasoning, and boil it gently for 10 minutes; skim off the fat, add the mustard, vinegar and lemon juice; give it one boil, and pour round the steaks, or whatever dish the sauce has been prepared for.

SALADS

Tomato Salad. Take one quart of best tomatoes, and drain in colander; cut the tomatoes quite fine, and add a finely minced onion, a level teaspoonful of salt and half a one of pepper, a heaping tablespoonful of sugar and one of vinegar. Mix well together, and serve.

Lettuce and Tomato Salad. Clean and wash the  lettuce, place in a bowl lined with a napkin, so as to absorb all the moisture, and put in the ice box. Skin the number of tomatoes needed, and put on ice. When ready to serve, dress the lettuce with

Tomato Salad in Bowl.

vinegar, oil (or melted butter), salt and pepper. Arrange the lettuce in the salad bowl, quarter, or slice the tomatoes, and arrange in the middle of the bowl, and spread over them a Mayonnaise dressing, and serve.

Lettuce and Tomato Salad No. 2. Clean and wash  the lettuce, shake, to free from excessive moisture, and place on ice. Skin the number of tomatoes required, and place on ice. When ready to serve, put three or four crisp lettuce leaves in each individual salad dish; place in the middle of each one a tomato cut in quarters; put on each tomato a spoonful of French or Mayonnaise dressing, and

Lettuce.

serve.

Cold Slaw. Put a tablespoonful of melted butter in a stewpan, and add to it a teaspoonful of flour; mix, and then put in a teacupful of vinegar. Beat an egg, and add to it a teaspoonful each of mustard, sugar, salt, and a half teaspoonful of pepper; beat all together, and stir in the boiling vinegar; boil one minute, and pour over sliced or chopped cabbage.

Cold Slaw No. 2. Slice cabbage very fine, and season with salt, pepper and sugar to taste. Pour vinegar over all, and mix thoroughly. This is a nice relish with raw or cooked oysters.

Cabbage Salad No. 1. Chop half of a medium sized head of cabbage very fine; add four teaspoonfuls of celery seed, or one head of celery cut fine. Beat in a bowl the yolks of two eggs, and add a teaspoonful each of sugar, butter, pepper, made mustard, and add two-thirds of a cupful of vinegar; set the bowl in hot water and stir until it thickens; set aside, and when cold, pour over the cabbage, and mix well.

Cabbage Salad No. 2. Take two quarts of finely chopped cabbage, and season with two level teaspoonfuls of salt, two of white sugar, one of black pepper, one of ground mustard; rub the yolks of four hard boiled eggs until smooth; add half a cupful of butter slightly warmed; mix thoroughly with the cabbage; then add a teacupful of good cider vinegar. Serve with whites of eggs, sliced and placed on the salad.

Cabbage Salad No. 3. One medium sized head of cabbage chopped fine; pepper and salt to taste. For a dressing beat the yolks of two eggs, add two tablespoonfuls of melted butter, and beat again; then add a teacupful of thick sour cream, two tablespoonfuls of sugar and half a cupful of vinegar, and beat for three minutes; pour on the cabbage, and mix.

Cucumber Salad. Needed: One large or two small cucumbers, ½ teaspoonful of pepper and salt mixed, 1 tablespoonful of best French vinegar, 3 tablespoonfuls of pure salad oil. Peel and slice the cucumber as finely as possible, sprinkle the pepper and salt over it; add vinegar and salt in the above proportions a moment before using.

Bean Salad. String young beans, cut into inch lengths and boil in salt and water until tender, drain well, and to a quart of beans, add a chopped onion; take three tablespoonfuls of vinegar, two of salad oil, or melted butter, salt and pepper to taste. Beat the vinegar and oil together, add the seasoning, and pour over the beans and onions; mix well, and set away for an hour or two before using.

Asparagus Salad. Drain the asparagus after taking it from the can, or if fresh, boil until tender in salted water, and dress like string bean salad.

Asparagus.

Potato Salad. Cut in half inch cubes two quart of cold boiled potatoes, a large Spanish onion, two heads of celery, and four hard boiled eggs; season with salt, pepper, and a little cayenne. Put in a stewpan a lump of butter the size of an egg; and when melted, add a tablespoonful of flour; cook, but do not brown; then add a cupful of milk or water. Beat the yolks of two eggs with a tablespoonful of sugar and a teaspoonful of mustard; add two-thirds of a cupful of vinegar, and stir all in with the sauce in the stewpan; let it come to boil, stirring all the time, and set away to cool. When cold, pour over the rest of the salad, mix well, and serve.

Potato Salad No. 2. Slice cold boiled potatoes thin, and mince an onion fine. Alternate layers of potatoes and onion, season each layer with salt, pepper, melted butter and a little vinegar. Let stand an hour or two before serving.

Salmon Salad. Procure two heads of nice crisp lettuce and wash each leaf separately, shaking to free from moisture. Arrange the lettuce on a round or oval dish about two inches deep, the darker leaves next the outside and the lighter ones in the middle. Take a can of best salmon, or its equivalent in fresh cooked salmon; with a fork pick in small flakes and place in the middle of the dish on the lettuce. Season the salmon with salt and a little cayenne, and pour over it a tablespoonful of vinegar and the juice of a lemon; then set aside in the ice box for an hour or two. When ready to serve, pour a teacupful of mayonnaise dressing over the fish; sprinkle a few capers on top of that, and serve.

Lobster Salad. A delicious lobster salad can be made by following the above rule and substituting lobster for salmon. A nice way is to arrange the lettuce in the form of shells on individual salad dishes and putting a spoonful of lobster in each one; then proceed with the dressing as you would in the larger dish.

Sardine Salad. Take two boxes of best sardines and arrange on a platter. For dressing take the yolk of four hard boiled eggs, put in a bowl and rub to a paste; add a tablespoonful of prepared mustard, three of vinegar, a teaspoonful of sugar and a little cayenne. Mix well together and pour over the sardines. Garnish with sliced lemon.

Egg Salad. Boil a dozen eggs for twenty-five minutes, slice and cover with a Mayonnaise dressing, garnish with lettuce leaves, capers, and olives.

Chicken Salad. Boil three chickens until tender, salting to taste; when cold, pick fine with the fingers, and add three heads of celery, cut fine with a knife (not chopped), and six hard boiled eggs sliced; mix all together thoroughly. For dressing, put in a sauce pan a pint of vinegar and a lump of butter the size of an egg; beat three eggs with two tablespoonfuls of made mustard, two of sugar, salt and pepper to taste; let the vinegar come to a boil; then stir in slowly the beaten

Salad Fully Garnished.

egg mixture, stirring until it thickens, but do not let it curdle, which it will do, if boiled too long. Set aside to cool. Do not add the dressing to the chicken and other ingredients, until just before serving.

Chicken Salad No. 2. For a pair of boiled fowls allow three heads of celery. Take all the skin from the chickens, pick all the meat from the bones, chop it fine, and put in with the cut celery; cut the white meat in half inch cubes and add to the other; boil the livers and sift them, and put in a bowl rubbed with a bit of onion; add the yolks of five hard boiled eggs rubbed to a paste, four tablespoonfuls of salad oil, or melted butter, two tablespoonfuls of prepared mustard, one of sugar, a heaping teaspoonful of salt, a little cayenne pepper, a level teaspoonful of grated lemon peel, and a teaspoonful each of vinegar and thick cream. Beat well together, and pour over, and mix well with the chicken just before serving.

Chicken Salad No. 3. A simple way to prepare a good chicken salad, is to remove the skin from a couple of boiled chickens, and cut the meat fine with a knife; cut up two or three heads of celery and add to the chicken; season with salt, pepper, and a little cayenne; pour over the whole a cold Mayonnaise dressing, mix, and serve.

Tongue Salad. Boil, skin and trim a tongue, cut in dice, and add the whites of six hard boiled eggs, cut in similar pieces: cut fine the white stalks of three heads of celery, and mix with the tongue and eggs. Make a dressing as follows: Beat together four eggs, six tablespoonfuls of vinegar, five of melted butter, one of prepared mustard, one of sugar, and two-thirds of a cup of cream; put over the fire in a double boiler, and cook until as thick as boiled custard. Set aside to cool; season with salt and a little cayenne, thin with lemon juice, if too thick; mix with the tongue and other ingredients, and serve at once.

Crab Salad. Take two small crabs, one large lettuce, 1 bunch watercress, 2½ tablespoonful of oil, 1 of vinegar, 1 hard boiled egg, a few slices of beet root or a tomato, pepper and salt. Pick all the meat from the shells and shred it finely. Wash and dry the lettuce and cress, and cut it up in a bowl, and mix first with the oil, next the pepper and salt, and lastly, the vinegar. Stir all well together, then add the crab, mixing it well with the salad. Pile on a flat dish and garnish with the egg cut in slices and the beet root, or tomato.

Mayonnaise Dressing. Put in a stew-pan a lump of butter the size of an egg and when melted, put in a tablespoonful of flour; then add a teacupful of milk or water and let it come to a boil; have ready three beaten eggs mixed with a tablespoonful of sugar, a teaspoonful of dry mustard and a teacupful of vinegar; salt and pepper to taste; stir in with the other ingredients in the sauce-pan, let come to a boil and set away to cool.

Salad Dressing. Take the yolks of two hard boiled eggs, mash fine in a bowl; add two tablespoonsful of white sugar, one teaspoonful of salt, one of mustard, and half a teaspoonful of white pepper. When thoroughly mixed, add two well beaten eggs, three tablespoonsful of melted butter, and half a cupful of vinegar. Set the bowl over the tea-kettle, or on the stove in a dish of hot water, and cook until it thickens. Remove from the stove and when cold stir in two-thirds of a cupful of thick sweet cream.

Sour Cream Dressing. Put a cupful of thick, sour cream in a bowl and set on the ice for several hours, or until it is very cold. When ready to serve, beat it with an egg beater for a few minutes; if it is as cold as it should be it will beat up into a stiff white foam. Now add to the cream, one teaspoonful of salt, a little cayenne, the juice of a small lemon, two or three tablespoonsful of vinegar, and beat for two or three minutes longer. This is a nice dressing for vegetables.

French Salad Dressing. Put six tablespoonsful of salad oil in a bowl; add to it three tablespoonsful of white wine vinegar, half a teaspoonful of salt, a little cayenne, and a few drops of onion juice; beat all together with a beater and it is ready to serve. This is a nice dressing for lettuce or tomatoes.

Tartare Dressing. For tartare sauce take mayonnaise dressing and stir into it half a small bottle of capers, or a few cucumber pickles chopped fine.

Summer Salad. Needed: Three lettuces, 2 handfuls of mustard and cress, 10 young radishes, a few slices of cucumber. Let the herbs be as fresh as possible for a salad. Wash and carefully pick them over, and drain them thoroughly by swinging them gently in a clean cloth. Cut the lettuces into small pieces, and the radishes and cucumbers into thin slices; arrange all these ingredients lightly on a dish, with the mustard and cress, and pour under, but not over, the salad, either of the dressings above, and do not stir it up until it is to be eaten. It should be garnished with hard boiled eggs cut in slices, beet root alternately, or sliced cucumbers, nasturtiums, and many other things that taste will always suggest. In making a good salad, care must be taken to have the herbs freshly gathered, and *thoroughly drained* before the sauce is added to them, or it will be watery and thin. Young spring onions, cut small, are by many persons considered an improvement to salads; but before these are added, the cook should always consult the taste of her employer. Slices of cold meat or poultry added to a salad make a convenient and quickly-made summer luncheon dish; or cold fish, flaked, will also be found exceedingly nice, mixed with it.

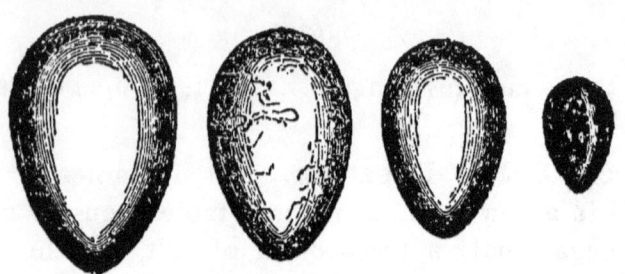

EGGS

Boiled Eggs. Have a sauce pan of boiling water; drop the eggs in carefully. To have the eggs soft, boil three minutes; medium, five minutes; hard, fifteen or twenty minutes.

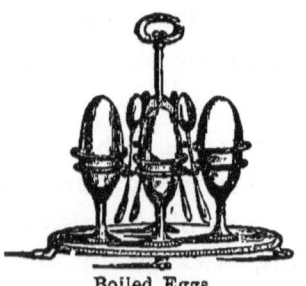
Boiled Eggs.

Hard Boiled Eggs. After boiling fifteen or twenty minutes, take out and put in cold water for a few moments. This will cause the shells to come off readily. They may be sent to the table in the shell, or served with a hot sauce. They are very nice cut in halves and served with a mayonnaise dressing.

Fried Eggs. Having enough fat in a frying-pan to nearly cover the eggs when frying, break each egg separately in a saucer, then slip into the hot fat. Do not turn the eggs over, but cook the top by basting the hot fat over the eggs. A good plan is to put muffin rings in the frying-pan and drop the eggs in, for this gives the eggs a nice shape. The rings can be lifted out with a fork as soon as the white is partly cooked.

Fried Eggs.

Deviled Eggs. Boil a dozen eggs for twenty minutes; put in cold water and take off the shell. With a sharp knife cut in halves lengthwise, take out the yolks carefully, put in a bowl and rub fine; season with pepper, salt, a little cayenne, a tablespoonful of prepared mustard, and three tablespoonsful of melted butter, mix all thoroughly together and fill the eggs with the mixture. Put the halves together and tie with thread or skewer together with short toothpicks; this is for ordinary use. For picnics, or cold spreads, a pleasing effect is produced by tying them with narrow colored ribbon, or gilt cord. If it is desirable to serve them hot, prepare as above, dip in beaten egg, roll in cracker dust, and fry in hot lard.

Eggs on a Plate. Put a lump of butter the size of an egg in a deep earthen plate, put in the oven, and when the butter is melted and the plate hot, break in half a dozen eggs, season with salt and pepper, and put back in the oven until the whites are set. Serve on the plate on which they are cooked.

Poached Eggs. Have enough boiling hot water in a pan to cover the eggs, but do not let it boil while putting in the eggs, as it will render the whites ragged and broken; break each egg separately, and slip carefully into the water, and when the whites are beginning to set, bring to a boil and begin to dip off the water until the tops are bare; boil until the whites are firm, take up carefully, put a small lump of butter, a little salt, and one shake of pepper on each egg, and serve.

Egg Baskets. Boil eggs for twenty minutes, take off the shells, and with a sharp knife cut in two crosswise; take out the yolks, rub fine, season with salt, pepper, melted butter and a little prepared mustard; put this mixture in the whites, cut a small slice from the bottom, so they will stand upright, arrange on the dish on which they are to be served and pour over them hot Old Zealand sauce (see sauces) as a dressing. Serve at once.

Scrambled Eggs. Put in a hot frying pan, two or three tablespoonfuls of butter; when hot, break in six or eight eggs and commence stirring at once, and continue until the eggs are cooked; turn into a dish, season with salt and pepper, and serve hot.

Scrambled Eggs No. 2. Have the frying pan hot, and put in two tablespoonfuls of butter; beat six eggs with half a cupful of milk, just enough to mix them, pour into the pan, commence stirring at once, and when done take up in a dish and serve at once.

Eggs with Creamed Beef or Codfish. Just before dishing the beef or fish, poach as many eggs as there are persons to be served, and place in the dish, pour the creamed meat over them and serve. Another way is to drop the eggs into the pan with the meat and let them cook until done; care must be used not to break the eggs in transferring from the pan in which they are cooked to the dish in which they are to be served.

Omelet. Have a smooth frying pan, heat it, and put in a tablespoonful of butter; beat six eggs until light, and pour into the frying pan. Let it cook until almost done through, then with a knife, double one-half over on the other half, and let cook for a moment longer. In transferring from the frying pan to the dish on which it is to be served, hold the frying pan in the left hand, slip a knife under the lower end of the omelet, lift a little, give the pan a little shake, and the omelet will be on the dish in good shape. An omelet can be equally well cooked by putting in the oven and baking instead of frying.

Oyster Omelet. Proceed as in plain omelet, and just before folding over, cover one-half with well drained oysters, season with salt and pepper and pour over them a tablespoonful of melted butter; fold the omelet and set in the oven for two or three minutes, until the oysters are cooked through. Serve at once.

Cheese Omelet. Beat together two eggs, two tablespoonfuls of grated cheese, and a scant half cupful of milk; when well beaten proceed as in plain omelet, and serve hot.

Ham or Beef Omelet. For ham or beef omelet, proceed as in plain, and as soon as it is "set" in the pan, sprinkle with cooked ham or beef, chopped fine; fold over and serve.

Mushroom Omelet. Chop half a can of mushrooms that have been thoroughly drained, mix with four well beaten eggs and proceed as in plain omelet, putting a little more butter in the pan than for plain.

Omelet Soufflee. Needed: Six eggs, 5 oz. of pounded sugar, flavoring of vanilla, orange-flower water, or lemon rind; 3 oz. of butter, 1 dessertspoonful of rice flour. Separate the yolks from the whites of the eggs, add to the former the sugar, the rice flour, and either of the above flavorings that may be preferred, and stir these ingredients well together. Whip the whites of the eggs, mix them lightly with the batter, and put the butter into a small frying pan. As soon as it begins to bubble, pour the batter into it, and set the pan over a bright but gentle fire; and when the omelet is set, turn the edges over to make it an oval shape, and slip it onto a silver dish, which has been previously well buttered. Put it in the oven, and bake from 12 to 15 minutes; sprinkle only powdered sugar over the souffle, and serve it immediately.

Rum Omelet. Beat the yolks of six eggs with six tablespoonfuls of milk; when well beaten add the whites, which must be beaten to a stiff froth, mix well together; put a lump of butter the size of an egg in the frying pan, and when hot pour in the eggs; when browned on the under side, set in the oven for five minutes; double as you take from the pan, cover with pulverized sugar and pour over all a gill of best Jamaica rum; burn the rum until the alcohol is exhausted, basting all the time.

Jam Omelet. Needed: Six eggs, four oz. of butter, 3 tablespoonfuls of apricot, strawberry, or any jam that may be preferred. Make the omelet by receipt No. 1 and leave flat in the pan. When quite firm, and nicely browned on one side, turn it carefully onto a hot dish, spread over the middle of it the jam, and fold the omelet over on each side; sprinkle sifted sugar over, and serve very quickly. A pretty dish of small omelets may be made by dividing the batter into three or four portions, and frying them separately; they should then be spread each one with a different kind of preserve, and the omelets rolled over. Always sprinkle sweet omelets with sifted sugar before being sent to table.

French Pancakes. Needed: Two eggs, 2 oz. of butter, 2 oz. of sifted sugar, 2 oz. of flour, ½ pint of new milk. Beat the eggs thoroughly and put them into a basin with the butter, which should be beaten to a cream; stir in the sugar and flour, and when these ingredients are well mixed,

French Pancakes.

add the milk; keep stirring and beating the mixture for a few minutes; put it on buttered plates, and bake in a quick oven for 20 minutes. Serve with a cut lemon and sifted sugar, or pile the pancakes high on a dish, with a layer of preserve or marmalade between each.

Snow Eggs. Needed: Five eggs, one pint of milk, pounded sugar to taste, flavoring of vanilla, lemon rind, or orange flower water. Put the milk into a sauce pan with sufficient sugar to sweeten it nicely, and the rind of half a lemon. Let this steep by the side of the fire for half an hour, when take out the peel; separate the whites from the yolks of the eggs, and whisk the former to a perfectly stiff froth, or until there is no liquid remaining; bring the milk to the boiling point, when drop in the snow a tablespoonful at a time, and keep turning the eggs until sufficiently cooked. Then place them on a glass dish, beat up the yolks of the eggs, stir to them the milk, add a little more sugar, and strain this mixture into a jug; place the jug in a sauce pan of boiling water, and stir it one way until the mixture thickens, but do not allow it to boil, or it will curdle. Pour this custard over the eggs, when they should rise to the surface. They make an exceedingly pretty addition to a supper, and should be put in a cold place after being made. When they are flavored with vanilla or orange flower water, it is not necessary to steep the milk. A few drops of the essence of either may be poured in the milk just before the whites are poached. In making the custard, a little more flavoring and sugar should always be added.

Scotch Eggs. Needed: Six eggs, 6 tablespoonfuls of forcemeat, No. 629, hot lard, ½ pint of good brown gravy. Boil the eggs for 10 minutes; strip them from the shells, and cover them with forcemeat. Fry the eggs a nice brown in boiling lard, drain them before the fire from their greasy moisture, dish them, and pour round them a quarter to half a pint of good brown gravy. To enhance the appearance of the eggs, they may be rolled in beaten egg and sprinkled with bread crumbs; but this is scarcely necessary if they are carefully fried. The flavor of ham or anchovy must preponderate in the forcemeat, as it should be very relishing.

Dutch Omelet. Break eight eggs into a basin, season with pepper and salt, add two ounces of butter cut small, beat these well together; make an ounce of butter hot in a frying pan, put the eggs in it, continue to stir it, drawing it away from the sides that it may be evenly done, and shake it now and then to free it from the pan; when the under side is a little browned, turn the omelet into a dish, and serve. This must be done over a moderate fire.

Eggs a La Suisse. Spread the bottom of a dish with two ounces of fresh butter; cover this with grated cheese, and break eight whole eggs upon the cheese without breaking the yolks. Season with red pepper, and salt if necessary; pour a little cream on the surface, strew about two ounces of grated cheese on the top, and set the eggs in a moderate oven for about a quarter of an hour. Pass a hot salamander over the top to brown it.

Curried Eggs. Slice two onions and fry in butter; add a tablespoonful of curry powder, and one pint of good broth or stock; stew till onions are quite tender; add a cup of cream thickened with arrowroot or rice flour, simmer a few moments, then add eight or ten hard boiled eggs cut in slices, and beat them well, but do not boil.

Creamed Eggs. Boil six eggs twenty minutes. Make one pint of cream sauce. Have six slices of toast on a hot dish. Put a layer of sauce on each one, and then part of the whites of the eggs; cut in thin strips, and rub part of the yolks through a sieve on the toast. Repeat this, and finish with a third layer of sauce. Place in the oven for about three minutes. Garnish with parsley, and serve.

VEGETABLES

Boiled Potatoes. Peel the potatoes and let stand in cold water for at least half an hour before boiling. Put in a kettle, cover with cold water and boil until done, which will take from thirty to forty minutes. When done, drain, and put back upon the stove, removing the cover to let the steam escape; then dish up and serve.

The Potato.

Baked Potatoes. Select large, smooth potatoes, wash and bake without removing the skins.

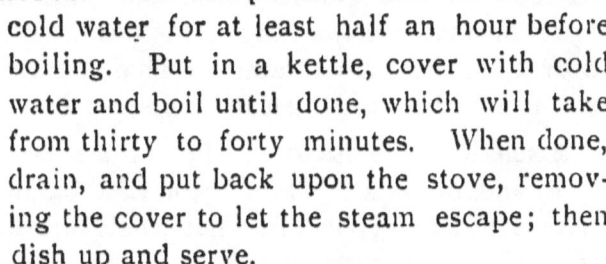

Mashed Potatoes.

Mashed Potatoes. Select small and irregular-shaped potatoes, which will not look so well cooked in other ways; peel, wash and boil until done; drain and wash thoroughly, season with salt and pepper, butter and milk or cream. Stir until light, put in a tureen, put small bits of butter over the top, and serve.

Potatoes Roasted with Meat. Peel and wash medium-sized potatoes, put in with roast meat and roast for thirty or forty minutes, basting frequently.

Potato Cakes. Take cold mashed potatoes and form into small cakes with the hands, put a spoonful of drippings into a hot frying-pan, put in the cakes and fry both sides to a nice brown; serve at once.

Baked Potato Balls. Take warm mashed potatoes, form into round balls with the hands, roll in flour, place in rows in a baking pan and bake in a quick oven for fifteen minutes, serve with drawn butter sauce.

Fried Potatoes. Slice cold potatoes (new ones are the best) and put in a frying-pan with hot melted butter, fry until brown and stir to keep from scorching; serve hot.

French Fried Potatoes. Peel and cut potatoes into narrow strips lengthwise, wash and drain, and dry upon a towel or napkin, then plunge into hot fat and fry to a nice brown. Take out with a wire skimmer, drain in a colander, sprinkle with salt and pepper and serve hot.

Escalloped Potatoes. Peel and slice small potatoes, wash and place a layer of them in a baking dish; season with salt and pepper, and put small bits of butter on the top. Continue these layers until the dish is full. Then pour in enough milk to almost cover the potatoes, put in the oven and bake for three-quarters of an hour.

Boiled Sweet Potatoes. Wash and trim the potatoes and boil from forty to fifty minutes. When done, place in the oven a few minutes to dry, serve whole.

Baked Sweet Potatoes. Prepare as above, and bake for about an hour. Large ones will require an hour and a quarter to bake well done.

Cold Sweet Potatoes. Sweet potatoes that are left over from a previous meal are nice when sliced and fried brown in hot butter.

Fried Potatoes with Eggs. Slice cold boiled potatoes and fry with small pieces of salt pork or good butter until brown, then break up two or three eggs and stir into them, just as you dish them for the table.

Vegetables

Saratoga Potatoes. Peel the potatoes and slice them with a slaw cutter, put them in cold water with a handful of salt and let them stand for an hour or more, then drain first in a colander, then on a napkin until dry. Fry in hot lard until a nice brown. These will keep several days; should they lose their crispiness before all are used, set in a brisk oven for a few moments.

Escalloped Onions. Boil six or eight large onions until tender. If the onions are very strong, change the water once while boiling. Separate them with a spoon and place alternately a layer of onion and a layer of bread crumbs in a pudding dish, season each layer with salt, pepper and melted butter, then pour over the whole enough milk to nearly cover them; put in the oven and bake to a nice brown.

Creamed Onions. Peel, wash and boil until tender, a quart of medium sized onions. When done, drain off the water and put in enough milk to almost cover them, season with salt and pepper, mix ½ a tablespoonful of flour with a lump of butter the size of an egg, stir this into the onions, when the milk boils, and boil a few minutes.

Fried Onions. Slice the onions fine and put in a frying pan containing about ½ a cupful of pork drippings, or butter and lard, equal parts, season with salt and pepper and fry to a nice brown; stir frequently.

Macaroni and Cheese. Boil macaroni in salt and water until tender, butter a pudding dish and put in a layer of macaroni, then layer of grated cheese, season with butter and pepper, then put in another layer of macaroni and so on until the dish is nearly full; finish

Macaroni.

with a layer of cheese, put in enough milk to nearly cover all and bake forty minutes.

Creamed Macaroni. Boil half a package of macaroni until tender, in slightly salted water. When done, drain and cut into two inch lengths and put in a pudding dish; pour over it a drawn butter sauce, and cover the top with rolled cracker, and bake for half an hour.

Boiled Cauliflower. Trim and clean a head of nice white cauliflower and boil in salted water for one-half hour, take out and drain, break apart carefully and arrange in the dish in which it is to be served and pour over melted butter or a drawn butter sauce, season with pepper and salt if necessary. Cabbage cut in quarters, boiled and drained, is very nice prepared in like manner.

The Cauliflower.

Baked Cauliflower. Boil a head of cauliflower whole in salt and water; and when tender drain carefully and put in a dish that will fit into one which is suitable to put on the table; pour over it a drawn butter sauce, sprinkle a little grated cheese over all, baste with melted butter and bake to a nice brown and serve.

Fried Egg Plant. Peel the plant and cut in slices about half an inch in thickness; sprinkle the slices with a little salt, and let it stand for an hour or two. Then dip first in beaten egg, then in cracker dust, and fry in hot butter; season with pepper and salt while frying. Serve at once.

Baked Egg Plant. Cut an egg plant in halves, season with salt and pepper; do not peel it, but cut the ends so it will stand; put in a baking pan, baste with butter, and bake about thirty minutes, using butter freely.

Green Vegetables. All green vegetables should be boiled in salted water until done. If you do dot wish to use them at once, put them in cold water and they will keep fresh in this way for several days; when ready for use, treat them as canned vegetables.

Boiled Cabbage. Cut a cabbage into six or eight pieces and boil until tender in salted water; drain, put into the dish in which they are to be served, season with salt and pepper, and melted butter.

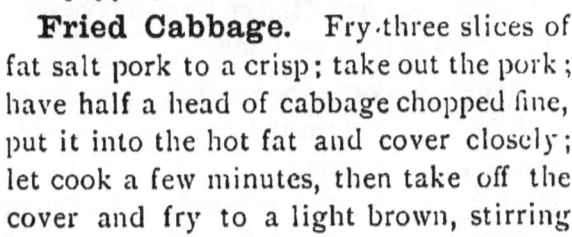

Fried Cabbage. Fry three slices of fat salt pork to a crisp; take out the pork; have half a head of cabbage chopped fine, put it into the hot fat and cover closely; let cook a few minutes, then take off the cover and fry to a light brown, stirring often, so as to have the color uniform.

The Cabbage.

Cabbage Cooked in Milk. Chop half a head of cabbage fine, put into a stew pan, cover with water, and boil until tender; then draw off the water, add milk to nearly cover the cabbage, add a lump of butter the size of an egg, salt and pepper to taste; simmer in the milk ten or fifteen minutes, and serve.

Mashed Turnips. Peel and wash the turnips, and cut into pieces the size of a medium-sized potato, boil until tender; when done, drain, mash fine and season with butter, pepper and salt.

String Beans. String the beans and cut into three or four pieces; boil in salted water until tender; drain and pour over them milk or sweet cream; add a small lump of butter, pepper and salt to taste, and boil five minutes longer; then serve.

The Turnip.

Deviled Tomatoes. Take large firm tomatoes and cut in slices one-half inch in thickness, and lay in a shallow dish; rub the yolk of a hard-boiled egg with one tablespoonful of vinegar, one of melted butter, one teaspoonful of sugar, a very little salt, mustard and cayenne; stir smooth, set upon the stove, and let come to a boil; then pour it on a well beaten egg, set in a vessel containing hot water, while you broil the tomatoes; lay them on a hot dish and pour the hot dressing over them.

Raw Tomatoes. Peel the tomatoes, slice and place in the dish in which they are to be served; season with salt, pepper, sugar and vinegar; or a mayonnaise dressing can be made and poured over them.

Stuffed Tomatoes. Take a dozen plump tomatoes, cut a thin slice off from the stem end, and lift out the heart and juice; drain off the juice and crush the pulp with a potato masher; mix with them one-fourth of a cupful of butter, two tablespoonsfuls of sugar, one and one-half cupfuls of bread crumbs, and with this mixture fill the tomatoes; put on the tops and arrange in a baking pan, and bake for forty-five minutes.

Green Peas. Boil until tender, drain nearly dry; season with butter, pepper and salt. A cupful of cream can be added if preferred.

Lima Beans and Shelled Beans. Lima beans and shelled beans are boiled until tender and seasoned the same as green peas.

Asparagus. Wash the asparagus and cut off the hard ends; boil until tender and season with butter, pepper and salt, and serve on dry toast.

Asparagus.

Green Corn Fritters. Grate two cupfuls of corn from the cob; mix with it one beaten egg, one cupful of sweet milk, soda the size of a pea, one tablespoonful of melted butter; add flour enough to make a batter. Fry on a hot griddle, or by adding a little more flour, they can be fried in spoonfuls in a kettle of hot lard.

Vegetables

Green Corn. Corn in the ear. Husk and pick off the silk carefully, and boil in salad water from thirty to forty minutes. A few minutes of cooking will suffice for canned corn. Season with butter, pepper and salt, and milk, if you choose.

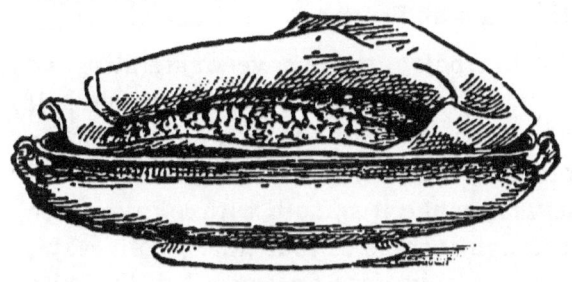
Green Corn.

Oyster Plant. Scrape and wash the root, and cut in thin slices. For soup add milk, and season the same as oyster stew. As a vegetable drain off nearly all the water, and add enough milk to nearly cover, add pepper and salt, and a good sized lump of butter, in which has been stirred a tablespoonful of flour. Do not put in enough flour to make the dressing thick, but just enough to render it creamy.

Mushrooms. Peel and wash a dozen heads of mushrooms, and whiten by plunging them alternately in hot and cold water. Let them drain, and when dry, put them in a sauce pan with a tablespoonful of melted butter; cook for a few minutes, then add a teaspoonful of flour, a little salt and pepper, and half a pint of stock; let cook slowly for fifteen or twenty minutes; remove the mushrooms and place on the dish on which they are to be served; add a little water to the sauce, and stir in the beaten yolks of two eggs and a teaspoonful of vinegar; cook for a minute or two, and pour over the mushrooms, and serve.

Boiled Hominy. Wash the hominy and put into a stone jar. Do not fill the jar much over half full with the hominy; then fill up the jar with cold water, place the jar in a kettle of boiling water, and cook for six hours. Let be served as a side dish, season with melted butter or cream. For breakfast it is served with cream and sugar.

Spinach. Cut off the roots, look over very carefully, and wash in several waters; boil for one-half hour, or until tender. Take up and drain in a colander, place in the dish in which it is to be served; make it smooth with a knife, then cut through it three or four times, both ways, with a sharp knife. Season liberally with hot melted butter, pepper and salt, if necessary. A cupful of scalded cream, or a drawn butter sauce, can be used as a dressing, instead of the melted butter, if preferred.

Spinach.

Boiled Rice. Put one cupful of rice, and cover with two cupfuls of cold water; boil until the rice has absorbed the water; then add a pint of milk, and boil for thirty or forty minutes longer, stirring carefully from time to time; season with salt. Put it in the dish in which it is to be served, and pour over it a little melted butter.

Parsnips. (Fried.) Scrape and wash clean, and boil until tender in salted water; take out of the kettle, drain and cut in halves; dip in a beaten egg and fry in hot butter, or lard.

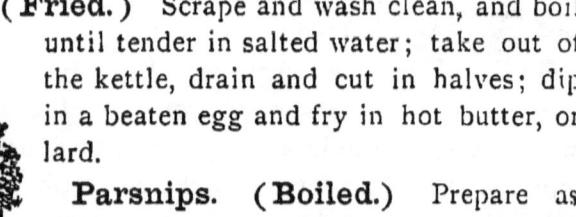
The Parsnip.

Parsnips. (Boiled.) Prepare as above and season with butter, pepper and salt, and serve hot.

Succotash. Take two cupfuls of green corn cut off the cob, and one cupful of green shelled beans; put in a stew pan, cover with water; add a teaspoonful of salt and boil until tender. When done, add one-half a cupful of cream, or milk, a small lump of butter, pepper and salt if necessary; cook for a few minutes and serve.

Vegetables

Hominy Croquettes. Mix together two cupfuls of cold boiled hominy, two eggs, a tablespoonful of melted butter, and a little salt, and a teaspoonful of flour; fry in small spoonfuls in hot lard. Serve with maple syrup, honey, or melted sugar.

Steamed Rice. Put in a pudding dish one cupful of rice, and three cupfuls of milk, or water; add a large teaspoonful of salt, and steam one and one-quarter hours. Serve the same as boiled rice.

Rice Croquettes. Take two cupfuls of cold rice, either boiled or steamed, and mix into it thoroughly two beaten eggs, and a tablespoonful of melted butter.

Potato Croquettes. You need mashed potatoes, salt and pepper to taste; when liked, a very little minced parsley, egg, and bread crumbs. Boil and mash the potatoes; add a seasoning of pepper and salt, and when liked, a little minced parsley. Roll the potatoes into small balls, cover them with egg and bread crumbs, and fry in hot oil or dripping until light brown; let them drain before the fire, dish them on a napkin, and serve.

Potato Croquettes.

Boiled Artichokes. Needed to each ½ gallon of water, allow 1 heaped tablespoonful of salt, a piece of soda the size of a 25c piece; artichokes. Wash the artichokes well in several waters; see that no insects remain about them, and trim away the leaves at the bottom. Cut off the stems and put them into *boiling* water, to which have been added salt and soda in the above proportion. Keep the sauce pan uncovered, and let them boil quickly until tender; ascertain when they are done by thrusting a Fork in them or by trying if the leaves can be easily removed. Take them out, let them drain for a minute or two, and serve on a napkin, or with a little white sauce poured

Artichokes.

over. A tureen of melted butter or oiled butter should accompany them. This vegetable, unlike any other, is considered better for being gathered two or three days; but they must be well soaked and washed previous to dressing, or if left till cold, they can be served with olive oil and vinegar.

Boiled Beets. When large, young and juicy, this vegetable makes a very excellent addition to winter salads, and may easily be converted into an economical and quickly made pickle. Beets are more frequently served cold than hot; when the latter mode is preferred, melted butter should be sent to table with it. They may also be stewed with button onions, or boiled and served with roasted onions. Wash the beets thoroughly; but do not prick or break the skin before they are cooked, or they will lose their beautiful color in boiling. Put them into boiling water, and let them boil until tender, keeping them well covered. If to be served hot, remove the peel quickly, cut the beet into thick slices, and send to table with melted butter. For salads, pickle, etc., let the root cool, then peel, and cut into slices.

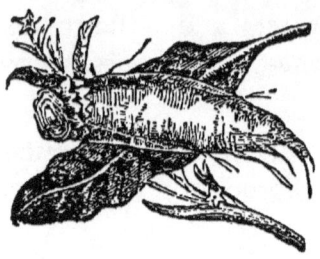

The Beetroot.

Boiled Brussels Sprouts. Clean the sprouts from insects, nicely wash them, and pick off any dead or discolored leaves from the outsides: put them into a saucepan of *boiling* water, with salt and soda in the above proportion; keep the pan uncovered, and let them boil quickly over a brisk fire until tender; drain, dish and serve with a tureen of melted butter, and maître d'hôtel sauce is sometimes poured over them. Another mode of serving is, when they are dished, to stir in about one and a half ounce of butter, and a seasoning of pepper and salt.

Brussels Sprouts.

They must, however, be sent to table very quickly, as, being so very small, this vegetable soon cools. Where the cook is very expeditious, this vegetable, when cooked, may be arranged on the dish in the form of a pineapple; and so served, has a very pretty appearance.

Stewed Red Cabbage. Needed, 1 red cabbage, a small slice of ham, ½ oz. of fresh butter, 1 pint of weak stock or broth, 1 gill of vinegar, salt and pepper to taste, 1 tablespoonful of pounded sugar. Cut the cabbage into very thin slices, put it into a stewpan, with the ham cut in dice, the butter, half a pint of stock, and the vinegar; cover the pan closely, and let it stew for 1 hour. When it is very tender, add the remainder of the stock, a seasoning of salt and pepper, and the pounded sugar; mix all well together, stir over the fire until nearly all the liquor has dried away, and serve. Fried sausages are usually sent to table with this dish; they should be laid round and on the cabbage, as a garnih.

Stewed Carrots. Take 7 or 8 large carrots, 1 teacupful of broth, pepper and salt to taste, ½ teacupful of cream, thickening of butter and flour. Scrape the carrots nicely; half boil, and slice them into a stewpan; add the broth, pepper and salt, and cream; simmer till tender, and be careful the carrots are not broken. A few minutes before serving, mix a little flour with about one ounce of butter; thicken the gravy with this; let it just boil up, and serve.

The Carrot.

Baked Mushrooms. For this mode of cooking, the mushroom flaps are better than the buttons and should not be too large. Cut off a portion of stalk, peel the top, and put them at once into a tin baking dish, with a very small piece of butter placed on each mushroom; sprinkle over a little pepper, and let them bake for about twenty minutes.

Have ready a *very hot* dish, pile the mushrooms high in the center, pour the gravy round, and send them to the table quickly on very *hot* plates.

Baked Spanish Onions. Put the onions, with their skins on, into a saucepan of boiling water, slightly salted, and let them boil quickly for an hour. Then take them out, wipe them thoroughly, wrap each one in a piece of buttered paper, and bake them in a moderate oven for two hours, or longer, should the onions be very large. They may be served in their skins and eaten with a piece of cold butter and a seasoning of pepper and salt; or they may be peeled, and a good brown gravy poured over them.

Stewed Cucumbers. Needed, 3 large cucumbers, flour, butter, rather more than ½ pint of good brown gravy. Cut the cucumbers lengthwise the size of the dish they are intended to be served in; empty them of the seeds, and put them into boiling water, with a little salt, and let them simmer for 5 minutes; then take them out, place them in another stewpan with the gravy, and let them boil over a brisk fire until the cucumbers are tender. Should these be bitter, add a lump of sugar; carefully dish them, skim the sauce, pour over the cucumbers, and serve.

The Cucumber.

A German Method of Cooking Potatoes. Needed: Eight to ten middling-sized potatoes, 3 oz. of butter, 2 tablespoonfuls of flour, ½ pint of broth, 2 tablespoonfuls of vinegar. Put the butter and flour in a stewpan; stir over the fire until the butter is of a nice brown color, and add the broth and vinegar; peel and cut the potatoes into long thin slices, lay them in the gravy, and let them simmer gently until tender, which will be in from 10 to 15 minutes, and serve very hot. A laurel leaf simmered with the potatoes is an improvement.

Stewed Spanish Onions. Peel the onions, taking care not to cut away too much of the tops or tails, or they would then fall to pieces; put them in a stewpan capable of holding them at the bottom without piling them one on the top of another; add the broth or gravy, and simmer *very gently* until the onions are perfectly tender. Dish them, pour the gravy round, and serve. Instead of using broth, Spanish onions may be stewed with a large piece of butter; they must be done very gradually over a slow fire or hot plate, and will produce plenty of gravy.

NOTE.—Stewed Spanish onions are a favorite accompaniment to roast shoulder of mutton.

Spinach Dressed with Cream. Needed: Two pailfuls of spinach, 2 tablespoonfuls of salt, 2 oz. of butter, 8 tablespoonfuls of cream, 1 small teaspoonful of pounded sugar, a very little grated nutmeg. Boil and drain the spinach, chop it finely, and put it into a stewpan with the butter; stir over a gentle fire, and when the butter has dried away, add the remaining ingredients, and simmer for about five minutes. Previously to adding the cream, boil it first, in case it should curdle. Serve on a hot dish, and garnish either with sippets of toasted bread or leaves of puff paste.

Baked Tomatoes. You need six tomatoes, some bread crumbs, a little butter, onion, cayenne and salt. Scoop out a small hole at the top; fry the bread crumbs, onion, etc., and fill the holes with this as high up as possible; then bake the tomatoes in the oven and take care that the skins do not break.

Boiled Vegetable Marrow. Have ready a saucepan of boiling water, properly salted, put in the marrows after peeling them, and boil them until quite tender. Take them up with a slice; halve, and, should they be very large, quarter them. Dish them on toast, and send to table with a tureen of melted butter, or, in lieu of this, a small pat of salt butter. Large vegetable marrows may be preserved throughout the winter by storing them in a dry place; when wanted for use, a few slices should be cut and boiled in the same manner as above; but when once begun, the marrow must be eaten quickly, as it keeps but a short time after it is cut. Vegetable marrows are also very delicious, mashed; they should be boiled, then drained, and mashed smoothly with a wooden spoon. Heat them in a saucepan, add a seasoning of salt and pepper, and a small piece of butter, and dish with a few sippets of toasted bread placed round as a garnish.

Vegetable marrows are delightful when sliced, and fried for ten minutes in butter. Before being fried they may be dipped in a batter of flour and water, seasoned with a little salt. Vegetable marrow may also be dressed as follows: Boil one, and when it is about ready, cut it in pieces, which place in a fresh saucepan, covered with soup stock, either white or brown; add a little salt in stewing. Serve in a deep dish when thoroughly tender. Vegetable marrows are very nice plain boiled, and served upon buttered toast. Peel them and cut them so as to be able to remove the seeds. Marrows will take from twenty minutes to an hour to boil, according to size and age. After being parboiled, they may be sliced down, dipped in egg, and then rubbed among bread crumbs and fried; serve them as hot as possible.

Butter Beans. With a knife, cut off the ends of pods and strings from both sides, being very careful to remove every shred; cut every bean lengthwise, in two or three strips, and leave them for half an hour in cold water. Much more than cover them with boiling water; boil till perfectly tender. It is well to allow three hours for boiling. Drain well, return to kettle, and add a dressing of half a gill of cream, one and a half ounces of butter, one even teaspoon of salt, and half a teaspoon of pepper. This is sufficient for a quart of cooked beans.

Vegetables

Mashed Squash. Peel, seed and slice fresh summer squashes. Lay in cold water ten minutes; put into boiling water, a little salt, and cook tender. Twenty minutes will suffice if the squash be young. Mash in a colander, pressing out all the water; heap in a deep dish, seasoning with pepper, salt and butter. Serve hot.

Baked Squash. Cut in pieces, scrape well, bake from one to one and a half hours, according to the thickness of the squash; to be eaten with salt and butter as sweet potatoes.

Fried Squash. Cut the squash into thin slices, and sprinkle with salt; let it stand a few moments; then beat two eggs, and dip the squash into the egg; then fry it brown in butter.

Pilaff. Two cups of water, one cup of rice. Put on the water with a little salt, and add the juice of one or two tomatoes to the water, or sufficient to color it. When the water boils, put in the rice, and boil until all the water is soaked up. Then add melted butter to taste, stir, cover and keep in a warm place, but not on the fire, till dinner is served.

To Preserve Vegetables for Winter Use. Green string beans must be picked when young; put a layer three inches deep in a small wooden keg or barrel; sprinkle in salt an inch deep, then put another layer of beans, then salt, and beans and salt in alternate layers, until you have enough; let the last be salt; cover them with a piece of board which will fit the inside of the barrel or keg, and place a heavy weight upon it; they will make brine.

When wanted for use, soak them one night or more, in plenty of water, changing it once or twice, until the salt is out of them; then cut them, and boil the same as when fresh.

Carrots, beans, beetroots, parsnips and potatoes keep best

in dry sand or earth in a cellar; turnips keep best on a cellar bottom, or they may be kept the same as carrots, etc. Whatever earth remains about them when taken from the ground, should not be taken off.

When sprouts come on potatoes or other vegetables, they should be carefully cut off. The young sprouts from turnips are sometimes served as a salad, or boiled tender in salt and water, and served with butter and pepper over.

Celery may be kept all winter by setting it in boxes filled with earth; keep it in the cellar; it will grow and whiten in the dark. Leeks may also be kept in this way.

Cabbage set out in earth, in a good cellar, will keep good and fresh all winter. Small close heads of cabbage may be kept many weeks by taking them before the frost comes, and laying them on a stone floor; this will whiten them, and make them tender.

Store onions are to be strung, and hung in a dry, cold place.

BREAD AND CAKES

Yeast. Take one gallon of water and in it boil two handfuls of hops. Then add one pint of grated potato, strain through a colander, and when lukewarm add one cup of salt, one of sugar, and of yeast. Let it raise and in a few hours transfer to jugs and cork up tight. A teacupful of this will make four loaves of bread.

Railroad Yeast. Dissolve two cakes of yeast in a quart of warm water and let it raise. Boil twelve or fourteen good sized potatoes, mash and mix in one-half teacupful of salt, one-half teacup of sugar; add one quart of cold water, and one of hot; stir in the water in which the yeast cake was dissolved, and let it rise. Use one pint of this yeast for every loaf of bread.

Salt Rising. Take two teacupsful of hot water and one of cold, put in a pitcher, or other deep vessel; add one teaspoonful of salt and one of soda; stir in enough flour to make a batter; set in a kettle of warm water, cover closely until it rises. If kept warm it will rise in from four to six hours.

Salt Rising Bread. Sift some flour in a bread pan, make a cavity in the center, and stir in slowly a quart of boiling water. Cool and thin the scalded mass with a quart of milk; add a tablespoonful of salt, stir in the salt

Cottage Loaf.

rising, cover with flour and set away to rise. When light, mix thoroughly, knead into loaves, put into baking pans and let it rise once more. When light, bake in a moderate oven from thirty to forty minutes, according to the size of the loaves.

Home Made Bread. Peel, boil and mash six or eight medium-sized potatoes; add a quart of water, strain through a colander and add enough flour to make a batter, and beat for two or three minutes; mix in thoroughly a tablespoonful of salt and a cupful of home-made yeast, or a cake of compressed yeast, cover, and set away in a warm place to rise. When light, knead in enough flour so that the dough will not stick to the hands. Let it rise once more, and when light shape into loaves with as little kneading as possible; put into baking pans and when light, bake from three-quarters to one hour in a moderate oven.

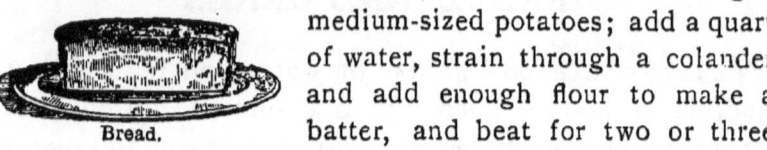
Bread.

Boston Brown Bread. Put in a stirring bowl a pint of sour milk; add a cupful of New Orleans molasses, two level teaspoonfuls of soda dissolved in a little hot water, and one of salt. Add two cups of corn meal and two of graham flour; mix all thoroughly together, put in a tin pail that will not be more than half full when the mixture is in it; cover tightly and boil for three hours; uncover, and place in the oven for ten or fifteen minutes to dry.

Graham Bread. Take one quart of white bread sponge, add a scant half cupful of molasses, and half a teaspoonful of soda dissolved in a little hot water. Stir in as much graham flour as can be worked in with a spoon, put in a baking pan, let it rise, and when light bake for one-half hour in a moderate oven.

Delicate Rolls. Take three pints of bread dough, and

work into it one cupful of butter, one-half cupful of sugar, and two eggs; mix these into the dough, and if the dough is too soft and sticky, add more flour, and set in a warm place to rise. When light, flour the bread board, turn out the dough, dust with flour, and cut into pieces the size of an English walnut. Grease or flour a large sized baking pan, work each roll smooth, and place in the baking pan in rows; set away to rise, and when light bake twenty minutes. When baked, brush with sweet cream. These are nice either hot or cold.

Parker House Rolls. Scald one quart of milk, and add to it one-half cupful each of sugar and butter, and one teaspoonful of salt; stir in enough flour to make a batter as thick as for pancakes. Let it cool, and when lukewarm stir in a half cupful of yeast or one cake of compressed yeast, dissolved in a little warm water. Set in a warm place to rise, and when very light add flour and knead into a dough, not too stiff, flatten with a rolling pin, and cut into cakes, about an inch thick, with a biscuit cutter. Roll out each cake separately, spread with butter, fold double, and let rise again, and bake for twenty-five minutes.

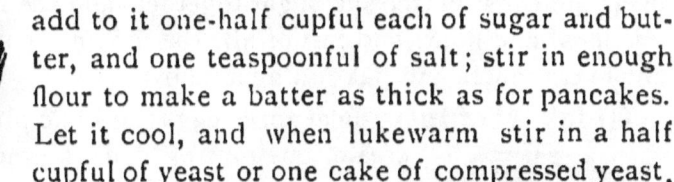
Twist.

Breakfast Rolls. Take a quart of ordinary light bread dough and work into it one teacupful of lard, cut into small bits, knead for five minutes, and set away to rise. When light, flour the bread board, lift the dough upon it, cut the dough into pieces the size of a small egg; knead each into a small loaf, place in a baking pan in rows, just touching each other, let rise, and when very light bake twenty minutes.

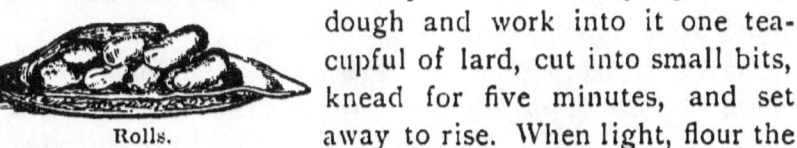
Rolls.

Graham Gems No. 1. Take one pint of sour milk, add to it two tablespoonfuls of molasses, one of melted butter, a teaspoonful of salt, and one of soda; stir in enough

Graham flour to make a very thick batter. Have the gem pans hot, and put a spoonful of the batter in each pan and bake for twenty minutes in a brisk oven.

Graham Gems No. 2. Beat two eggs, add one-half cupful of sugar, one of milk, two of Graham flour, one of wheat flour, two tablespoonfuls of butter, and three teaspoonfuls of baking powder; stir all thoroughly together and bake for twenty to twenty-five minutes.

Corn Gems. Take two cupfuls of cornmeal, two of flour, two of sweet milk, one-half cupful of butter, one-half cupful of sugar, two eggs, and three teaspoonfuls of baking powder. Beat the eggs, butter and sugar together, add the milk, then the meal and flour, and last of all, the baking powder; stir for five minutes and bake in gem pans.

Quick Muffins. Beat three eggs, add one pint of sour cream, one pint of flour, a pinch of salt, and one teaspoonful of soda, dissolved in a little warm water; beat until very light and bake in muffin rings or gem pans.

Muffins.

White Muffins. Take one teacupful of milk, add two beaten eggs, one half cupful of sugar, and two tablespoonfuls of melted butter, then sift in three teacupfuls of flour, to which has been added three teaspoonfuls of baking powder. Stir all together, beat for three minutes, and bake in a quick oven in muffin rings or gem pans.

Sally Lunn. Beat two eggs, and add a lump of soft butter the size of an egg, put in three teaspoonfuls of sugar, one-half pint of milk, one pint of flour, and sift in three teaspoonfuls of baking powder; stir all together, and bake in shallow tins for twenty minntes.

Steamed Corn Bread. Take two cups of sweet milk, one of sour, and add to it two cupfuls of corn meal, one of flour, one of sugar, and one teaspoonful of soda, dissolve in a little warm water. Steam for two hours.

Bread and Cakes

Baking Powder Biscuits. Put one quart of flour in a sieve, add to it two heaping teaspoonfuls of good baking powder; sift and rub in one tablespoonful of lard or butter; add a teaspoonful of salt and moisten with a pint of milk or water. Knead quickly, roll and cut into cakes and bake in a quick oven for fifteen or twenty minutes. Serve hot.

Biscuits.

Rusks. Beat two eggs, add one-half cupful of sugar, three tablespoonfuls of butter, one cupful of sweet milk, three of flour, and two teaspoonfuls of baking powder. Stir all together, bake in shallow buttered tins in a quick oven.

Fritters. Take two beaten eggs, one pint of sweet milk, butter the size of an egg, and two teaspoonfuls of baking powder; mix with flour, as stiff as you can stir with a spoon. Drop small spoonfuls into boiling hot lard, fry to a nice brown.

Albany Breakfast Cakes. Take ten eggs, beat for three minutes, add one-half cupful of melted butter, three pints of warm milk, two teaspoonfuls of salt, one of soda dissolved in a little hot water. Make a thick batter with white Indian meal; pour to the depth of an inch into buttered tins, and bake in a quick oven from thirty to forty minutes.

Fried Cakes. Beat one egg, add one cupful of sugar, one-half cupful of cream, and one and one-half cupfuls of sour milk, one teaspoonful of soda dissolved in a little warm water, grate in half a nutmeg, mix in enough flour to make a soft dough, cut in bars an inch wide and half an inch thick, twist and fry in hot lard.

Spider Corn Cakes. Beat two eggs, and one-half cup of sugar, two cups of sweet milk, and one of sour, three tablespoonfuls of melted butter, and one and one-third cupfuls of corn meal, one third of a cupful of flour, and one teaspoonful of soda; mix all the ingredients together, heat a spider hot, greasing well, pour in the mixture, and bake in a hot oven from twenty-five to thirty minutes.

Flannel Cakes. Take two eggs and stir them into a pint of sour milk, put in an even teaspoonful of soda and flour enough to make a thin batter. Bake on a hot greased griddle.

Graham Griddle Cakes. Mix together one pint of Graham flour, one-half pint of corn meal, one-half pint of flour, two tablespoonfuls of molasses, one-half teaspoonful of salt, one egg, one pint of buttermilk, one teaspoonful of soda. Bake on a well greased hot griddle.

Green Corn Griddle Cakes. Six ears of green corn, grated; stir in two eggs, one pint of milk, one pint of flour, two tablespoonfuls of melted butter, a little salt, one teaspoonful of baking powder. Beat well and bake on a hot griddle.

Waffles. Take one pint of sour milk, three tablespoonfuls of melted butter, three eggs, beaten separately, a teaspoonful of soda, dissolved in a little warm water,

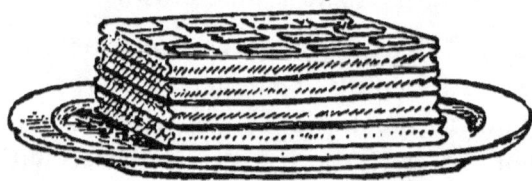
Waffles.

add a little salt, and stir in enough flour to make a stiff batter. Bake upon waffle irons.

Pop-Overs. Take one pint of sifted flour, one level teaspoonful of salt. Beat three eggs light, add one pint of milk, and gradually stir into the flour mixture; **beat six minutes** after all are together; put into gem pans, **and bake from** twenty to twenty-five minutes

Pop-Overs.

Bread Griddle Cakes. Soak a pint of stale bread in a pint of sour milk over night. In the morning mash fine with a spoon; add another pint of milk, a little salt, two teaspoonfuls of soda dissolved in a little water, and flour enough to make a batter as thick as for ordinary griddle cakes.

Buckwheat Cakes. Take one pint of buttermilk, one pint of water, one-half cake of yeast, a little salt, and stir in enough buckwheat flour to make a batter; let it rise over night, and in the morning add two tablespoonfuls of molasses, and a teaspoonful of soda dissolved in a little water. Bake on a hot griddle well greased.

Breakfast Cakes.

Toast. Cut stale bread into slices, toast to a nice brown; butter, set in the oven for a moment, and serve hot.

Cream Toast. Take one quart of milk, add a lump of butter the size of an egg, a level teaspoonful of salt; put in a double heater, and let it come to a boil. When boiling hot stir in a tablespoonful of flour, wet with a little milk. Place the toasted bread in a deep dish, pour the cream over it, and serve at once.

Spanish Toast. Beat two eggs, add one cup of milk, a teaspoonful of flour, and a little salt; dip slices of bread in the mixture, and fry to a nice brown in hot lard or drippings. Sift powdered sugar on each slice, and serve hot.

Vienna Rolls. Sift two or three times one quart of flour, two teaspoonfuls of baking powder, and half a teaspoonful of salt; work in one tablespoonful of butter; add one pint of milk, stirring into a dough of the usual consistency; roll to the thickness of half an inch, cut into circular forms and fold over once, moistening a little between the folds, if necessary, to make them stick; butter the baking pan well, and do not let the rolls touch each other when placed thereon; moisten the tops of the rolls with a little milk, or butter melted in milk, and bake in a hot oven.

Chicago Muffins. Mix together one and one-half pints of flour, half a pint of corn meal, two teaspoonfuls of baking powder, one tablespoonful of sugar, and one teaspoonful of salt. Work in one tablespoonful of butter; heat, and add three eggs, and one pint of milk, and beat the whole quickly in a firm batter. Have the griddle hot and well greased to receive the muffin rings and cook to a nice brown. Muffin rings should not, as a rule, be filled to more than half of their capacity, and as soon as the batter rises to the top the muffin is generally ready to be turned.

Jolly Boys. Mix together thoroughly, while dry one and one-half pints of rye meal, half a pint of flour, half a teacupful of corn meal, two pinches of cinnamon, a little salt, and two teaspoonfuls of baking powder. Add one egg, well beaten; two tablespoonfuls each of molasses and sugar, and cold water enough to make a thick batter. Fry in hot lard a heaping tablespoonful at a time, and cook until well browned.

CAKE

Rich Bride or Christening Cake. Needed, 5 lbs. of the finest flour, 3 lbs. of fresh butter, 5 lbs. of currants, 2 lbs of sifted loaf sugar, 2 nutmegs, ¼ oz. of mace, ¼ oz. of cloves, 16 eggs, 1 lb. of sweet almonds, ½ lb. of candied citron, ½ lb. each of candied orange and lemon peel, 1 gill of wine, 1 gill of brandy. Let the flour be as fine as possible, and well dried and sifted; the currants washed, picked and dried before the fire; the sugar well pounded and sifted; the nutmegs grated; the spices pounded; the eggs thoroughly whisked, whites and yolks separately; the almonds pounded with a little orange-flower water; and the candied peel cut in neat slices. When all these ingredients are prepared, mix them in the following manner: Begin working the butter with the hand till it becomes of a cream-like consistency; stir in the sugar, and when the whites of the eggs are whisked to a solid froth, mix them with the butter and sugar; next, well beat up the yolks for 10 minutes, and adding them to the flour, nutmegs, mace and cloves, continue beating the whole together for half an hour or longer, till wanted for

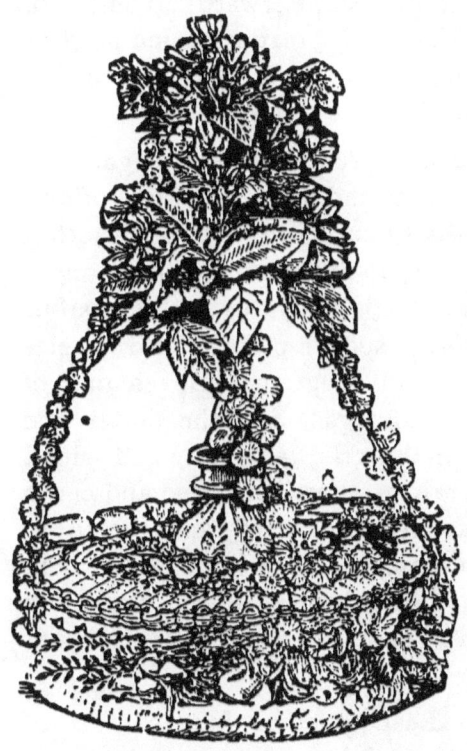

the oven. Then mix in lightly the currants, almonds and candied peel, with the wine and brandy; and having lined a hoop with buttered paper, fill it with the mixture, and bake the cake in a tolerably quick oven, taking care, however, not to burn it; to prevent this, the top of it may be covered with a sheet of paper. To ascertain whether the cake is done, plunge a clean knife into the middle of it, withdraw it directly, and if the blade is not sticky and looks bright, the cake is sufficiently baked. These cakes are usually spread with a thick layer of almond icing, and over that another layer of sugar icing, and afterward ornamented. In baking a large cake like this, great attention must be paid to the heat of the oven; it should not be too fierce, but have moderate heat to bake the cake through.

Fruit Cake. Take three cupfuls of brown sugar, one of butter, one pound of raisins, one of currants, one-half pound of citron, one quart of flour, one teaspoonful of currant jelly, eight eggs beaten separately, two teaspoonfuls of sour milk, one teaspoonful of soda, a piece of lard the size of a walnut, one tablespoonful of ground cloves, one of cinnamon, and two grated nutmegs. Stir the butter and sugar to a cream, then stir in the milk, lard, jelly and spices, then stir in the fruit (the raisins must be stoned and cut in two, the currants picked, washed and dried, and the citron shaved fine), then the soda dissolved in a little water, next the flour, and last of all the beaten whites of the eggs; mix all thoroughly together, and bake for three hours in pans lined with buttered paper.

Fruit Cake No. 2. Beat together four cupfuls of sugar, with one and one-half cupfuls of butter, then stir in six beaten eggs, two cupfuls of sweet milk, one pound of stoned and chopped raisins, one pound of chopped or sliced citron, six and one-half cupfuls of flour, and two teaspoonfuls of soda, dissolved in a little warm water; line the baking pans with buttered paper and bake from two to three hours.

Pork Cake. Chop one pound of fat pork very fine, and pour over it a pint of boiling hot water, then stir in three cupfuls of brown sugar, one of molasses, one tablespoonful of ground cinnamon, one of ground cloves, one pound of stoned raisins, eight cups of flour, and two teaspoonfuls of soda dissolved in a little water; stir four or five minutes and bake same as fruit cake.

Clove Cake. Stir together one cup of soft butter with one of sugar and molasses, add one cupful of strong black coffee, in which has been dissolved a teaspoonful of soda, two teaspoonfuls of ground cloves, two of cinnamon, four cupfuls of flour, and two well beaten eggs; mix well, and bake in a moderate oven

The Clove.

Bread Cake. Beat together one cupful of butter with two of sugar, add two well beaten eggs, two cupfuls of stoned raisins, two-thirds teaspoonful of soda in one of milk, and last of all stir in three cupfuls of light bread dough; work until thoroughly mixed, line a baking pan with buttered paper, put in the dough, set in a warm place to rise, and when light bake in a moderate oven for an hour or more.

Watermelon Cake. For the white part, stir to a cream two cupfuls of sugar, with one of butter; then stir in one cupful of sweet milk; mix two teaspoonfuls of cream tartar, and one of soda, with three and one-half cupfuls of flour; stir in with the other ingredients; then add the beaten whites of eight eggs. For the red part: One cupful of red sugar, and one-half cupful of butter, stirred to a cream, add one-third cupful of sweet milk, two cupfuls of flour, in which has been mixed one teaspoonful of cream-tartar, and a half teaspoonful of soda; then the beaten whites of four eggs, and a cupful of small seedless raisins. Have an oval, or round baking pan, put a layer of the white dough in the bottom, then all the red in the middle, and the rest of the white dough around the sides and on top; bake in a moderate oven. You can use a baking pan with a tube if preferable.

Andalusian Cake. Beat three eggs for five or six minutes; add a cupful of fine granulated sugar, and beat two or three minutes longer; then stir in one cupful of flour, a teaspoonful of baking powder and to suit the taste; bake at once in a quick oven.

Raisin Cake. Beat together one cupful of butter, with two of sugar, add a cupful of molasses, three well beaten eggs, one cupful of buttermilk, one of stoned raisins, five of flour, one and one-half teaspoonfuls of soda, two of cinnamon, two of cloves, one grated nutmeg, stir well together and bake as you would fruit cake.

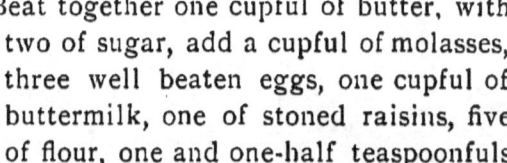
Almonds and Raisins.

Dried Cherry Cake. Beat to a cream one cupful of sugar with one-half cupful of butter, add one-half cupful of sour milk, one cupful of dried cherries, one teaspoonful of soda, spice to taste, and flour enough to make a stiff batter; bake in paper lined tins in a moderate oven for about one hour.

Measured Pound Cake. Four cupfuls of flour, three of sugar, two of butter, one and one-half of sweet milk, nine eggs, two teaspoonfuls of baking powder; beat the butter and sugar together, stir in the milk, then the yolks of the eggs well beaten, next sift in the flour and baking powder together, and last of all stir in the whites, beaten to a stiff froth. Bake in a moderate oven for about forty-five minutes.

Pound Cake.

French Cake. Beat three eggs and one and one-half cupfuls of sugar to a cream, add one-half cupful of soft butter, and beat from three to five minutes longer, put in a cupful of sweet milk and beat again, measure off three cupfuls of flour and add to it two teaspoonfuls of cream of tartar and one of soda, sift twice and add in two parts to the mixture, stirring in thoroughly each time, line a round baking pan with buttered paper and bake in a moderate oven. A nice addition to this cake is a large cupful of nut meats or two cupfuls of raisins or currants. This cake is fully as good if made two or three days before using.

Black Cake (very rich.) Stir together a pound of sugar and a pound of butter for fifteen minutes, then stir in two wineglassfuls of brandy and two of wine, then beat in the beaten yolks of twelve eggs; put in two wineglassfuls of sour cream, one teaspoonful of soda, four grated nutmegs, one tablespoonful of cinnamon, one of mace, one of clove, three pounds of raisins, stoned and chopped, three pounds of currants, washed and dried; and three pounds of citron or two citron, and one-half each of orange and lemon peel; when these are well mixed in, stir in a pound of flour, and last of all the beaten whites of twelve eggs. Bake in a moderate oven for about four hours. This cake is very rich; is nice enough for any entertainment, and will keep for months. It should be made at least two or three weeks before using.

The Nutmeg.

Apple Cake. Stir together one and one-half cupfuls of sugar, with a large half cupful of butter; add two eggs, the whites and yolks beaten separately, one-half cupful of sweet milk, two cupfuls of flour, one teaspoonful of cream tartar, sifted in the flour, and a half teaspoonful of soda, dissolved in the milk. Put in jelly-cake tins, cover the top with sliced apples and bake; when done put a little melted butter, or thick whipped cream on the apple, sift powdered sugar over all, and serve at once.

Spice Cake. Stir for five minutes two cupfuls of sugar with one of soft butter, add four beaten eggs, and stir for five minutes longer, then mix a cupful of sweet milk, a grated nutmeg, a tablespoonful of cinnamon, one of mace, one of clove; measure three cupfuls of flour and mix with it two teaspoonfuls of cream tartar and one of soda; sift twice and stir in with the rest of the ingredients. Bake from forty to sixty minutes in a moderate oven.

Cinnamon.

Spice Cake No. 2. Mix two cupfuls of sugar, with two-thirds of a cupful of butter, add three beaten eggs, a cupful of sour or buttermilk in which has been dissolved a teaspoonful of soda and three and one-half cupfuls of flour; add spices to taste. Bake in shallow square tins; when done cover with the yolk of an egg, beaten with powdered sugar. Cut in squares to serve.

Dried Apple Cake. Soak three cups of dried apples over night in warm water. In the morning chop or cut them into small bits, put in a stew pan with two cupfuls of N. O. molasses and simmer for two hours; add two beaten eggs, one cupful of sugar, one of milk, one-half cupful of butter, two teaspoonfuls of soda, spice to taste, and flour enough to make a stiff batter. Bake as you would fruit cake.

Pound Cake. Put together a pound of sugar, and three-fourths of a pound of butter, and beat for ten minutes, add the beaten yolks of eight eggs; mix three teaspoonfuls of baking powder with a pound of flour. Put in with the sugar, butter and yolks a grated nutmeg, and part of the flour, and stir until smooth, then add the beaten whites of the eggs, and the rest of the flour. Bake in a moderate oven.

Imperial Cake. Rub to a cream one pound of sugar, and three-quarters of a pound of butter, add ten well beaten eggs, a pound of flour, a pound of almonds blanched, and cut fine; one-half pound of stoned raisins, one-half pound of citron, sliced fine, rind and juice of a lemon, and one grated nutmeg. Mix all well together, and bake slowly.

Wine Cake. Beat together two cupfuls of sugar, with one-half cupful of butter, and three eggs; add two cupfuls of sifted flour, one teaspoonful of baking powder, and one gill of wine. Mix into a firm batter, put in deep mould, and bake in a moderate oven. Frost.

Sponge Cake. Stir together two cups of sugar, two and one-half cupfuls of flour, two teaspoonsful of cream tartar. When well mixed, stir in six well-beaten eggs. Line a baking pan with buttered paper, pour in the dough and bake in a moderate oven.

Sponge Cake.

Sponge Cake No. 2. Stir together two cupfuls of sugar, two of flour, and three teaspoonfuls of baking powder. Then mix in separately, the well-beaten whites of four eggs, and the yolks of five; last of all, stir in one-half cupful of cold water. Bake as above.

White Sponge Cake. Stir together one and one-half tumblers of sugar, with one tumbler of flour and one teaspoonful of cream tartar. When these are thoroughly mixed, add the whites of ten eggs beaten to a stiff froth. Line a baking pan with buttered paper, pour in the dough and bake in a moderate oven. Be careful not to jar the cake while baking, as it will cause it to fall.

Water Sponge Cake. Stir together one cupful of sugar, one cupful of flour, one teaspoonful of baking powder, and a pinch of salt. When these are mixed, stir in two well-beaten eggs and one-half cupful of boiling water; bake in paper-lined tins in a moderate oven.

Angel Food. One and one-fourth cupfuls of powdered sugar, one cupful of flour, one-half teaspoonful of cream tartar, whites of nine large, or ten small eggs. Sift the flour four or five times before measuring. Beat the whites two or three minutes, add the cream tartar, then beat them to a very stiff froth; add the sugar and when well beaten in, add the flour, and mix well. Line a baking pan with buttered paper, turn in the mixture and bake in a moderate oven, being careful not to jar the pan, as it will cause the cake to fall.

Chocolate Cake. Shave off one-half cupful of Baker's chocolate, put in a stirring bowl, and set the bowl in boiling water until the chocolate is dissolved. While it is dissolving add one-half cupful of milk; when dissolved set in a cool place. When cold, add two cupfuls of sugar, one-half cupful of butter, one-half cupful of milk, the well-beaten yolks of three eggs and the whites of two. When these are well mixed, stir in two and three-fourths cupfuls of flour, and three teaspoonfuls of baking powder. Bake in layers and frost between.

Tip-Top Cake. Beat together one and one-half cupfuls of sugar, two eggs, one tablespoonful of butter, one cupful of milk, $2\frac{1}{2}$ cupfuls of flour, and two tablespoonfuls of baking powder. Beat for three minutes, pour into a shallow square tin and bake in a rather quick oven.

Cream Cake. Beat together one cup of sugar and two eggs, then add one cupful of sweet cream, one and two-thirds cupfuls of flour and three teaspoonfuls of baking powder. Stir all together and bake in rather a brisk oven.

Snow-Flake Cake. Mix together one and one-half tumblers of powdered sugar, one tumbler of flour, and half a teaspoonful of cream tartar. When they are well mixed, add the well-beaten whites of eight eggs. Bake as you would sponge cake.

Golden Cake. Beat together one cupful of butter with two cupfuls of sugar; add one cupful of milk and beat again. Then stir in two and one-half cupfuls of flour, the well-beaten yolks of six eggs, and three teaspoonfuls of baking powder. Stir all together and bake in a loaf or layers.

Silver Cake. Beat together one cupful of butter with two cupfuls of sugar, two-thirds of a cup of milk, two and one-half cupfuls of flour and three teaspoonfuls of baking powder. Last of all, stir in the well-beaten whites of six eggs.

These cakes can be combined by baking in layers and putting in one of golden, and one of silver, alternately, or they can be baked in a loaf and a marble effect produced by putting in alternately, spoonfuls of each.

Soft Ginger Cake. Take a teacup and put into it four tablespoonfuls of hot water, three of melted butter, and fill up the cup with molasses. Put into the stirring bowl one teaspoonful of ginger and one of soda, and to this add the mixture in the cup. Stir in enough flour to make a stiff cake dough. Pour into square tins and bake carefully.

Molasses Cake. Put together two cupfuls of molasses, two of brown sugar, one of sour milk, one teaspoonful of soda, one cupful of butter, two beaten eggs, 5¼ cupfuls of flour. Beat all together, line a dripping-pan with buttered paper, and put in the dough. Sift white sugar over the top before baking and bake in a slow oven. This is excellent and will keep for weeks.

White Cake. Beat together one cupful of granulated sugar with ¼ of a cupful of butter; beat for ten minutes, then add ½ cupful of sweet milk and 1½ cupfuls of flour; last of all, stir in the whites of two eggs beaten to a froth, and two teaspoonfuls of baking powder. Bake slowly.

Delicate Cake. Beat to a cream one-half cupful of butter, one and one-half cupfuls of sugar; then add one cupful of milk, three of flour, three teaspoonfuls of baking powder and the whites of three eggs beaten to a froth. Bake in two layers. Put frosting between and on top.

White Cream Cake. Stir together two cupfuls of white sugar, two tablespoonfuls of butter, one teacupful of sour cream, one teaspoonful of soda. When these are well mixed, stir in three cupfuls of flour. Last of all, add the well-beaten whites of eight eggs. Bake in shallow baking pans in a moderate oven.

Cold Water Pound Cake. Beat together three eggs and 1½ cupfuls of sugar; add one-half cupful of soft butter, one-half cupful of cold water, two cupfuls of flour, and two teaspoonfuls of baking powder. Stir all together, flavor with lemon, and bake in a moderate oven.

Loaf Cake. Beat three cupfuls of sugar together with one-half cupful of butter; add six beaten eggs and four cupfuls of light bread dough. Mix well together, put in a pan lined with buttered paper and set in a warm place to rise. When light, bake in a moderate oven as you would bread.

Raised Cake. Take two cups of dough and stir into two cups of sugar, two-thirds of a cup of butter, three eggs, and a small teaspoonful of soda. When thoroughly mixed, put in two shallow baking pans, set in a warm place to rise. When light, bake in a moderate oven for about half an hour.

Marble Cake. WHITE PART: Stir together one and one-half cupfuls of sugar and one-half cupful of butter; then add one cupful of sweet milk, one teaspoonful of cream tartar, one-half teaspoonful of soda, and two cupfuls of flour; last of all, stir in the well-beaten whites of four eggs.

Dark Part: Stir together one cupful of brown sugar, one-half cupful of molasses, one-half cupful of soft butter, the beaten yolks of four eggs, one-half cupful of milk, one teaspoonful of cream tartar, one-half teaspoonful of soda, two of cinnamon, and grate in half a nutmeg: then stir in two cupfuls of flour. Line the baking pan with buttered paper and put in alternately, spoonfuls of the light and dark mixtures. Bake in a moderate oven.

Dolly Varden Cake. The whites of three eggs with one teacupful powdered sugar and half a teacupful of butter; two teacupfuls flour with one and a half teaspoonfuls baking powder. Cream the butter and sugar, add the eggs, mix in the flour with half a teacupful of milk, and flavor with lemon. Make a frosting of the yelks of the eggs and one teacupful of sugar.

Neufchatel Cheese Cake. One Neufchatel cheese, one teacupful sugar; grate the rind of one lemon and use with it half of the juice, half a teacupful each of rolled cracker crumbs and currants, four eggs, one tablespoonful melted butter, half a teacupful cream or rich milk, half a nutmeg grated, and one saltspoonful of salt. Mix the cracker crumbs dry with the cheese, first removing the wrapper and taking off the thin skin on the outside of the cheese; crumble the cheese and cracker crumbs well together, beat the eggs well with the sugar and add, following with the butter and cream. If the cream is very rich the butter may be omitted. Lastly, add lemon, nutmeg and currants. The currants must be washed, dried and dusted with cracker dust or flour. Mix all well together and put into well-buttered patty-pans that have been lined with puff-paste. Bake fifteen or twenty minutes in a quick oven. **They will puff up, but must not be permitted to get too brown.**

LAYER CAKES

Fruit Layer Cake. Stir together two cupfuls of sugar with two-thirds of a cupful of butter; add one cupful of sweet milk, three cupfuls of flour, one teaspoonful of soda, and two of cream tartar; mix thoroughly and divide in two equal parts. To one-half add the beaten whites of three eggs; to the other half, add the beaten yolks of three eggs, one tablespoonful of molasses, two tablespoonfuls of brandy, one teaspoonful of cinnamon, one-half teaspoonful of cloves, one-half teaspoonful of allspice, quarter of a pound of citron sliced fine, one cupful of chopped raisins, and one-quarter of a cupful of flour. Stir all well together, and bake in jelly cake tins. The dark layers will have to bake longer than the light ones. In arranging the loaf have a dark layer at the bottom, a light one next, and so on, having a light layer for the top. Put frosting between each layer, and on the top and sides.

Gaelic Fruit Cake. Cream two teacupfuls of sugar and one of butter; add gradually one teacupful of milk, then the beaten yolks of nine eggs, four teacupfuls of flour sifted and mixed while dry with two teaspoonfuls of baking powder. While beating in the flour add the whites of the eggs whipped to a froth. Flavor to taste. In putting the cake in the pan place first a thin layer of cake, then sprinkle in a portion of the following three kinds of fruit mixed together: One pound of raisins seeded and chopped, half a pound of currants, and one-fourth pound of citron sliced thin. Follow with a layer of cake, then a layer of fruit, and so on, finishing with a thin layer of cake. Bake in a moderate oven for two hours. It is perhaps needless to add that the currants should be washed and dried before using.

Layer Cakes

The Palm Tree.

Cocoanut Cake. One-half cupful of butter and two cupfuls of sugar rubbed to a cream; stir in a cupful of sweet milk, then three cupfuls of flour and four teaspoonfuls of baking powder; last of all, the whites of five eggs beaten to a stiff froth. Bake in three or four layers. Grate the meat of a fresh cocoanut, be careful to first remove all the shell. Make a frosting of the whites of two eggs and a large cupful of powdered sugar; put a layer of frosting and then one of the grated cocoanut between each layer of cake, cover the top and sides with frosting, and sprinkle thickly with the cocoanut. Prepared cocoanut can be used if the other is not obtainable.

Jelly Cake. Stir together one cupful of sugar, one-half cupful of butter, three-fourths of a cupful of sweet milk, two beaten eggs, two cupfuls of flour, and two teaspoonfuls of baking powder. Bake in three layers, spread jelly between and put a frosting on top.

Jelly Cake No. 2. Beat together two eggs and one cupful of sugar; add two tablespoonfuls of melted butter, four of cold water, one cupful of flour, and one and one-half teaspoonfuls of baking powder. Bake in layers; spread jelly, cocoanut, orange, or lemon frosting, or any other suitable mixture between the layers.

Jelly Roll. One cupful of sugar, one of flour, three eggs, and one teaspoonful of baking powder; beat well, and spread on a long narrow baking tin; bake quickly and turn out on a cloth, spread with jelly and roll up. This is a very favorite cake for children parties. Its excellence, of course, depends on the quality of the jelly.

Cream Cake. Stir together two cupfuls of sugar, a lump of butter the size of an egg, three eggs, two and one-half cupfuls of flour and two teaspoonfuls of baking powder. Beat well and bake in two layers in jelly pans.

Cream for Cake. Take one cupful of thick sweet cream that has been on ice, or in a very cold place for some time; whip to a stiff froth, add sugar and flavoring to taste; spread between the layers and serve.

Cream Cake No. 2. Take two teacupfuls of flour and stir into it thoroughly two teaspoonfuls of cream tartar; then add two teacupfuls of sugar, and mix well; then add six beaten eggs, two tablespoonfuls of melted butter, and one-half cupful of cold water in which has been dissolved a teaspoonful of soda. Bake in three layers.

Cream for Cake. Take a little over two cupfuls of sweet milk, put in a double boiler and let come to a boil. Beat together two eggs, one cupful of sugar, and two tablespoonfuls of corn starch, or flour; stir this mixture into the boiling milk and when the consistency of thick cream, take off the fire, flavor with lemon, and when cool spread between the layers of cake. This cake is best when used fresh.

Fig Cake. Two cupfuls of sugar and six eggs, beaten together for five minutes; then stir in one cupful of sweet milk, three cupfuls of flour and two teaspoonfuls of baking powder. Bake in two or three layers.

Figs.

Fig Dressing. Chop one pound of figs very fine, adding a little hot water from time to time, to moisten; put in enough so they will spread nicely, but not enongh to make them sloppy; add enough sugar to sweeten, or a frosting can be made and a layer can be put on top on each of the figs.

Caramel Cake. Make any of the above layer cakes and spread between each layer and on top, a frosting made as follows: Two cupfuls of sugar, two-thirds of a cupful of sweet milk and a lump of butter the size of an egg. Boil for fifteen minutes, being careful not to let it scorch; beat until cool, and flavor with vanilla.

Lemon Cake. Make a cake after any of the foregoing rules for layer cake and make a dressing for it as follows: Put in a bowl the juice and grated rind of a lemon; add a well-beaten egg, three-fourths of a cupful of sugar, two tablespoonfuls of corn starch, and pour over the whole a cupful of boiling water. Set the bowl in hot water until the corn starch is cooked. When cool spread between the layers of cake.

Pineapple Cake. Make a cake after the rule given for cocoanut cake, and for the dressing to put between the layers, prepare a pineapple as follows: Pare the pineapple and chop, or grate, very fine; put in a stewpan with enough sugar to make a thick syrup when boiled. Save a large tablespoonful of the pineapple to put with the frosting, and spread the rest, when cool, between the layers of cake. Make a frosting of the beaten white of one egg, the tablespoonful of pineapple, and enough sugar to make a thick frosting; spread on the top and sides of the cake.

Ice Cream Cake. One and one-half cupfuls of sugar, and one-half cupful of butter; stir the butter and sugar to a cream; add the whites of four eggs, one at a time, without previously beating, one-half cupful of sweet milk, two and one-half cupfuls of flour, and two teaspoonfuls of baking powder. Stir well, and bake in layers. ICE CREAM: To prepare the ice cream, take two cupfuls of white sugar, add a little water and boil to a soft wax; then beat in the whites of two eggs, and tartaric acid the size of a pea dissolved in a few drops of water. Spread between the layers and on the top and sides.

Chocolate Cake. Two cupfuls of sugar and one-half cupful of butter; stir the butter and sugar to a cream, add one cupful of sweet milk, and when that is well stirred in add three cupfuls of flour, and three teaspoonfuls of baking powder, then add the beaten whites of five eggs; bake in three or four layers. For chocolate dressing grate one-quarter of a cake of chocolate, add a cupful of sugar and water enough to dissolve, set in hot water, and let come to a boil; when cold add the beaten white of an egg. Spread between the layers and on the top and sides.

DROP CAKES, COOKIES AND FRIED CAKES

Ginger Drops. Dissolve a teaspoonful of pulverized alum in a cupful of boiling water, add two cupfuls of molasses, one of melted butter or pork drippings, two beaten eggs, two teaspoonfuls of soda and two of ginger, stir in flour enough to make a thick batter; drop in small spoonfuls in a baking pan and bake in a rather quick oven.

Ginger Drop Cakes. One cupful of molasses, one-half cupful of melted butter, one-half cupful of warm water, three cupfuls of flour, one teaspoonful of soda, and two of ginger; stir all well together, line a dripping pan with buttered paper, drop in small spoonfuls and bake in a quick oven.

Cup Cakes. Rub one-half pound of butter, and three-quarters of a pound of sugar to a cream; then stir in five beaten eggs, one cupful of milk, one teaspoonful of baking powder, and one-half pound of flour; when well mixed put in small moulds or patty pans, filling them about half full and bake in a brisk oven.

Lady's Fingers. Eight ounces of powdered sugar, one-half gill of water, nine eggs, and ten ounces of flour; separate the yolks from the whites, and put the whites in a bowl on ice. Put the sugar and water in a sauce pan on the fire, add the yolks and beat with en egg beater until the mixture is warm, not hot; take the pan off the fire and beat for ten minutes, until cold, whip the whites to a stiff froth and mix lightly with the other composition, then stir in the flour without beating. Make a cornucopia of a sheet of foolscap, sewing up the side where it laps over, so that it will be firm, cut off the lower point enough to make an opening as large as one's finger; line a baking pan with buttered paper, put some of the cake mixture in the cornucopia and squeeze out in finger lengths upon the buttered paper, sift powdered sugar over them and bake for eight minutes.

Savoy Biscuits. Make the same batter as for lady's fingers, and flavor with vanilla. Bake in gem or patty pans, fastened together by the dozen. Prepare the pans by brushing them with melted butter, fill the pans about half full, and powdered sugar sifted over them before baking.

Savoy Biscuits. These cakes bake very quickly, and should be a light brown color when done.

Sugar Cookies. One cupful of butter, one cupful of cream; two cupfuls of sugar, three eggs, and one teaspoonful of soda. Beat the eggs for one minute, add the sugar and beat again, then put in the butter (soft and melted), the cream and the soda dissolved in a very little water, and flour enough to make a very soft dough; roll out, cut with a cake cutter, and bake in a brisk oven.

Sugar Cookies No. 2. Rub to a cream two cupfuls of sugar and one of butter, add a cupful of sweet milk, and two teaspoonfuls of soda and flour enough to roll without sticking. Cut in round or square cakes, and bake in a quick oven.

Jumbles. Beat together three eggs, and one and one-quarter cupfuls of sugar, add a cupful of soft butter, three tablespoonfuls of sour milk, one-quarter teaspoonful of soda, and flour enough to mix stiff; when rolled out, sift sugar over the top, cut in rings and bake in a quick oven.

Almond Cookies. One-half pound butter, one-half pound of sugar, one and one-quarter pound of flour, five beaten eggs, one heaping teaspoonful of baking powder, flavor with almond extract; mix to a smooth dough; roll to a quarter of an inch in thickness, brush with the beaten white of an egg and sprinkle thickly with chopped almonds; bake in a quick oven.

The Almond.

Cocoanut Cookies. Stir together two cupfuls of sugar, one cupful of butter, two eggs, one teaspoonful of soda dissolved in a little milk, and the meat of one medium sized cocoanut grated fine, add flour enough to roll, and bake in a quick oven.

Lemon Cakes. One pound of sugar, one-half pound of butter, one pound and three ounces of flour, three eggs; the grating of two lemons; mix the butter, sugar, lemon grating and eggs together, mix in the flour, and set on ice or in a cool place for two or three hours, then roll out, cut in small round cakes, brush with beaten egg, and bake in a quick oven.

Card Cakes. Take one cupful each of sugar, butter, molasses, and sour milk; add two teaspoonfuls of soda, two of ginger, two of cinnamon, and a pinch of salt; mix in enough flour to roll out, cut in cakes four inches wide and five inches long; when in the pan mark with a knife across the top, about half an inch apart. Bake in a quick oven.

Ginger Cookies. One cupful of molasses, one of sugar, one of sour milk, one of butter or fried meat fat, one teaspoonful of soda, one tablespoonful of ginger; stir well together and add enough flour to make a soft dough; cut in round or square cakes, and bake in a quick oven.

Ginger Cookies No. 2. One cupful of molasses, one of sugar, one of butter or pork drippings, one-half cupful of boiling water, a small tablespoonful of soda, dissolved in the hot water, and a tablespoonful of ginger; add enough flour to roll out without sticking and bake in a quick oven.

Ginger Snaps. One coffee cupful of New Orleans molasses, one of butter, and one of sugar. Put in a sauce pan, set on the stove and let come to a boil; then take off and add a teaspoonful of soda and a tablespoonful of ginger; mix in enough flour to roll out easily, roll out very thin, and bake in a quick oven.

Little Currant Cakes. Stir to a cream three cupfuls of sugar, and three-fourths of a cupful of butter, add one cupful of buttermilk, four beaten eggs, five cupfuls of flour, one teaspoonful of soda, and a heaping cupful of currants; mix well and bake in buttered patty pans.

A Currant Bush.

Hermits. One cupful of butter, one and one-half cupfuls of nice brown sugar, three eggs, one cupful of stoned and chopped raisins, one teaspoonful of soda dissolved in two tablespoonfuls of milk, nutmeg, cinnamon and cloves to taste, and flour enough to roll out; cut in squares and bake in a moderately quick oven.

Cream Puffs. Stir together in a saucepan one cupful of butter with two of flour; when well mixed add half a pint of boiling water, stir smooth, and when it boils set aside to cool, when cool, add five eggs and beat for two or three minutes; cover the bottom of a baking pan with buttered paper and drop the mixture on it in small spoonfuls, or it can be put in muffin rings. Bake for twenty-five or thirty minutes in a brisk oven.

Cream for Filling. Boil one pint of milk, heat together 1 cupful of sugar, 2 eggs and ½ cupful of flour, stir this into the boiling milk and let it cook for three minutes; flavor with lemon or vanilla; cut a circular piece out of the top of each puff, fill with the custard and replace the top.

Eclairs. One pint of milk, 6 ounces butter, 8 ounces corn starch, ten eggs. Boil the milk and butter together, add the corn starch and boil for three minutes. After removing the paste from the fire, let cool, and then add the eggs one at a time and beat thoroughly; bake in oval-shaped patty pans; when done, cut open and fill with whipped cream, flavored to taste; make an icing for the tops flavored the same as the whipped cream.

Chocolate Eclairs. Make the same as above, fill the center of the cakes with vanilla custard, and ice with chocolate icing.

Transparent Puffs. Mix together 1 pint of water, 2 ounces butter, 6 ounces corn starch, then beat in 5 whole eggs and the whites of five. Beat well and bake in patty pans or in small spoonfuls on buttered paper.

Doughnuts. Beat 2 eggs and 1 cupful of sugar together, add 4 tablespoonfuls of melted lard, 1 cupful of sour milk, 1 teaspoonful of soda, a pinch of salt, seasoning to suit taste and flour enough to make a soft dough; roll out, cut in rings by using two sizes of cake cutters and fry them in hot lard.

Doughnuts.

Raised Doughnuts. Measure off 2 quarts of flour, put in a large stirring bowl and make a cavity in the middle, scald a pint of milk and when tepid add a heaping cupful of sugar, ½ of a cupful of butter and a cake of yeast; pour this in the cavity in the flour and stir in enough flour to make a sponge, cover and set away in a warm place to rise, letting it stand all night. In the morning put in a ½ teaspoonful of soda dissolved in a little water and knead in the rest of the flour. Let it rise again until light, knead again, roll out and cut into shape, and let them lie on the pastry board eight or ten minutes before frosting. Fry in hot lard.

Frosting. Beat the whites of 2 eggs to a stiff froth, stir in 1½ cupful of sugar and a teaspoonful of extract of lemon or vanilla.

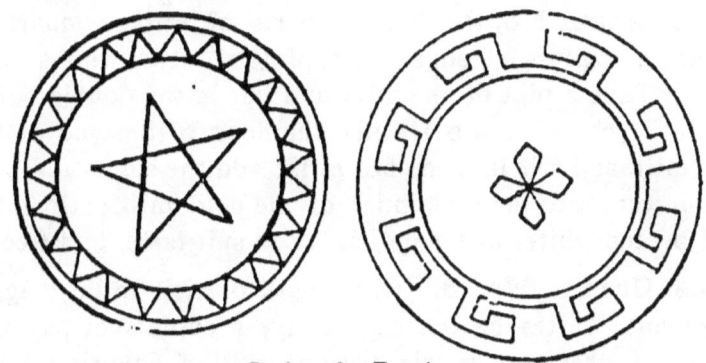

Designs for Frosting.

Boiled Frosting. Put in a stewpan 2 cupfuls of sugar and ½ a cupful of milk, set on the stove and boil for five minutes; care must be taken to prevent scorching. When boiled, take off the fire and beat until it creams; spread on the cake at once.

Boiled Frosting No. 2. Boil 1 cupful of sugar with ½ a cupful of water; boil without stirring until the syrup is thick, take from the fire and when partially cool add the beaten white of 1 egg.

Lemon Icing. One cupful of sugar, the juice of 1 lemon, and 1 beaten egg; put on the stove and let come to a boil, stir until cool and use.

CREAMS AND CUSTARDS

Ice Cream No. 1. Put 1 quart of milk in the double boiler; let come to a boil and then stir in 1 coffee cupful of sugar, and 3 beaten eggs. Put in the freezer and when partly frozen add ½ of a pint of rich sweet cream, then finish freezing.

Ice Cream No. 2. Three quarts of milk, 1 quart of cream, 3 cupfuls of sugar, ½ cupful of flour, whites of 6 eggs. Take a pint of the milk and put in the double boiler and let it come to a boil; mix the flour with some of the cold milk and stir into the hot milk, add the sugar and pour the mixture into the remainder of the cold milk; stir in the well beaten whites of 6 eggs, flavor to suit taste, and freeze.

Ice Cream No. 3. One quart of rich milk, 7 eggs, yolks and whites beaten separately, 4 cupfuls of sugar, 2 quarts of sweet cream, six teaspoonfuls of flavoring. Put the milk in a double boiler and heat almost to boiling; beat the yolks very light, add the sugar and heat a little longer; then, little by little, add the boiling milk, beating all the while; stir in the well beaten whites of the eggs, return to the boiler and cook until it is as thick as boiled custard, stirring steadily all the time. Take off the fire and when quite cold stir in the cream and flavoring, and freeze.

Chocolate Ice Cream. Make a gallon of ice cream after any of the foregoing rules. Shave two bars of good chocolate in a little milk, sweeten to taste, and add to the ice cream when partly frozen, and then finish freezing.

Berry Ice Cream. Any kind of berries may be used for this. Mash thoroughly in a large bowl 1 quart of berries with 1 pound of sugar, rub through a colander, add 1 quart of sweet cream, and freeze. Very ripe peaches may be used instead of berries.

Berries.

Coffee Ice Cream. To 3 quarts of pure cream add one pint decoction of very strong coffee and 2 pounds of sugar, and freeze.

The Coffee Plant

Lemon Ice. Take the juice of 4 lemons, 1 pound of sugar and 1 quart of boiling water. Let cool, and just before freezing add the beaten whites of three eggs, and freeze.

Orange Jelly. Grate the peel of one orange, and pour over it one pint of boiling water; when cool add the juice of four oranges, two cupfuls of sugar, one box of gelatine dissolved in a pint of water, strain and put into a mould.

Orange Jelly.

Pineapple Jelly. Pare a medium-sized pineapple, grate, add to it one quart of water and boil for fifteen or twenty minutes; add to it one and one-half cupfuls of sugar, and two-thirds of a box of gelatine, dissolved in a little cold water. Strain through a flannel bag and put into moulds and set in a cold place.

Lemon Jelly. Put one box of gelatine in a bowl, and

pour over it one coffee cupful of cold water, and let stand over night. In the morning grate the rinds of two lemons, the juice of four, and pour over it one pint of boiling hot water, two cupfuls of sugar, add to it the gelatine and one cupful of cold water   Strain. This must be made three or four hours before wanted.

Boiled Custard. One quart of milk, four eggs, two tablespoonfuls of sugar; scald the milk, beat the eggs and sugar together, add to the milk, boil for five minutes and flavor with lemon or vanilla.

Custard in Cups.

Floating Island. Put one quart of milk in a double boiler, beat the yolks of six eggs, one teacupful of sugar, and add to the boiling milk; flavor with two teaspoonfuls of lemon. Beat the whites of six eggs to a stiff froth, add two tablespoonfuls of sugar; pour the custard into a dish, put the beaten eggs or island on the top, and set in the oven for a few minutes, until slightly browned.

Blanc Mange. Put into a double boiler one quart of sweet milk, and let come to a boil. Beat together four eggs, four tablespoonfuls of corn starch, one-fourth of a cup of milk, and add to the boiling milk. Cook for a few minutes, dip cups in cold water, then fill with the custard; when firm turn out and serve with cream and sugar. Raisins, currants or candied fruit make a nice addition.

Blanc Mange.

Chocolate Blanc Mange. Put into the double boiler one quart of milk. Dissolve one bar of Baker's chocolate add to it two beaten eggs, four tablespoonfuls of sugar, and three heaping tablespoonfuls of corn starch. Add to the boiling milk and boil for ten minutes. Rinse a mould with cold water, pour in the blanc mange and when firm turn out and serve with cream and sugar.

Chocolate Blanc Mange No. 2. Put two quarts of milk in a double boiler and let come to a boil; grate one-half cake of Baker's chocolate and boil for one hour. Take one box of Cox's gelatine, dissolve and add to the milk, sweeten with two cups of sugar, flavor with vanilla, strain and put into a mould.

Charlotte Russe. Put two cupfuls of milk into a sauce pan, and let come to a boil. Take the yolks of four eggs, four tablespoonfuls of sugar, beat together, stir into the boiling milk, and when thickened set the custard away to cool. Take one-half of a box of gelatine, and add to it one cupful of warm water, and set it on the back of the stove, but do not let it get hot. Beat the whites of five eggs to a stiff froth, add one and one-half cupfuls of pulverized sugar. Whip two cupfuls of cream, and add it to the custard; add flavoring to the beaten whites of the eggs and mix them with the custard, and last of all add the gelatine, and stir in thoroughly; take the dish in which the Charlotte russe is to be served, line with white sponge cake or lady fingers, pour the custard into it and set into the ice chest. This should be made two or three hours before serving.

Spanish Cream. Dissolve one-half of a box of gelatine in a little warm water. Put one and one-half pints of milk in a double boiler, beat the yolks of three eggs with two-thirds of a cup of sugar, add to the milk and boil for a few minutes, then add the gelatine. Take from the fire and stir in the beaten whites of four eggs, and put into a mould, and when cold serve with whipped cream.

Russian Cream. Jelly: To one package of gelatine add one pint of cold water, when dissolved add one pint of hot water, two cups of sugar, and the juice of six lemons, stir slowly until well dissolved, then strain into moulds.

Cream: Cover one package of gelatine with cold water, when dissolved add one cup of new milk, one cup of sugar, heat to boiling point, stirring frequently. Then set away to cool. Whip one quart of thick cream until light, beat the whites of six eggs and add both to the mixture. When cool flavor with vanilla. Place the jelly in the bottom of the moulds, and when stiff and cold add the cream; turn out of the moulds and serve in slices.

Whipped Cream. Needed: To every pint of cream allow 3 oz. of pounded sugar, 1 glass of sherry, or any kind of sweet white wine, the rind of ½ a lemon, the white of 1 egg. Rub the sugar on the lemon rind and pound it in a mortar until quite fine, and beat up the white of the egg until quite stiff; put the cream in a large bowl, with the sugar, wine, and beaten egg, and whip it to a froth; as fast as the froth rises, take it off with a skimmer, and put it on a sieve to drain, in a cool place. This should be made the day before it is wanted, as the whip is then so much firmer. The cream should be whipped in a cool place, and in summer, over ice, if it is obtainable. A plain whipped cream may be served on a glass dish, and garnished with strips of angelica, or pastry leaves, or pieces of bright colored jelly; it makes a very pretty addition to the supper table.

Stewed Apples and Custard. You need seven good sized apples, the rind of ½ a lemon or 4 cloves; ½ lb. of sugar, ¾ pint of water, ½ pint of custard.

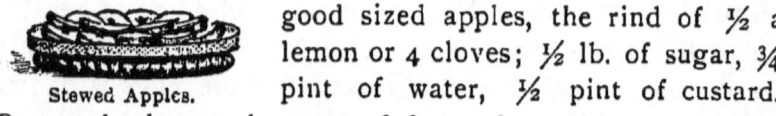
Stewed Apples.

Pare and take out the cores of the apples, without dividing them, and, if possible, leave the stalks on; boil the sugar and water together for 10 minutes; then put in the apples with the lemon rind or cloves, whichever flavor may be preferred, and simmer gently until they are tender, taking care not to let them break. Dish them neatly on a glass dish, reduce the syrup by boiling it quickly for a few minutes, let it cool a little; then pour it over the apples. Have ready quite half a pint of custard; pour it round, but not over, the apples when they are quite cold, and the dish is ready for table. A few almonds, blanched and cut into strips, and stuck in the apples, would improve their appearance.

Stewed Pears. Take six or eight pears, water, sugar, two ounces of butter, the yolk of an egg, one-half ounce of gelatine. Peel and cut the pears in any form that may be  preferred, and steep them in cold water to prevent their turning black; put them into a saucepan with sufficient cold water to cover them, and boil them, with the butter and enough sugar to sweeten them nicely, until tender; then brush the pears over with the yolk of an egg, sprinkle them with sifted sugar, and arrange them on a dish. Add the gelatine to the syrup, simmer it quickly for about five minutes, strain it over the pears, and let it remain until set. The syrup may be colored with a little prepared cochineal, which would very much improve the appearance of the dish.

Stewed Pears.

Preserved Quinces. Pare and quarter the fruit; boil in enough water to keep them whole; when they are tender take them out, and to each pound of quinces add one pound of white sugar; let them stand with the sugar on until the next day, when the syrup will be as light and clear as amber; put them in the pan and let them boil twenty minutes; they never get hard. The water they were boiled in may be used to make a jelly of the parings; add one pound of white sugar to each pint of juice, and boil half an hour.

The Quince.

Jelly with Oranges. Take one quart of any clear

Compote of Oranges.

yellow jelly, six oranges, a little syrup, preserved cherries, angelica. Peel the oranges and divide them into quarters, taking off all the white; coat a plain mould with the jelly, then lay in the oranges, each piece dipped in clear syrup, in the manner shown in the illustration, putting the angelica, cut into leaves, in the corners of the mould, and the cherries round the top and bottom, and between the pieces of orange; fill up with jelly, and set on ice.

Orange Custards. Needed: The juice of ten large oranges, a teacupful of sifted sugar, the yolks of twelve eggs, one pint of cream. Sweeten the orange juice with the sugar, and set it over the fire; stir constantly till hot, when skim it carefully, and set aside to cool. When nearly cold add the yolks of eggs beaten very light, and the cream. Put all into a saucepan, and stir over a very slow fire until thick. Pour into cups, and serve cold. If desired, the whites of the eggs, beaten stiff, with a teacupful of pounded sugar, may be used, a heaped tablespoonful on the top of each cup of the custard.

Rice Snowballs. Needed: Six ounces of rice, one quart of milk, flavoring of essence of almonds, sugar to taste, one pint of custard. Boil the rice in the milk, with sugar and a flavoring of essence of almonds, until the former is tender, adding, if necessary, a little more milk, should it dry away too much. When the rice is quite soft, put it into teacups, or *small* round jars, and let it remain until cold; then turn out the rice on a deep glass dish, pour over a custard, and on the top of each ball, place a small piece of bright colored preserve or jelly. Lemon peel or vanilla may be boiled with rice instead of the essence of almonds, when either of these is preferred; but the flavoring of the custard must correspond with that of the rice.

PUDDINGS

English Plum Pudding. One pound of suet chopped very fine, one pound of flour, one pound of bread crumbs, one pound of sugar, two pounds of raisins, stoned and chopped, two pounds of currants, picked, washed and dried, one pound of figs, chopped fine, one-half pound of mixed citron and orange peel, sliced fine, one ounce of mixed spice, three tablespoonfuls of molasses, four beaten eggs, a tablespoonful of salt, one pint of brandy; mix all together with about a quart of milk, place in a pudding bag and boil in water for seven or eight hours. Boil steadily to prevent the pudding from absorbing the water.

Plum Pudding.

English Plum Pudding No. 2. Three cupfuls of flour, one cupful of bread crumbs, two and one-half cupfuls of beef suet, chopped very fine, four cupfuls of raisins, stoned and chopped, four cupfuls of currants, picked, washed and dried, two cupfuls of sugar, two ounces of citron, chopped fine, the juice of one lemon, and four beaten eggs. Dredge a pudding cloth with flour, put in the pudding, tie loosely, plunge in boiling water and boil for eight hours.

Fig Pudding. One pound of figs, chopped fine, one quart of grated bread, one cupful of powdered sugar, one-half cupful of butter, four beaten eggs and two cupfuls of sweet milk; stir all together, place in a pudding dish and steam for one and one-half hours. Serve with sauce.

Fruit Pudding. One cupful of molasses, one cupful of sweet milk, one-half cupful of butter, one cupful of stoned and chopped raisins, one-half cupful of currants, two and one-half cupfuls of flour, one-half teaspoonful of soda, one-half of a grated nutmeg and a pinch of salt. Mix well, and steam two hours.

Fruit Pudding No. 2. Line a bowl with thin slices of bread and fill with fruit; very ripe peaches are the best. Take one tablespoonful of gelatine and add one-half cupful of cold water; let soak for one-half hour, then add two cupfuls of sweet milk, one cupful of sugar, put in a saucepan and let come to a boil, pour over the fruit and bread and set in a refrigerator. Serve cold with whipped cream.

Tapioca Pudding. Two tablespoonfuls of tapioca put to soak over night in enough water to cover it. Put a quart of milk in a double boiler, beat the yolks of eggs and one cupful of sugar; stir into the boiling milk and boil until it thickens. Put the tapioca into a pudding dish, pour the hot custard over the tapioca, mix the two together thoroughly and bake for one half hour. Beat the whites of four eggs to a stiff froth with two-thirds of a cupful of powdered sugar; spread over the custard, return to the oven and leave there until the frosting is a golden brown. Serve either hot or cold.

Tapioca Ice. One cupful of tapioca soaked over night; in the morning place upon the stove and when it begins to boil put in a large cupful of sugar and boil until it is clear. Clear a good sized pineapple free from all specks and chop fine; pour the tapioca boiling hot over the pineapple and stir together. The hot tapioca will sufficiently moisten the pineapple; pour into moulds or cups, and when cold serve with cream and sugar.

Suet Pudding. Two-thirds of a cupful of suet chopped fine, one cupful of molasses, one cupful of sweet milk, one cupful of stoned raisins, one-half cupful of sugar, three cupfuls of flour, one teaspoonful of soda, one grated nutmeg. Mix all together thoroughly, put in a pudding dish and steam three hours. Serve with sauce.

Puddings

Suet Pudding No. 2. Two-thirds of a cupful of suet chopped fine, two-thirds of a cupful of molasses, one-half cupful of sour milk, one and one-half cupfuls of flour, one teaspoonful of soda, one of cloves, one of cinnamon, one beaten egg, one cupful of stoned raisins; stir together and boil or steam for three hours.

Graham Pudding. One cupful of molasses, one cupful of sweet milk, one cupful of stoned raisins, one beaten egg, one tablespoonful of melted butter, one teaspoonful of soda, two cupfuls of Graham flour; put in a pudding dish, steam for two hours, and serve with sauce.

Charlotte Pudding. Grease a pudding dish with butter, put in a layer of bread crumbs; then a layer of sliced apples, pour over them a cupful of milk in which has been dissolved a piece of butter the size of an egg. Bake one hour.

Charlotte Pudding.

Chocolate Pudding. One quart of milk and three ounces of grated chocolate, scalded together; when cold, add the beaten yolks of five eggs and one cupful of sugar. Bake twenty-five minutes. Beat the whites of five eggs to a stiff froth with one-half cupful of powdered sugar; spread upon the pudding, place in the oven and brown.

Sponge Pudding. Three cupfuls of flour, one and one-half cupful of butter, one cupful of milk, four eggs, one teaspoonful of soda, two teaspoonfuls of cream tartar. Beat the butter, sugar and yolks of the eggs together, put the cream tartar into the flour and soda into the milk, mix all together and last add the beaten whites of the eggs and steam two hours.

Corn Starch Pudding. Put into a double boiler one quart of milk and let come to a boil. Beat together five tablespoonfuls of corn starch, two eggs, and one cupful of sugar; stir into the boiling milk and cook for five minutes;

pour into a mould or cups and serve cold with whipped cream.

Queen of Puddings. One pint of bread crumbs, one cupful of sugar, four eggs, a piece of butter the size of an egg, one quart of milk; put the bread crumbs into the milk, stir in the yolks of the eggs and the sugar beaten together, add the butter and bake for one hour. Cover the top of the pudding with a layer of jelly or fruit; make a frosting with the whites of four eggs and two-thirds of a cupful of powdered sugar; spread this over the jelly and place in the oven and brown.

Puff Pudding. One quart of milk, four beaten eggs, four tablespoonfuls of flour and a little salt; stir all together and bake half an hour. Serve with sauce.

Baked Rice Pudding. Put two cupfuls of rice into two quarts of milk and bake an hour. Beat together four eggs, two-thirds of a cupful of butter, two cupfuls of sugar; stir into the partially cooked rice, add more milk, if necessary, and bake another hour.

Rice Pudding without Eggs. Put into a pudding dish one cupful of rice and three pints of milk, add one teacupful of sugar and bake for three hours; stir thoroughly every ten or fifteen minutes. This is sometimes called creamed rice.

Snow Pudding. Pour one pint of boiling water over one-half box of gelatine, add the juice of one lemon, and one and one-half cupfuls of sugar. Strain, and when nearly cold stir in the whites of three eggs, beaten to a stiff froth. Serve with a boiled custard.

Black Pudding. One cupful of molasses, one of butter, one of sugar, one of sour milk, three of flour, four eggs, one grated nutmeg, and one teaspoonful of soda. Beat the butter and sugar together, add the eggs and molasses, then the sour milk and the soda dissolved in a little hot water, stir in the flour, put it in a buttered pudding dish, and steam two hours. Serve with wine sauce.

Steamed Indian Pudding. Mix together two cupfuls of meal, one of flour, one of suet chopped fine, one of stoned raisins, one of molasses, one of sweet milk; add one-half teaspoonful of soda dissolved in a little hot water, and a pinch of salt. Put in a buttered pudding dish, and steam three hours.

Egg Pudding. Take one quart of milk, put in a double boiler and let come to a boil; mix nine tablespoonfuls of flour with one pint of cold milk, and stir into the boiling milk and let it remain on the fire until well cooked. Beat the yolks of twelve eggs, six tablespoonfuls of sugar, and three of melted butter. Take the boiler from the fire and stir in the eggs, sugar, etc., beat the whites of the eggs and stir them in. Butter a pudding dish, pour in the mixture, set the dish in a pan of hot water, put the whole in the oven and bake in a moderate oven for one hour. Serve with sauce.

Cabinet Pudding. Take a two quart pudding dish and cover the bottom with a layer of stale cake, sprinkle over it a spoonful of chopped citron and bits of butter, then another layer of cake, citron and butter, util the dish is two-thirds full. Beat together three eggs, a wineglassful of brandy, the rind and juice of a lemon, a half cupful of sugar, unless the cake is very sweet, and one quart of milk; pour over the contents of the pudding dish and bake one-half hour

Cabinet Pudding.

Baked Indian Pudding. Boil one quart of milk, and stir into it two-thirds of a cupful of meal and let it cook a few minutes, then take from the fire, and when cool stir in one-half cupful of sugar, one-half cupful of molasses, one half cupful of butter, one egg, one teaspoonful of ginger, and one-half teaspoonful of cinnamon, and a pinch of salt. Put in a buttered pudding dish, and bake one hour.

Minute Pudding. Let one quart of milk come to a boil, add a little salt, then stir into the milk four tablespoonfuls of flour, and three beaten eggs; cook for four or five minutes. Serve with cream and sugar.

Tapioca Pudding with Apples. Put one cupful of tapioca into half a pint of water, and let it stand a couple of hours, where it will be quite warm, but not cook. Peel six tart apples, take out the cores, place them in a pudding dish, and fill with sugar. Beat together two eggs, two tablespoonfuls of melted butter, one-half of a cupful of milk, two-thirds of a cupful of sugar; stir this into the tapioca and pour the whole over the apples. Bake one hour, and serve with sauce.

Apple Dumpling. Measure four cupfuls of flour, put in two teaspoonfuls of cream tartar, and two of soda, sift two or three times, then rub in a lump of butter the size of a walnut, then stir in two cupfuls of sour milk, turn out on the board and work into a smooth dough, roll out to half an inch in thickness, and cut in three or four inch squares, put some sliced apple in the middle of each one, bring the corners together, pinch up the openings and cook. These dumplings are very nice, either boiled, baked or steamed, and will require about one-half hour to cook. Serve with cream and sugar if baked, and with a boiled sauce if steamed or boiled.

Apples.

SAUCES FOR PUDDINGS

Sauce for Suet Pudding. One-half cup of butter, one cup of sugar, beaten to a cream; add the beaten yolk of one egg, grate in half a nutmeg, then stir in a tablespoonful of boiling water, and flavor with a little wine or brandy. Place where it will keep warm and just before serving add the well-beaten white of one egg.

The Lemon.

Lemon Sauce. Take one large tablespoonful of butter, one of flour, and one cupful of sugar; beat all together to a cream, then pour over it one cupful of boiling water, taking from the fire; add two tablespoonfuls of melted butter. Flavor with lemon.

Fruit Sauce. Boil fruit, berries, or any other kind until soft, rub through a sieve and add enough sugar to sweeten them; boil until clear. This is a nice sauce for corn starch pudding, blanc mange, or plain steamed puddings.

Strawberries.

Custard Sauce. Put one pint of milk into a double boiler and let come to a boil. Beat the yolks of five eggs, one small tablespoonful of corn starch, one cupful of sugar; stir it into the boiling milk and cook for three or four minutes; flavor with lemon or vanilla, and use when cold.

Caramel Sauce. Put one cupful of sugar into a small saucepan and add to it a lump of the size of an egg; let it boil for ten minutes; then add one and one-half cupfuls of water, and one beaten egg, stirring all the time.

Plain Sauce. Beat together one cupful of sugar with the yolks of two eggs; then add the whites beaten to a stiff froth; flavor with a wine glass of wine, or half of a grated nutmeg; add a small teacupful of boiling water, and stir constantly.

Wine Sauce. Put a teacupful of water into a saucepan and let it boil; beat together one cupful of sugar, two tablespoonfuls of butter, one tablespoonful of flour and the yolk of one egg; stir into the boiling water, and when cooked and slightly cool, add one gill of wine.

Vinegar Sauce. One and one-half cupfuls of sugar, two tablespoonfuls of flour wet in a little water, two tablespoonfuls of vinegar, one fourth of a nutmeg grated, a pinch of salt; mix well together and pour over the whole one and one-half pints of hot water, and let boil ten minutes.

Brandy Sauce. Take one tablespoonful of baked flour, 3 oz. fresh butter, 1 tablespoonful moist sugar, ¾ pint of boiling water, 1 wineglassful of brandy. Work the flour and butter together with a wooden spoon, then stir in the boiling water and sugar, boil gently for 10 minutes, then add the brandy.

Cherry Sauce. (For Sweet Puddings. German Recipe.) You need one pound of cherries, one tablespoonful of flour, one ounce of butter, one-half pint of water, one wineglassful of port, a little grated lemon rind, four pounded cloves, two tablespoonfuls of lemon juice, sugar to taste. Stone the cherries, and pound the kernels in a mortar to a smooth paste; put the butter and flour into a sauce pan; stir them over the fire until of a pale brown; then add the cherries, the pounded kernels, the wine, and the water. Simmer these gently for

Cherries.

a quarter of an hour, or until the cherries are quite cooked, and rub the whole through a hair sieve; add the remaining ingredients, let the sauce boil for another five minutes, and serve. This is a delicious sauce to serve with boiled batter pudding, and when thus used, should be sent to the table poured over the pudding.

Raspberry Sauce. (For Simple Puddings.) You need 4 eggs, 2 teaspoonfuls of flour, ¼ lb. of loaf sugar, 1 pint of fresh raspberry juice. Beat the eggs well, and smooth the flour with a little water; then put all into a saucepan, add the sugar and raspberry juice. Put the pan onto the fire, and lightly whisk the contents till they thicken. They will become light and frothy, and should be served at once.

Zwetschen Sauce. (Piquant Sauce for Plain Puddings.) Take one-half pound of best French prunes, one glass of wine, juice of one lemon and part of rind, one-half teaspoonful powdered cinnamon, sugar to taste. Simmer the prunes in a saucepan with just enough water to cover them, until soft. Then remove them from the pan, take out the stones, crack them, and save the kernels; then return the fruit to the pan, add the other ingredients, simmer for seven or eight minutes, then strain through a coarse sieve, adding more wine or water, if too thick.

A Good Sauce for Various Boiled Puddings. Use ¼ lb. of butter, ¼ lb. of pounded sugar, a wineglassful of brandy or rum. Beat the butter to a cream until no lumps remain; add the pounded sugar, and brandy or rum; stir once or twice until the whole is thoroughly mixed, and serve. This sauce may either be poured round the pudding or served in a tureen, according to the taste or fancy of the cook or mistress.

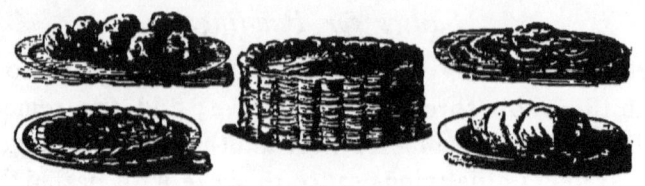

PASTRY

General Instructions

In pastry making, the quality to be desired is lightness, and this depends on the amount of air in the pastry before and the expansion of the air after it is put in the oven. Therefore the best pastry is that which contains the greatest quantity of the coldest air before it is baked. The foldings and the rollings, with which we are all familiar, has this increase of air in view. The difference between flaky and short crust is that in one there are thin layers of air and pastry alternating, and in the other the air fills small cavities all over the pastry.

To make the air cold, pastry should always be made in a cold place, with cold water, on ice if possible, and paste that is set aside to wait between rollings or before baking should stand on ice or on a cold stone. Cooks with a hot hand should mix paste with a knife. Pastry should be rolled lightly, the rolling pin often lifted and little pressed upon. It should not be turned over or thrown about. Any pieces that are left over should be laid on over the other and rolled flat, not rolled into a ball as the common practice is. Eggs are used to increase the tenacity of the paste, and so hold more air, or if, as sometimes happens, the white is whisked to a froth, it contains a great deal of air which it carries with it into the paste. Baking powder has the same effect in pastry and in bread, where its action has been more or less fully described. If it is used, it should be for pastry baked at once and little handled—that is for short rather than for flaky crust.

SHORT CAKES

Crust No. 1. Take one quart of flour, and add to it two teaspoonfuls of soda and two of cream tartar, sift two or three times, and rub into it a lump of butter the size of an egg; add a pint of sour milk, and work smooth with as little kneading as possible; roll out to half an inch in thickness, place in a shallow square baking pan and bake in a brisk oven for twenty minutes. When done, split open, butter, and put fruit between the layers and on top. Another nice way is to make the crust as above, and divide in two equal parts; roll out one-half to fit the baking tin, and spread with butter, then roll out the other half and put on top of the first half, then spread a little butter on top of the last half. This will make the crust nice and flaky, and also cause it to come apart without splitting with a knife.

Crust No. 2. Beat together one egg, one-half cupful of sugar, a lump of butter the size of an egg, two cupfuls of sweet milk, two teaspoonfuls of baking powder, and flour enough to make a batter as for cake; bake in layers in a quick oven for almost twenty minutes.

Fruit for Short Cake. Strawberries, raspberries, blackberries, very ripe peaches and oranges make a nice filling for short cake. The fruit should be mashed or sliced, sweetened and put between the crust, and on top. Jam, marmalade, and almost any kind of preserved fruit can be used, if fresh fruit is not obtainable.

Roll Puddings. Make a crust as for short cake, roll out thin, and spread with raspberries, peaches, chopped apples, or any fruit that is suitable; sweeten the fruit and roll over and over, pinch the ends and side opening together, and either boil or bake. Two hours will be required to boil it, while one and one-half hours will be sufficient for baking. Serve with sauce.

PIES

Pie Crust. Take one quart of flour and rub into it a cupful of butter or lard, add a teaspoonful of salt, and enough very cold water to make a stiff dough. Mix with as little handling as possible, and put on ice or in a cool place, an hour or two before using; roll out thin, put in the filling, and spread a little butter on the upper crust, before baking.

Puff Paste. Take one pound of flour, and one pound of butter. Rub the flour and one-half the butter together, and add enough cold water to make a stiff dough, roll this out till one-half inch in thickness, then put on one-half of the remainder of the butter in a lump; fold the corners of the dough over the butter, and roll out carefully until about a quarter of an inch thick, put on the rest of the butter, fold the corners over this again, and roll out again in as long a strip as possible, fold backward and forward, and roll out as before. Do this four or five times, letting rest one-half hour between each rolling.

Tart Paste. Take one-half cupful of water, one-half cupful of lard, the beaten white of one egg, three tablespoonfuls of powdered sugar, and one teaspoonful of cream tartar, and one-half teaspoonful of soda; add flour enough to make a moderately stiff dough.

Fruit Pies. Rub the plates or tins on which they are to be baked with a very little butter; roll the crust out thin, line the plate, and put in the fruit, being careful not to put in too much, as that would cause the pie to run over. Sweeten to taste, and if the fruit is juicy, stir a little flour through it before putting it in the crust. Berries, cherries, gooseberries, rhubarb, plums, etc., do not need any seasoning, except sugar. Apple and peach pies are improved by placing bits of butter on the fruit before putting on the upper crust. The edge of under crust should be wet with a little flour and water before putting on the upper crust. Pies should be baked in a moderate oven, the usual time being from forty to sixty minutes.

Mince Meat. One pound of chopped apples, one pound of stoned raisins, one pound of suet chopped very fine, one-half pound of mixed citron and orange peel chopped fine, one-half ounce of mixed spice, one pound of sugar, one teaspoonful of salt; mix all together thoroughly, add enough water to moisten, and cook for one hour. Then add one-half pint of good whiskey or brandy. When making the pies, add a little more sugar, if not sweet enough.

Mince Meat No. 2. Cook until tender, four pounds of lean meat or tongues, chopped very fine; then add two pounds of chopped suet, seven pounds of chopped apples, two pounds of currants, picked, washed and dried, three pounds of stoned raisins, one pound of citron chopped fine, four pounds of brown sugar, two chopped lemons, peel and all, one-half ounce of mace, one tablespoonful of cinnamon, one tablespoonful of allspice, one tablespoonful of cloves, two tablespoonfuls of salt, and two oranges chopped fine; add enough cider to moisten and cook all together for one hour.

Mock Mince Pie. One and one-half pints of cold water; add five soda crackers rolled fine, one-half cupful of cider or vinegar, one cupful of molasses, one and one-half cupfuls of sugar, one cupful of raisins, stoned and chopped, one teaspoonful each of cinnamon, cloves and nutmeg, one tablespoonful of butter, one beaten egg. Boil all together, except the cracker, for fifteen minutes; then add the cracker, **and make the pies with two crusts.**

Lemon Cream Pie. The juice and grated rind of one lemon, one cupful of sugar, the yolks of two eggs, two tablespoonfuls of flour; mix all together and pour over the whole a cupful of boiling water. Set the dish containing the mixture into another of hot water and boil until well cooked. Make the pie with an under crust only, and bake until done; then add a frosting made of two beaten whites of eggs, and two tablespoonfuls of white sugar; spread evenly over the pie, put back into the oven and brown slightly.

Pumpkin Pie. Cut up a small sized pumpkin, cook until done, then stew down until little moisture is left; then press through a colander or sieve. Take four cupfuls of the pumpkin, add to it one cupful of molasses, two cupfuls of sugar, two tablespoonfuls of ginger, two of cinnamon, two of flour, three pints of milk, a teaspoonful of salt, and five well-beaten eggs; mix all together thoroughly, and bake with under crust only.

Potato Cream Pie. One pound of mashed potatoes, one-half pound of white sugar, six ounces of butter, three-quarters of a cupful of milk, four beaten eggs, and a little brandy. Boil good mealy potatoes and mash them through a sieve; mix butter with them while warm, then the sugar, milk, and flavoring; separate the eggs, and beat both yolks and whites quite light, stir them into the pie just before baking, and sift powdered sugar over the pie when done.

Squash Pie. Pare the squash and remove the seeds, stew until soft and dry; then press through a sieve or colander, stir into the squash enough sweet milk to make it a batter; season with cinnamon, ginger, and nutmeg to taste; sweeten with sugar, and add three beaten eggs for each quart of milk. Fill very full pie plates, lined with crust, and bake for one hour.

Orange Pie. Grate one orange, add one cupful of sugar, one of water, two tablespoonfuls of melted butter, two tablespoonfuls of flour, three eggs, reserving the white of one for frosting, one teaspoonful of tartaric acid. Mix all together thoroughly and bake with under crust only When done, spread over it a frosting made of the white of one egg and two tablespoonfuls of powdered sugar. Put back into the oven and brown slightly.

Transparent Pie. Beat together one whole egg and the yolks of two others; add two tablespoonfuls of melted butter, one cupful of sweet milk, one cupful of brown sugar, one-half of a grated nutmeg. Beat all together and bake with under crust only. When done, cover with a frosting made of one cupful of sugar and the whites of two eggs; flavor with lemon and put back into the oven for two or three minutes.

Apple Cream Pie. One pint of stewed apples, one cupful of sugar, one cupful of milk, two tablespoonfuls of melted butter, two beaten eggs, a little grated nutmeg, and half a glass of wine; mix together and bake with two crusts.

Custard and Cocoanut Pie. Line your pie plate with pie crust, and fill it with a mixture of three beaten eggs, one pint of milk, two-thirds of a cupful of sugar; flavor with a little mace, and bake it in a medium hot oven. For cocoanut pie use the same custard as for custard pie, but add grated cocoanut, either fresh or prepared.

Chocolate Cream Pie. One quart of milk, one coffee cupful of sugar, four tablespoonfuls of flour, one bar of bitter chocolate grated, two tablespoonfuls of melted butter, the yolks of five beaten eggs. Boil the milk with the chocolate in it; mix the flour and sugar together, and stir into the boiling milk; then add butter and yolks of eggs, and take the mixture off the fire immediately. Bake in thin crusts of puff paste. Whip the whites of five eggs to a stiff froth while the pies are baking, add a cupful of sugar, and flavor with vanilla. Spread over the hot pies, and put back into the oven until slightly brown.

Sour Milk Pie. One cupful of sour milk, one cupful of sugar, one cupful of raisins stoned and chopped, two eggs, all kinds of spice. Bake between two crusts.

Cream Pie. Put one pint of milk in the double boiler, and let come to a boil. Beat together the yolks of two eggs, one-half cupful of sugar, two tablespoonfuls of flour or corn starch; stir this into the boiling milk, and cook until thick. Flavor with lemon or vanilla. Line a pie plate with puff paste, and bake first; then pour the boiled custard into the baked crust; then spread over it a frosting made of the beaten whites of the eggs, and a tablespoonful of powdered sugar; put the pie back in the oven, and brown slightly.

Sweet Potato Pie. Boil nice bright sweet potatoes, and when well done peel, mash, and put through a colander. For every cupful of the sweet potato use one cupful of milk, one egg, add sugar, cinnamon, and nutmeg to taste. Bake with under crust only.

Orange Tarts. Needed: Oranges, sugar, puff-paste. Pare some oranges very thin, soak them in water for three days, changing the water frequently. Boil them until soft. When cold, cut a thick slice from the top and bottom, and the rest in thin slices; line tart dishes with puff paste, and fill them with layers of sugar and orange alternately.

Sand Tarts. Cream together one pound of brown sugar and half a pound of butter. Beat the yolks of three eggs very light, and add butter and sugar; sift one pound of flour in dry state with two teaspoonfuls of baking powder, mix with the eggs, butter and sugar until a paste firm enough to roll has been formed. Roll out thin and cut into squares; spread the whites of the eggs over the top; sift over this granulated sugar and crown with half a pound of blanched almonds, rolled and spread over the surface. Bake in a quick oven.

Neapolitaines. Make enough puff paste for a pie; roll into a sheet half an inch thick and cut into strips three inches by one and one-half. Bake in a quick oven. When cold, spread with jam or jelly half the strips, and stick the others over in pairs with jelly between. Cover with frosting.

Rhubarb Pie. Pour boiling water over two teacupfuls of chopped rhubarb, drain off the water after four or five minutes, and mix with the rhubarb a teacupful of sugar, the yolk of an egg, a piece of butter and a tablespoonful of flour, moistening the whole with three tablespoonfuls of water. Bake with the lower crust only, and make a meringue of the white of the egg with three tablespoonfuls of sugar; spread over the top of the pie, and return to the oven to brown.

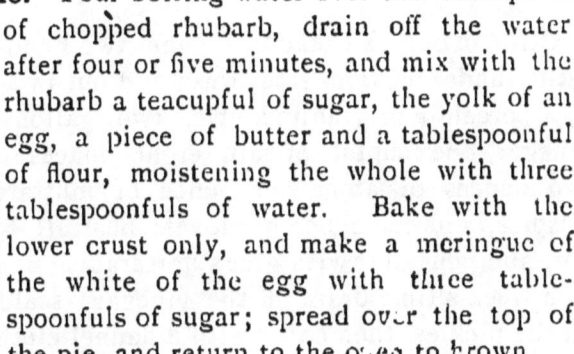
Rhubarb.

PICKLES AND PRESERVES

Cucumber Pickles. Take two hundred cucumbers rather under medium size; wash and put in a stone jar. Put in a porcelain or granite kettle, two gallons of good cider vinegar, one cupful of salt, eight ounces of horseradish, two ounces of alum, one ounce of mustard, one ounce of allspice, and one ounce of cloves; heat all together boiling hot, and pour over with green horseradish or cabbage leaves. In a week's time drain off the vinegar, scald, and put back on the pickles, then cover with a flannel cloth.

Ripe Cucumber Pickles. Pare and cut the cucumbers, and scrape out the seeds. Put the pieces in a stone jar, and cover with salt and water, not too strong; let stand for a day or two, changing the water once or twice; take out, and drain; then let stand in fresh water for a few hours; then boil them in vinegar until tender; skim out carefully, and put in a stone jar. Make a syrup of one quart of vinegar, four pounds of sugar, one ounce of cassia buds, and a tablespoonful of ground cinnamon; boil until the syrup is clear, and pour over the cucumbers. This amount of syrup is enough for three quarts of the cucumbers after they are boiled.

Chow Chow. Chop one peck of green tomatoes fine. Sprinkle a large cupful of salt over them, and let stand over night. In the morning put in a sieve and drain; then take six large green peppers, six large onions, six or eight stalks of celery, and chop all fine, and put in a porcelain kettle with the chopped tomato; put in with them two teaspoonfuls each of ground mustard, cinnamon and cloves; add a half teaspoonful of mace, two pounds of brown sugar, and enough vinegar to cover all. Simmer for two hours, stirring occasionally. Put up in glass or stone jars.

Sweet Chow-Chow. One gallon cabbage, two quarts green tomatoes, one pint of onions, one-fourth cup green peppers; chop all fine and add one and one-half pounds of sugar, one tablespoon mustard, one tablespoon ginger, two tablespoons cloves, two tablespoons salt, three tablespoons cinnamon, or three or four sticks cinnamon. Put all in three quarts vinegar and boil until cabbage is tender.

Mustard Pickles. Take two quarts small green cucumbers, two quarts of small green tomatoes, cut in halves or quarters; one quart of very small onions, two quarts of cauliflower, cut in small pieces. Let them stand over night in a weak brine, and in the morning cook each separately until tender. Put all together in a stone jar, and pour over them a mixture made as follows: Put on the fire one gallon of good cider vinegar, and let come to a boil; mix together one large cupful of flour, one pound of ground mustard, and three cupfuls of sugar; stir into the boiling vinegar, let it cook for two or three minutes; then pour the vegetables in the jar. These pickles will keep for a year.

Green Tomato Pickles. Slice one-half bushel of green tomatoes as thin as possible, and let stand in strong salt and water for twenty-four hours; take out carefully, and put in fresh cold water, and let stand for twelve hours; take out and drain; put on more cold water, and let stand for twelve hours longer; take out and drain, and boil in fresh water until it is tender enough to cut easily with a fork or spoon; take out carefully, and drain once more. Make a syrup of one-half gallon of vinegar, eight pounds of nice brown sugar, one-half tablespoonful of every kind of spice, one tablespoonful of whole mustard seed. Let all boil together for ten minutes; then put in the tomatoes about a quart at a time, and boil for fifteen minutes; skim out carefully, and put in a stone jar; put more tomatoes in the vinegar, and proceed as before until all are cooked; then boil down the syrup a few minutes, and pour over the tomatoes. These pickles are delicious, and will keep for months.

Ripe Tomato Pickles. Weigh off seven pounds of nice, firm, medium sized tomatoes; take off the skins by scalding; stick six or eight whole cloves in each one, and place in a jar. Put two quarts of good cider vinegar in a preserving kettle, add five pounds of nice brown sugar, a few sticks of cinnamon, and a tablespoonful of bruised ginger root; let all boil together for fifteen minutes; then pour boiling hot over the tomatoes; cover with a plate, and put a weight on to keep the fruit under the vinegar.

Tomato Preserves. Cut six lemons in slices, and boil until tender in three pints of water; then skim out, and put in ten pounds of sugar, and let it boil until the sugar is all dissolved; then put in ten pounds of peeled and sliced tomatoes, and boil for one-half hour; put back the lemons, and boil for ten or fifteen minutes longer. Put in jars, and cover closely. Partly ripe tomatoes are better than ripe ones for these preserves. A little ginger root boiled with the lemons improves the flavor.

Sliced Green Tomato Pickle. One-half peck green tomatoes (unpeeled), one pint sugar, one and one-half pints vinegar, one tablespoon cinnamon; one tablespoon whole allspice, handful whole cloves, little nutmeg and dry mustard, two or three small green peppers, three large onions. Boil one-half hour, or till tender.

Tomato Chutney. Cut up and peel twelve large tomatoes, six onions chopped fine, one cup vinegar, one cup sugar, handful of raisins, chopped fine, salt to taste, one-half teaspoon of cayenne, one-half teaspoon white pepper. Boil one hour and a half, bottle or put in stone jar.

Spiced Tomatoes. Put in a porcelain kettle one pint of good cider vinegar, four pounds of sugar, one-half ounce of cloves, and one ounce of cinnamon in a thin muslin bag and let boil until clear, then put seven pounds of whole tomatoes (peeled) and boil for two hours. Put in a stone jar. It will keep for months.

Tomato Catsup. Scald and peel ripe tomatoes, cook until soft, and press through a sieve. To one gallon of the tomato add one pint of vinegar, two tablespoonfuls of salt, two tablespoonfuls of mustard, one of allspice, one of cinnamon, one teaspoonful of black pepper, one of ground cloves, and one red pepper pod without seeds. Simmer an hour or more, put in jugs and cork tight.

Chili Sauce. Five large onions, eight green peppers, thirty ripe tomatoes, all chopped fine; add to them five tablespoonfuls of sugar, three of salt, and eight cupfuls of vinegar; mix all together, and boil two and one-half hours. Put in glass jars.

Pickled Lily. Chop very fine one peck of green tomatoes, two small heads of cabbage, three green peppers, four onions, six large cucumbers; put all in a large stone jar, and sprinkle over it a teacupful of salt and let stand over night. In the morning drain and scald in one quart of vinegar and two quarts of water; take out with a skimmer, and drain in a sieve. Make a syrup of three quarts of vinegar and four pounds of sugar, and let all boil together for thirty minutes. Put up in glass or stone jars.

Pickled Nasturtiums. (A very Good Substitute for Capers.) Use to each pint of vinegar, one ounce of salt, six peppercorns, nasturtiums. Gather the nasturtium pods on a dry day, and wipe them clean with a cloth; put them in a dry glass bottle, with vinegar, salt and pepper, in the above proportions. If you cannot find enough ripe to fill a bottle, cork up what you have got until you have some more fit; they may be added from day to day. Bung up the bottles, and seal or rosin the tops. They will be fit for use in ten or twelve months; and the best way is to make them one season for the next.

Pickled Gherkins. Let the gherkins remain in salt and water for three or four days, when take them out, wipe perfectly dry, and put them into a stone jar. Boil sufficient vinegar to cover them, with spices and pepper, etc., in the above proportion, for ten minutes; pour it, quite boiling, over the gherkins, cover the jar with vine leaves, and put over them a plate, setting them near the fire, where they must remain all night. Next day drain off the vinegar, boil it up again, and pour it hot over them. Cover up with fresh leaves, and let the whole remain till quite cold. Now tie down closely with bladder to exclude the air, and in a month or two they will be fit for use.

Gherkin.

Citron or Melon Preserves. Take thick watermelon or citron rind, and cut in strips about three inches long, and one-half inch thick, until you have five pounds, and let them stand in cold water for two or three hours. Make a syrup of five pounds of best white sugar, and two quarts of water, and squeeze in the juice of six lemons, and add the grated rind of three; let boil for fifteen minutes, then strain; heat again and stir in the beaten white of an egg, and skim off as it rises; the syrup should be of a nice lemon color, and as clear as amber; put in the citron, which should be drained and dry, and cook until tender. Skim out the fruit carefully, and add to the syrup a pound of best raisins, boil for two or three minutes, and pour over the fruit. Great care must be taken to remove every particle of stem from the raisins and to wash them thoroughly, so that there will be no dark specks in the clear syrup.

Walnut Ketchup. Use one-half a sieve of walnut shells, two quarts of water, salt, one-half pound of shalots, one ounce of cloves, one ounce of mace, one ounce of whole pepper, one ounce of garlic. Put the walnut shells into a pan, with the water and a large quantity of salt; let them stand for ten days, then break the shells up in the water, and let it drain through a sieve, putting a heavy weight on the top to express the juice; place it on the fire, and remove all scum that may arise. Now boil the liquor with the shalots, cloves, mace, pepper and garlic, and let all simmer till the shalots sink; then put the liquor into a pan, and, when cold, bottle, and cork closely. It should stand six months before using; should it ferment during that time, it must be again boiled and skimmed.

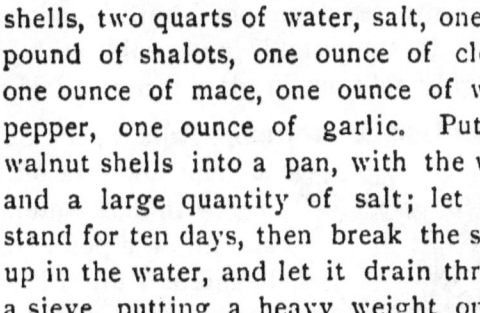
The Walnut.

Blackberry Pickle. Seven pounds of fruit, five pounds white sugar, one pint of best cider vinegar, and cook until the berries are done. Skim out the berries, boil the juice until thick as good syrup, pour over berries, cover and keep in cool, not cold, place. These will keep a long time, and need not be sealed up, as they will keep without. Raspberry jam will keep, too, if cooked thoroughly in common earthen jars, simply covering to keep free from dust.

Pineapple Preserves. Have your pineapples as ripe as they can be procured; pare and cut in thin slices and cut each slice in quarters; be very careful to remove every particle of the skin, for if all is not removed it will cause the preserves to look specky. Weigh the fruit and allow a pound of sugar for every pound of fruit. Put a layer of the pineapple in a large earthen dish, then a layer of sugar, and so on until all the fruit is in the dish; put a layer of sugar on top, and let stand over night. In the morning drain off the juice and put in a preserving kettle; stir in the beaten white of an egg and skim as it comes to a boil. Let it boil for ten minutes, then pour boiling hot over the pineapple, and let it stand and grow cold with covering. When thoroughly cold put in glass jars and seal.

Brandied Peaches. Take a peck of nice peaches not too ripe and take off the skins by scalding with hot water. Weigh the fruit and allow a pound of sugar to every pound of fruit. Make a syrup of the sugar, allowing two-thirds of a cupful of water to each pound of sugar. Let the syrup come to a boil, skim and when clear put in the fruit and let them cook until they can be pierced with a straw; then take out one at a time, and place carefully in a jar. Let the syrup boil a few minutes, then put in two quarts of brandy and boil for a few minutes longer, then pour over the peaches. Put up in glass jars, if preferred.

Preserved Fruit. In preserving, those fruits that are naturally sweet, require only three-fourths of a pound of sugar to one of fruit, while those fruits that are very acid require pound for pound. Small fruits are boiled down with the syrup until the syrup is thick and clear, then taken from the fire and put in jars; while the larger fruits, such as pears, quinces, plums, and peaches, are boiled in the syrup until they look clear and are tender, then skimmed out carefully and put in a jar. Allow the juice to boil until thick,

Pickles and Preserves

then pour over the fruit. Cover with paper wet in brandy.

Pickled Apples. Peel, quarter, and core nice sweet apples until you have five pounds; put them in a stewpan, cover with water, and cook until tender; lift out carefully with a skimmer and put on an earthen dish. Make a syrup of three pounds of sugar, and one pint of vinegar, add some stick cinnamon, and a few cloves; boil until clear, then put in the apples and cook slowly for twenty or thirty minutes. put in glass cans.

Plum Catsup.  Put in a preserving kettle six pounds of plums, three and one-half pounds of sugar, and one quart vinegar; boil until the plums are reduced to a pulp; cool and press through a sieve, then add cinnamon, cloves, nutmeg and allspice to taste. Put up in glass jelly cups.

Grape Catsup. Five pounds of grapes, boiled to a pulp and sifted, add two pounds of sugar, one pint of vinegar, one tablespoonful each of cinnamon, cloves, allspice, and one teaspoonful of pepper. Boil two hours and put up in glass.

Canned Fruit. In canning fruit be sure to have it good and fresh. If at all decayed or fermented, it will cause the fruit to work after it is canned. Allow one cupful of sugar to a quart can of peaches, pears, cherries and raspberries, and two cupfuls to strawberries, grapes, gooseberries and fruit that is very tart. Make a syrup of the sugar and some water, and let it boil before putting in the fruit. The more juicy the fruit is, the less water will be required. Boil the fruit until cooked through, but not long enough to become mussy; have your can full of hot water, and when ready to fill with fruit, pour out the water and set it in a basin partly filled with hot water, put in the fruit with a fruit tunnel, and when filled wipe off the can with a damp cloth, put on the rubber and top hot and screw down; tip the can bottom side up and if no juice escapes it is airtight, but if there is a flow of juice press down the lower edge of the cover with an iron spoon handle; if this is not effectual add another rubber, or change the cover. In canning strawberries plunge them in the hot syrup and boil briskly at least thirty or forty minutes; this will prevent them from losing their shape and color after they are canned. Pears should be put in cold water as soon as peeled, to prevent discoloration.

Fruit Jellies. Boil the fruit with as little water as possible, and squeeze in a jelly bag. Allow a pound of sugar to a pint of juice, and boil until it jellies, which is usually in fifteen or twenty minutes. Pour in cans or glasses, and leave uncovered until cold. If the jelly fails to thicken as much as is desirable when cold, set the glasses in the sun for two or three days, leaving off the covers.

Jams. Crush the fruit with a potato masher, and allow a pound of sugar to a pint of the crushed fruit. Bring to a boil slowly to prevent scorching, and boil until thick and clear. Put up in glass.

Orange Marmalade. Take two dozen sour oranges, and take off the peel, cut in halves across the sections, take out the seeds, and weigh. Take as many pounds of sugar as you have pounds of fruit, and put in a **preserving kettle** with enough water to dissolve. Bring to a boil slowly, to prevent scorching, and boil for ten or fifteen minutes. While the syrup is boiling, grate half a cupful of the yellow part of the orange peel, and when the syrup has boiled the requisite time, put in the orange and grated peel. Boil fifteen minutes longer, and put in glass jars or cups.

Syrup for Spiced Fruit. One pint of vinegar, three and one-half pounds of sugar, cinnamon, cloves, and allspice, tied in a thin muslin bag and boiled in the syrup. Pears, peaches, cherries, plums, grapes, can all be spiced or pickled in this syrup; it always gives satisfaction. Allow about seven pounds of fruit to the above rule.

Apple Marmalade. Take green fruit, sour, equal quantities of apples and sugar, cook the apples (a peck before they are cored) with a little water, and two lemons. When thoroughly cooked then sift, add sugar, boil fifteen minutes, and can. Much better than the ripe fruit, and it looks clearer. Common sour apples that are juicy, or crab apples, are the best for this.

Canning. The proportions of sugar fruit used in canning and preserving vary greatly. The amount of sugar given below is about an average for canning when a very rich preserve is not desired. These canned fruits are excellent for pies, etc.

Sugar to a Quart Jar.

Cherries,	6 ounces.	Grapes,	6 to 8 ounces.
Strawberries,	6 to 8 "	Peaches,	4 "
Raspberries,	4 "	Pineapples,	4 to 6 "
Blackberries,	5 to 6 "	Crab apples,	6 to 8 "
Quinces,	8 to 10 "	Plums,	4 "
Pears,	4 to 6 "	Pieplant,	8 to 10 "

CANDY

Cream Candy. Take one pound of white sugar, one cupful of water, one-half teaspoonful of cream tartar, two teaspoonfuls of vinegar, two teaspoonfuls of vanilla, butter the size of an egg; boil until it hardens when dropped into water. Pour upon a buttered platter and when nearly cold, pull.

Sugar Candy. Take two cupfuls of "A" coffee sugar, one-third cupful of good vinegar, two-thirds of a cupful of water; boil without stirring until it crisps in cold water. Turn out upon a buttered platter and pour the desired flavor over it. When sufficiently cool pull until white and light, pulling directly from you without twisting. Have the hands clean and dry; do not use butter on them. This rule is varied by using different flavorings, and makes excellent candy by pouring it over nuts or popcorn.

French Creams. Take two cupfuls of granulated sugar, add to it one-half a cupful of milk, set upon the stove and bring slowly to a boil and boil for five minutes; take off the fire and set in a pan of cold water, stir rapidly until it creams. Shape into balls with the hands and nuts on top of some of the creams.; or it can be arranged in layers and figs or dates placed between; then cut in squares. Fine chocolate creams can be made of this mixture by dipping the balls into melted chocolate, leaving until cold upon buttered white paper.

French Creams No. 2. Break the white of an egg into a glass and add an equal quantity of milk or water; then stir in enough XXXX confectioners' sugar to make sufficiently stiff to roll into shape; about a pound and a half will be needed; use different flavorings to make a variety.

Chocolate Caramels. One cupful of grated chocolate, one cupful of brown sugar, one cupful of molasses, one-half cupful of sweet milk; boil until it hardens when dropped in water. Then add a piece of butter the size of an egg, and one cupful of chopped English walnut meats; pour into a buttered pan, and when partly cold cut in squares.

Kisses. Two cupfuls of powdered sugar, the whites of three eggs, two cupfuls of cocoanut, two teaspoonfuls of baking powder; mix all together, drop upon buttered paper, and bake until slightly brown in a brisk oven.

Crystalized Popcorn. Put into an iron kettle one tablespoonful of butter, three tablespoonfuls of water and one teacupful of white sugar; boil until ready to candy, then throw in three quarts of nicely popped corn, stir briskly until the candy is evenly distributed over the corn. Care should be taken not to have too hot a fire, or the corn will be scorched while crystalizing. Nuts of any kind may be treated in the same way.

Molasses Candy. Take four cupfuls of sugar, two cupfuls of molasses and one-half cupful of vinegar; boil until it crisps in cold water, then stir in one tablespoonful of baking soda. Pour into well buttered dishes, leave until sufficiently cool, then pull.

Nougat. Almonds and other nuts for nougat should be blanched, drained and skinned some time before they are chopped. The nougat is made by melting pounded sugar in a copper sugar boiler, putting a dessertspoonful of lemon juice to each pound, then adding double the weight of sugar in almonds, either colored or white, filberts, or pistachios, and a little sweet liquor. The almonds or nuts should be hot when put into the syrup. For lining moulds, small pieces of the nougat should be pressed in with a lemon till the mould is covered, when the nougat should be turned out.

BEVERAGES

Coffee. In preparing tea and coffee, it is of the first importance to begin right. See that the teakettle is clean, and the water pure. A teakettle that is filled with lime, or other sediment, is unfit for use, and water that has stood in the house over night, or for some hours, is impure. To begin then, rinse the teakettle thoroughly and fill with fresh water, put on the fire, and bring to a boil quickly. For coffee, procure of a good reliable dealer a mixture of one-third Mocha, to two-thirds Java, freshly roasted and ground. Allow a tablespoonful of ground coffee for every person to be served, and put in an extra spoonful for every five or six persons. If an ordinary pot is used, mix the coffee with an egg, put it in the coffee pot and add to it about a cupful of cold water; set it on the stove and bring to a boil quickly. The moment it begins to boil, add boiling water (about two quarts to five spoonfuls of ground coffee) and set it on the back part of the stove where it will keep hot, but on no account allow it to boil, as that destroys the aroma. The coffee will be ready to serve in six or eight minutes after the hot water has been added. If a drip coffee pot is used, the coffee must be ground very fine. Good directions usually accompany the different kinds of coffee pots in use.

Beverages

However, great care must be taken to keep the strainer, whether made of cloth or wire, clean and free from all obstruction. If made of wire, it should be washed and cleaned with a brush, at least once a day.

Tea. Procure a good quality of tea of whatever kind preferred. Scald the teapot (an earthen or granite one is the best) and use about a teaspoonful for each person. Use boiling water, but do not boil the tea. Steep for a few minutes before serving. Black and uncolored teas are considered purer and less liable to affect the nerves than green teas.

The Tea Plant.

Iced Tea. Make a pitcherful of tea two or three hours before wanted. It should be made stronger than if it were to be served hot, as the melting ice weakens it. About ten or fifteen minutes before serving, add to the tea a quantity of chopped ice. Put a lump of ice in each cup or glass, and serve.

Russian Tea. Russian tea is made by adding a slice of lemon to each cup of tea, whether hot or iced.

Chocolate. Take two quarts of good rich milk, put in a double boiler, and let come to a boil. Grate fine a little more than a quarter of a cake of bitter chocolate, dissolve with a little milk, and add to the boiling milk; sweeten to taste; simmer for a few minutes after adding the chocolate, and serve.

The Cocoa Bean.

Broma and Cocoa. Broma and Cocoa can be made the same as chocolate. Equal parts of milk and water can be used in preparing these drinks, if pure milk is considered too rich, but they will be found lacking in flavor, as nothing brings out the rich flavors of these compounds like pure milk.

Raspberry Shrub. Place red raspberries in a stone jar, cover them with good cider vinegar and let stand over night. In the morning strain, and to each pint of juice, add one pint of sugar; boil for five minutes, skim, and let cool; then bottle and cork tightly.

Hop Beer. Put in a boiler one pound of hops, a handful of thoroughwort, and a small bunch of dandelion root; add two gallons of water and boil for one hour. Strain and cool; then add four pounds of sugar and one cake of yeast. Put in jugs and leave out the corks. When it has stopped working, cork, and set in a cool place. This is an excellent spring tonic. Drink a small glassful three or four times a day.

Raspberry Vinegar. To every three pints of the best vinegar allow four and one-half pints of freshly gathered raspberries; to each pint of liquor allow one pound of pounded loaf sugar, one wineglassful of brandy. Let the raspberries be freshly gathered; pick them from the stalks, and put one and one-half pint of them into a stone jar, pour three pints of the best vinegar over them, and let them remain for twenty-four hours, then strain the liquor over another one and one-half pint of fresh raspberries. Let them remain another twenty-four hours, and the following day repeat the process for the third time; then drain off the liquor without pressing, and pass it through a jelly bag (previously wetted with plain vinegar), into a stone jar. Add to every pint of the liquor one pound of pounded loaf sugar; stir them together, and when the sugar is dissolved, cover the jar; set it upon the fire in a saucepan of boiling water, and let it boil for an hour, removing the scum as fast as it rises; add to each pint a glass of brandy, bottle it, and seal the corks. This is an excellent drink in cases of fevers and colds; it should be diluted with cold water, according to the taste or requirements of the patient. To be boiled one hour.

Egg Wine. One egg, one tablespoonful and one-half glass of cold water, one glass of sherry, sugar, and grated nutmeg to taste. Beat the egg, mixing with it a tablespoonful of cold water; make the wine and water hot, but not boiling; pour on it the egg, stirring all the time. Add sufficient lump sugar to sweeten the mixture, and a little grated nutmeg; put all into a very clean saucepan, set it on a gentle fire, and stir the contents one way until they thicken, but *do not allow them to boil.* Serve in a glass with sippets of toasted bread or plain crisp biscuits. When the egg is not warmed, the mixture will be found easier of digestion, but it is not so pleasant a drink.

Almond Milk. Needed: Two ounces of sweet almonds, one-half ounce of bitter almonds, two ounces of loaf sugar, one tablespoonful of orange flower water, one pint of spring water. Blanch the almonds and pound them with the sugar and orange flower water, in a mortar, adding a few drops of water occasionally whilst pounding, to prevent too much oiliness. When the mixture looks creamy and smooth, pour it into a clean basin, add the cold spring water, and stir it with a silver or thin wooden spoon. Leave it for two hours, then strain and keep it either on ice or in a very cool place, as it is likely otherwise to turn sour. Almond milk is served with an equal quantity of water.

Ching-Ching. A good orange, a few drops of essence cloves, ditto peppermint, 3 or 4 lumps of sugar, a tumblerful of ice.

Orangeade. Peel of 3, juice of 15 oranges, ¾ lb. loaf sugar, 2 quarts of water. Peel the three oranges thinly and boil the peel with the sugar in a pint of water. Press all the juice from the oranges through a fine hair sieve into a jug. Add the strained syrup and the rest of the

cold water, mix, and stand it on ice for an hour. Serve it from cut glass jugs or decanters, and large claret glasses.

Lemon Syrup. Two lbs. of loaf sugar, 2 pints of water, 1 oz. of citric acid, ½ drachm of essence of lemon. Boil the sugar and water together for a quarter of an hour, and put it into a basin, where let it remain till cold. Beat the citric acid to a powder, mix the essence of lemon with it, then add these two ingredients to the syrup; mix well, and bottle for use. Two tablespoonfuls of the syrup are sufficient for a tumbler of cold water, and will be found a very refreshing summer drink. Two tablespoonfuls of syrup to a tumblerful of cold water.

Pineapple Water. One large, ripe pineapple, 1 pint of boiling syrup, juice of 1 lemon. Peel the pine, slice and mash it well in a basin, then pour on the syrup and lemon juice; stir well and cover. Let it stand 2 hours, then filter through a fine silk sieve and add a quart of spring water.

Strawberry Water. One lb. of fine strawberries, ½ lb. of loaf sugar, juice of 1 lemon. Crush the sugar finely, and sift over the strawberries, which should be red and ripe. Add half a pint of cold water, filter through a sieve, add a quart of spring water, and the strained juice of a lemon.

Currant Water. One lb. of fine red currants, ½ lb. of raspberries, 1 lb. of crushed loaf sugar water. Pick the fruit, add half a pint of water, and crush with a wooden spoon, then put the pulp into a preserving pan with half the sugar. Stir till it is beginning to simmer, then filter through a hair sieve. Make the rest of the sugar into a syrup with 3 gills of water, pour it to the fruit syrup, add a pint and a half of water. Let it cool, then decant like wine for use.

To Make Essence of Coffee. To every ¼ lb. of ground coffee allow 1 small teaspoonful of powdered chicory,

3 small teacupfuls, or 1 pint of water. Let the coffee be freshly ground, and, if possible, freshly roasted; put it into a percolator, or filter, with the chicory, and pour *slowly* over it the above proportion of boiling water. When it has all filtered through, warm the coffee sufficiently to bring it to the simmering point, but do not allow it to boil; then filter it a second time, put it into a clean and dry bottle, cork it well, and it will remain good for several days. Two tablespoonfuls of this essence are quite sufficient for a breakfastcupful of hot milk. This essence will be found particularly useful to those persons who have to rise extremely early; and having only the milk to make boiling, it is very easily and quickly prepared. When the essence is bottled, pour another 3 teacupfuls of *boiling* water slowly on the grounds, which, when filtered through, will be a very weak coffee. The next time there is essence to be prepared, make this weak coffee boiling, and pour it on the ground coffee instead of plain water; by this means a better coffee will be obtained. Never throw away the grounds without having made use of them in this manner; and always cork the bottle well that contains this preparation, until the day that it is wanted for making the fresh essence. Prepared coffee essence can now be bought at a reasonable price, and of good quality. It needs to be mixed with *boiling* water or milk, to be filtered once, then brought to the boiling point, and allow 2 tablespoonfuls for a breakfastcupful of hot milk.

Koumiss (sometimes called Milk Beer). Into one quart of new milk put one gill of fresh buttermilk and three or four lumps of white sugar. Mix well and see that the sugar dissolves. Put in warm place to stand ten hours, when it will be thick. Pour from one vessel to another until it becomes smooth and uniform in consistency. Bottle and keep in warm place twenty-four hours; it may take thirty-six in winter. The bottles must be tightly corked, and the corks tied down. Shake well five minutes before opening.

It makes a very agreeable drink, which is especially recommended for persons who do not assimilate their food, and young children may drink it as freely as milk. Instead of buttermilk, some use a teaspoon of yeast. The richer your milk, which should be unskimmed, the better will be your koumiss.

Mulled Buttermilk. The well beaten yelk of an egg added to boiling buttermilk and allowed to boil up; or add to the boiling buttermilk a little thickening of flour and cold buttermilk.

Baked Milk. Put the milk in a jar, covering the opening with white paper, and bake in a moderate oven until thick as cream. May be taken by the most delicate stomach.

Elderberry Syrup. Take elderberries perfectly ripe, wash and strain them, put a pint of molasses to a pint of the juice, boil it twenty minutes, stirring constantly; when cold, add to each quart a pint of French brandy; bottle and cork it tight. It is an excellent remedy for a cough.

Strawberry Syrup. Take fine ripe strawberries, crush them in a cloth, and press the juice from them; to each pint of it put a pint of simple syrup, boil gently for one hour, then let it become cold, and bottle it; cork and seal it. When served reduce it to taste with water, set it on ice, and serve in small tumblers half filled.

Blackberry Cordial. Secure ripe berries and crush them; to each gallon of juice add one quart of boiling water; let it stand twenty-four hours, stirring it a few times; strain and add two pounds of sugar to each gallon of liquid; put in jugs and cork tightly. It may be used in two months; is excellent for summer complaint, and can be taken by delicate invalids.

DISHES FOR INVALIDS

Beef Tea. Procure two pounds of lean beef, chop into small bits and put into a glass fruit jar; screw on the cover, and put the jar in a kettle of cold water; bring to a boil and boil for two or three hours; pour off the juice and season to taste.

Beef Broth. Cut some pieces of lean beef into small pieces, cover with cold water, and boil until the meat comes to pieces; then strain through a colander and let the broth stand until cold. Take off any particles of fat that are on top, season with salt and pepper, and add small squares of toasted bread. Rice, sage, and tapioca, may be used instead of toast, if preferred. Other meat broths are made in the same manner.

Rice for Invalids. Take a tablespoonful of rice and a pint of milk; put them in an earthen dish and bake in the oven for two hours. Keep the dish covered for the first hour, then take off the cover and stir occasionally. Sweeten if preferred. This is an excellent diet for persons recovering from bowel trouble.

Cornmeal Gruel. Let a pint of water come to a boil; then stir in one tablespoonsful of cornmeal, wet with a little water. Let it boil a few minutes, and season with salt. Milk can be added, if preferred.

Toast Water. Toast a slice of bread very brown, break it into pieces, and pour over it a cupful of boiling water. When cold it makes a nourishing drink.

Corn Coffee. Roast an ear of dry corn until the tips of the kernels are black. Break the ear in pieces, put in a bowl; then pour over it a pint of boiling hot water. Drink cold.

Jelly Water. Put in a tumbler a tablespoonsful of currant jelly, and a tablespoonful of wine; mix them well together, then fill the glass with ice water. If the patient is feverish, leave out the wine.

Flaxseed Lemonade. Steep two tablespoonfuls of flaxseed in one quart of hot water, for ten minutes. Stir in and add the juice of three lemons, a large cupful of sugar, and a wineglassful of wine. Drink either hot or cold. This is an excellent drink for persons suffering with colds or lung troubles.

Appetizers. Patients can often be induced to taste the following, when nothing else will tempt them: Scrape raw beef very fine and season with salt and pepper. It can be made into a sandwich, if preferred. Second: Roast over the coals a small slice of salt pork until almost burnt. A little taste of this often creates an appetite.

To Make Gruel for Invalids. Take 1 tablespoonful of Robinson's patent groats, 2 tablespoonfuls of cold water, 1 pint of boiling water. Mix the prepared groats smoothly with the cold water in a basin; pour over them the boiling water, stirring it all the time. Put it into a very clean saucepan; boil the gruel for 10 minutes, keeping it well stirred, sweeten to taste, and serve. It may be flavored with a small piece of lemon peel, by boiling it in the gruel, or a little grated nutmeg may be put in; but in these matters the taste of the patient should be consulted. Pour the gruel in a tumbler, and serve. When wine is allowed to the invalid, 2 tablespoonfuls of sherry or port make this preparation very nice. In cases of colds, the same quantity of spirits is sometimes added instead of wine. Fine oatmeal may be used, but it then requires rather longer boiling.

The Invalid's Mutton Chop. A well broiled chop is a very digestible thing to give to an invalid. It should be cut fairly thin and thoroughly well cooked. None of the skin should be eaten of this or any meat. A fresh tomato is a wholesome and digestible accompaniment. To vary a diet of chops, of which most invalids tire, one may be cut from the loin, the next day the bone can be taken out and the chop rolled up and skewered, and a third, 1 or 2 tiny cutlets from the neck might be served. The greatest care must be taken that the meat should not have the slightest taint, which is most likely to be in the under part or in the marrow. The under cut of a loin of mutton is a very good and tender piece of meat to serve to an invalid.

Whey. To a pint of warm new milk add a teaspoonful of prepared rennet. Let it stand, and then strain it through a piece of muslin. This can sometimes be taken when milk cannot. It is a useful drink in feverish complaints.

White wine whey is made by pouring a wineglassful of sherry into a breakfast cupful of boiling milk, and then straining through muslin.

Treacle posset is made of boiling milk, with 1 or 2 tablespoonfuls of treacle, in the same way. Alum whey and tamarind whey are also occasionally made.

Irish Moss or Carrageen. This seaweed has a reputation as a remedy for chest diseases. It should be first soaked and washed in cold water, and then boiled for a quarter of an hour in fresh water, allowing half an ounce of moss to a pint and a half of water. Strain, and when cold it will set to a jelly. If required as a drink, it should have double the quantity of water, or milk can be used.

Iceland Moss. Wash the moss very thoroughly. Put it in cold water, and let it nearly boil. Throw this first water away, as it will be bitter. Then put the moss on again with water, allowing 1 oz. of moss to a pint and a half of water. Boil it for 15 or 20 minutes, and strain it while hot. It should be sweetened, and flavored with lemon or spice. Milk can be used instead of water. It is a slightly bitter drink, or if a sufficient quantity of the moss is used it cools into a jelly.

Cream of Tartar Drink. Dissolve half an ounce of cream of tartar in half a pint of syrup of sugar and water, add 20 drops of essence of lemon, and keep it in a bottle to be diluted with water, or soda water, as required. It will keep a long time.

Baked Beef Tea. One pound of fleshy beef, one and one-half pints of water, one-half saltspoonful of salt. Cut the beef into small square pieces, after trimming off all the fat, and put it into a baking jar, with the above proportion of water and salt; cover the jar well, place it in a warm, but not hot, oven, and bake for three or four hours. When the oven is very fierce in the daytime, it is

The Marjoram. a good plan to put the jar in at night, and let it remain till the next morning, when the tea will be done. It should be strained, and put by in a cool place until wanted. It may also be flavored with an onion, a clove, and a few sweet herbs, etc., when the stomach is sufficiently strong to take these.

Panada for Invalids. These are rather different from what is understood by panada in the ordinary routine of cooking. They are useful in invalid cookery because whatever they are made of is finely divided. The following recipe is given by Dr. F. V. Pavy: Take the white part of the breast and wings freed from skin, of either roasted or boiled chicken, or the under side of cold sirloin of roasted beef; or cold roasted leg of mutton, and pound in a mortar with an equal quantity of stale bread. Add either the water in which the chicken has been boiled, or beef tea, until the whole forms a fluid paste, and then boil for ten minutes, stirring all the time.

Panada. (Another Mode.) Take of pearl barley or rice two ounces, wash and put it in a saucepan with half a pound of veal or mutton cut in small pieces, and half a pint of water. Simmer it all very gently for two hours, or set it in the oven all night. Then pound it in a mortar and rub it through a fine sieve. Add a little cream to make it as thin as desired, with seasoning to taste, and serve it hot or cold; or to the meat and barley pounded add a handful of bread crumbs and the yolk of one or two eggs. Poach it in dessertspoonfuls and serve with any vegetable and a little milk sauce.

Restorative Jelly. Three ounces of isinglass, two ounces of gum arabic, two ounces of sugar candy, a bottle of sherry. Put them in a jar, cover it closely, and let it stand all night; then set it in a saucepan of water, and let it simmer until it is dissolved.

Sago, Cream, and Extract of Beef. Two ounces of sago, one-half pint of water, one-half pint of cream, yolks of four eggs, one quart of beef tea. Wash the sago until the water poured from it is clear. Then stew the sago in half a pint of water until it is quite tender and very thick; mix with half a pint of good cream and the yolks of four eggs, and mingle the whole with one quart of beef tea, which should be boiling. Useful in cases of lingering convalescence after acute disease.

The Invalid's Cutlet. One nice cutlet from a loin or neck of mutton, two teacupfuls of water, one very small stick of celery, pepper and salt to taste. Have the cutlet cut from a very nice loin or neck of mutton; take off all the fat; put it into a stewpan, with the other ingredients; stew *very gently* indeed for nearly two hours, and skim off every particle of fat that may rise to the surface from time to time. The celery should be cut into thin slices before it is added to the meat, and care must be taken not to put in too much of this ingredient, or the dish will not be good. If the water is allowed to boil, the cutlet will be hard. It is better cooked in a jar set in a saucepan of water, as it must then be below boiling point.

Eel Broth. One-half pound of eels, a small bunch of sweet herbs, including parsley; one-half onion, ten peppercorns, three pints of water, two cloves, salt and pepper to taste. After having cleaned and skinned the eel, cut it into small pieces, and put it into a stewpan with the other ingredients; simmer gently until the liquid is reduced nearly half, carefully removing the scum as it rises. Strain it through a hair sieve; put it by in a cool place, and when wanted, take off all the fat from the top, warm up as much as is required, and serve with sippets of toasted bread. This is very nutritious broth, and easy of digestion.

Covered Silver Dish.

Calf's Foot Blancmange. One calf's foot, one quart of milk, one egg, sugar, nutmeg and lemon, or seasoning to taste. Get a calf's foot that has been already cooked, such as is sold in first-class markets and put it on the fire with milk enough to cover it, a strip of lemon peel, a piece of nutmeg, and sugar to taste. Let it cook very slowly for three or four hours, and then strain it. While still hot stir in the yolk of an egg, and set it in small moulds. This blancmange can be made savory by using a little salt, peppercorns, parsley, nutmeg or cloves, onion and celery instead of the sugar. The lemon peel may be added in any case. The egg may be omitted if not liked; a little cream might also be added. It is directed that small moulds shall be used. For an invalid, it is better to set just as much as is wanted for one meal rather than to cut a piece out of a large quantity.

Arrowroot. Use milk or water as preferred. Put a heaping teaspoonful of ground arrowroot into a cup, and mix with a little cold milk. Stir into a pan containing a pint of either cream or water that has been brought to a boil, adding a little salt. Let it simmer for a few minutes, and then pour out. May be sweetened or flavored with grated nutmeg if desired. Should be made only as it is wanted.

Herb Teas. Made by infusing the dried or green stalks and leaves in boiling water, and letting stand until cold. Sweeten to taste.

Jellied Chicken. Cook six chickens in a small quantity of water, until the meat will part from the bone easily; season to taste with salt and pepper. Just as soon as cold enough to handle, remove bones and skin; place meat in a deep pan or mould just as it comes from the bone, using gizzard, liver and heart, until the mould is nearly full. To the water left in the kettle add three-fourths of a box of good gelatine (some add juice of lemon) dissolved in a little warm water, and boil until it is reduced to a little less than a quart, pour over the chicken in the mould, leave to cool, cut with a very sharp knife and serve. The slices will not easily break up if directions are followed.

Slippery Elm Bark Tea. Break the bark into bits, pour boiling water over it, cover, and let it infuse until cold. Sweeten, ice, and take for summer disorders, or add lemon juice and drink for a bad cold.

THE DINNER TABLE

General Rules. Whether the table is to be covered with the most costly viands or the most simple fare, whether it be for prince or tradesman. there is yet equal necessity that the cloth should be spotless and good, the cutlery well cleaned and sharp, the silver polished brightly, and the glass clear. These are luxuries within the reach of all. We say "luxuries" because we all know the *comfort* of a well-laid table, and yet there are many who do not trouble themselves about the usual everyday laying of the cloth, only making a point of this being carefully done when guests are expectd. We would venture to suggest that if the mistress of a household would see that her table was properly laid every day she would find it less trouble than the anxiety of having it so only now and then, and much of the annoyance which the occasional dropping in of a friend at meal time often causes could be spared. Besides, though perhaps this point should not be discussed here, why should our ordinary family table differ so widely, as we confess it does too often, from the table we like our friends to see us preside at? It is because we have let "only ourselves" take a broader, wider meaning than it should have. "Only ourselves" stands too often as the apology for a dirty cloth, unpolished cutlery and silver, and smeared glass, to say nothing of perhaps negligent cookery into the bargain. And is it not a notable fact that when we do give a dinner-party, we strive our utmost to carry off the affair with ease and nonchalance, and are vexed if the secret be discovered—more than vexed—that to do this has been a source of worry and hard work ever since we projected the scheme? It is seldom, too, that we succeed in keeping the secret to ourselves, and our friends sometimes maliciously enjoy it.

The sideboard for all meals should be covered with a clean white cloth and all that is wanted for each meal—in addition to what is placed upon the table—that can be brought into the dining-room, should there be ready for use, with the addition of knives, forks, glasses, etc., in case such may be required, but as the sideboard will have to be laid differently for different meals, it will be best to arrange it separately for each. A sideboard should be an ornamental as well as useful piece of furniture, and may be as carefully and prettily laid out as the table itself.

Everything needed in laying a cloth should be first brought into the room in which the table is to be laid, and what you are about to partake of should be your guide as to what you require. For instance if fish is to be served then fish-eaters must be placed to each person, or failing these, two extra forks may be given. In the same way when **soup** is to be served then put on the necessary spoons at the right side, while the other courses must determine what knives and forks will be needed. The same rule applies to the glasses put upon the table, always to the right hand of each person. If you give three wines then put three glasses of the proper kinds, if only one, then put one glass, and if none, only the tumblers which may serve for either water or beer. It is only in hotels that everything is laid irrespective of what may be ordered. Salt is a necessary accompaniment to every meal and it is a great convenience to have plenty of small salt-cellars, one to each person, or one between two. To avoid the trouble of passing, pepper, mustard, etc., may also be placed upon the table or handed round by the servants, but as the serving of one meal does not apply to another one must prepare differently the different tables— Breakfast, Lunch, Dinner, Tea or Supper.

Table Cloths and Napkins. Anybody knowing how to lay a cloth properly and tastefully, prettily and neatly, knows something decidedly worth knowing. The first, or almost the first, attention bestowed by a young wife upon her household affairs should be directed to the laying of the meal cloth. Just as she begins, so, doubtless, she will go on. The laying of the cloth is a most important item in household management; it exercises a certain moral influence upon the inmates of the house in the degree of care or thought that is bestowed upon it. This is a point which, we hope, will not be lost sight of by our readers.

The serviettes or table napkins should be neatly and tastefully folded when first put on the table, although afterward in ordinary family use they may be put into rings. We give instructions and illustrations showing a few ways of making these useful articles an ornament to the table, on the following pages. It is a good plan to place them upon the table first so that one can apportion the space allowed for each person and make the napkins equi-distant, and in laying a dinner-table the roll or piece of bread is put in the folds.

FANCY WAYS OF FOLDING NAPKINS

The Sachet. First fold the napkin in three, then turn the upper fold to the middle in a hem (No. 1).

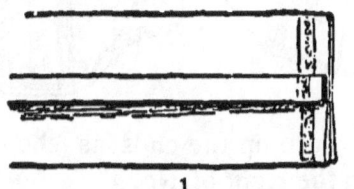

Next fold over the napkin end to end, leaving the hem inside (No. 2). Fold from the outer edge over and over,

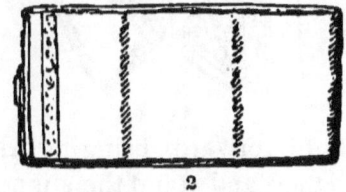

repeating the same on the other side. Next fold back A in a diamond shown by dotted line (No. 3) on each side, and put

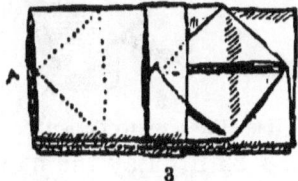

the corners under the hem crossing the center (No. 4).

The Palm Leaf. Fold the napkin diagonally across (No. 5).

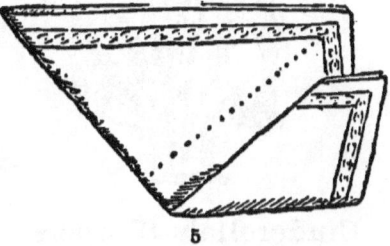

Next the two sides a short distance from the center (No. 6).

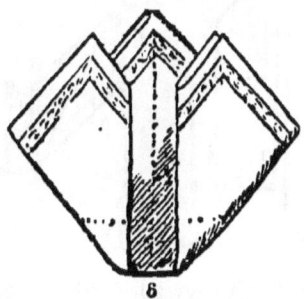

Fold over the base at the

dotted line shown in No. 7.

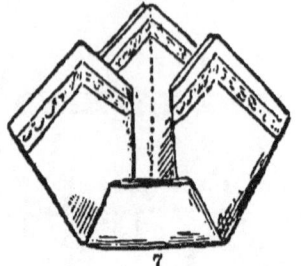

Lastly, pleat the base as a fan, and set it in a ring or glass (No. 8).

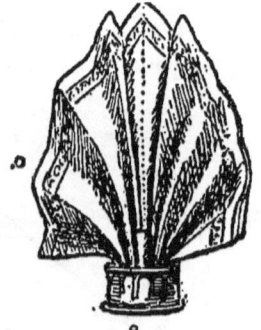

Cinderella's Slipper.

First fold the napkin in three, then again once over to make

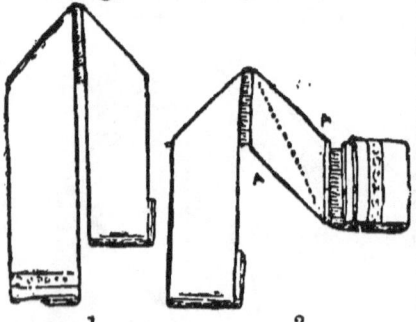

it half the width, fold over at center and turn up the ends,

next *under* at the dotted lines as in No. 1.

Again fold over at dotted line shown on the right in No. 2, on both sides.

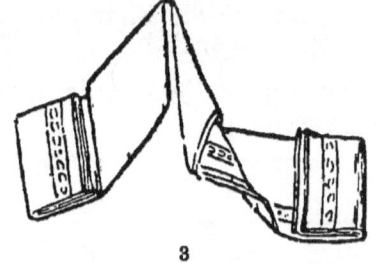

Turn up the ends as shown on the right of No. 3.

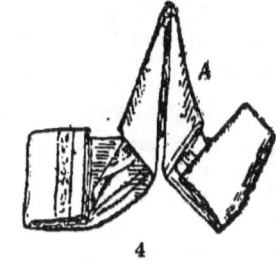

Fold forward, bringing **AA** together, and stand the slipper as shown in No. 5.

Isn't this a pretty design?

The Fan.

Lay the napkin flat upon the table, and make

a deep pleat at each side as in No. 1.

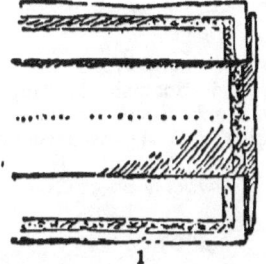

Next fold the two sides together as in No. 2.

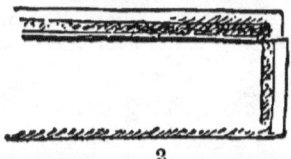

Next pleat from end to end in inch deep folds, backward and forward, as in No. 3.

Then pinch down the folds in points between each fold, as in No. 4.

A WORD OF ADVICE

The first thing to be thought of is the dinner, and varying that very good old maxim, "Cut your cloak according to your cloth," we should say, choose your dinner according to your cook. When fortunate enough to possess a good one, one need not be afraid of trying a few experiments; otherwise it is a dangerous thing, and if any contretemps occur, it is the mistress; and not the cook, who suffers.

No hostess is likely to be quite happy or at ease, with any fear on her mind as to how the next course will turn out.

Far better is it to have a simple dinner, which one knows will be properly cooked and served, than to risk *any*thing more elaborate, for it is almost impossible to appear unconcerned when one is harassed by petty cares, and a good hostess is one who is able herself to enjoy, without anxiety, the dinner she is giving to her friends.

SIMPLE FAMILY DINNERS

For Each Month of the Year

For January.

Consomme with egg.
Bread Sticks.
Boiled Corned Beef or Ham.
Boiled Potatoes.
Cabbage Salad.   Stewed Corn.
Dessert.
Apple Pie.   Cream Cheese.
Grapes.
Tea.   Coffee.

For February.

Oyster Soup. Celery.
Roast Turkey.   Cranberry Sauce.
Mashed Potatoes.
Canned Peas.   Oyster Plant Fritters.
Dessert.
Lemon Pie,
Cake or Whipped Cream.

For March.

Creamed Tomato Soup.
Roast Beef.   Browned Potatoes.
Mashed Turnips, Pickled Beets.
Dessert.
Orange Tapioca with whipped cream.

For April.

Celery Soup.
Roast Veal with Dressing.
Potato Balls.
Lettuce Salad, Maccaroni with cheese, (or Spinach.)
Dessert.
Lemon Jelly with custard sauce.

For May.

Bouillon, served in cups.
Roast Spring Lamb with mint sauce.
Baked Potatoes.
Green Peas.   Stewed Tomatoes.
Dessert.
Chocolate Blanc Mange.

For June.

Cream of Rice Soup.
Broiled Spanish Mackerel.
French Fried Potatoes.
Asparagus.   Dressed cucumbers.
Dessert.
Strawberry Short Cake.

For July.

Potato Soup.
Fried Spring Chicken.   Cream Gravy.
Baked Potatoes.
Summer Squash.   Sliced Tomatoes.
Dessert.   Ice Cream and Cake.

For August.

Asparagus Soup.
Boiled Leg of Mutton, caper sauce.
Boiled Potatoes.
String Beans.   Fried Egg Plant.
Dessert.   Sponge Pudding.

For September.

Vermicelli Soup.
Fricassee of Chicken, with dumpling.
Cauliflower with cream dressing.
Mashed Potatoes.   Lobster Salad.
Raspberry Pie.   Cheese.

For October.

Bean Soup.
Roast Pig with dressing.
Apple Fritters.   Green Corn.
Baked Sweet Potatoes.
Graham Pudding.   Wine Sauce.

For November.

Mock Turtle Soup.
Roast Goose.   Stewed Gooseberries.
Boiled Potatoes.
Baked Winter Squash. Boiled Turnips.
Pumpkin Pie.   Suet Pudding.
Cheese.

For December.

Raw Oysters.
Broiled Prairie Chicken, currant jelly.
Escalloped Potatoes dressing.
Fried Parsnips, Cabbage with Mayonnaise dressing.
English Plum Pudding.

For Lent.

Egg Soup.
Broiled Codfish or Salmon Steak, with Old Zealand Sauce.
Baked Potatoes.
Macaroni with Tomatoes, Rice Croquettes.
Plum Cake.   Preserved Pears.

NOTE :—For a family of six, from three pints to two quarts of soup are required; and from three to five pounds of meat, poultry or fish are required for the same number of persons if only one kind of meat is served.

RULES FOR DINNER GIVING

Rule 1.—Let your family dinner hour be at a given hour, and let that hour *be* the dinner hour. Allow no shirking here from any one, unless accident or circumstances render such compulsory. *Then* you stand some chance of being able to turn your cookery talents, if you have any, to account.

Rule 2.—Always arrange your dinner, having a kind of mind's-eye menu, satisfactorily beforehand, before you attempt either to give directions concerning it or to help, it may be, in its preparation. Without this, you *may* give your family or your guests an eatable dinner now and then, but as a general rule, it will be a failure.

Rule 3.—For a "hot dinner" let the plates be hot, not warm merely, but *hot*. The best dinner you can give guests will be spoiled if you serve it to them on plates in which almost before they begin to eat the gravy floats about in small, island-like patches.

Rule 4.—Give due attention to the customary order of courses. You do not want your fish, for instance, ready before the soup, causing the former to look flabby, and most likely break and lose its trim appearance.

Rule 5.—Be careful in dishing vegetables, that they are perfectly drained from water. Turnips or other edibles of the kind swimming about in a sea of dingy water are enough to cause the excellence of the cookery or the other viands to be put in the shade.

TABLE ETIQUETTE.

These very simple and practical rules are especially intended for the training of children, and as such, will be kindly received by busy parents. They will also be found useful as reminders for those grown up people who may have forgotten some of the necessary requisites of "Good Table Manners"—the infallible touch stone of a lady or a gentleman's breeding.

Make a point to be on time at family meals. Exactitude is the politeness of kings—and of well bred people.

Never come to the table in a neglected attire, or in your shirt sleeves, or with hair unkempt, or with hands and face of doubtful cleanliness. Your home is a temple, not a pig-stye.

If there are ladies in the party do not sit down before they are themselves seated.

Sit down square to the table, not sideways, or leaning back in your chair as if to take a nap instead of a meal.

Never allow your elbows to rest on the table. Let your hands—when not busy—rest on the edge of the table.

Do not tuck your napkin under your chin, or between the buttons of your waistcoat; put it across your lap.

If you sport a beard or mustache, use your napkin frequently to wipe away any unnoticed drop or crumb.

Never use your napkin to mop your face with.

Never cut your bread with a knife; bread is made to be broken, not cut, when once off the loaf.

Make no noise with your mouth when eating or drinking, especially when eating soup.

Never attempt to talk with a mouth half full.

Eat without haste; do not take huge mouthfuls.

Keep your elbows as close to your side as possible when cutting your meat or carrying spoon or fork to your mouth.

Do not throw your head back when drinking, nor drink a full glass at a time without stopping for breath.

Take care that all the ladies in the party except possibly your own daughters—are served before you.

If you have ladies by your side, attend, unobtrusively, to their wants, offering to fill their glasses, pass the bread, the salt, etc.

Never, under any circumstances, use your knife for any other purpose except cutting your meat. Knives are not to be put in contact with mouths.

Try your best to eat all vegetables—peas included—with the help of your fork. A famous society man who stood as a model of good manners, claimed that he could bring everything to his mouth by means of a fork—except tea, coffee and soup

Bring your spoon to your mouth sideways, not point foremost, and absorb its contents noiselessly.

Never pour the contents of your cup in your saucer, under pretence of cooling the beverage. Be patient awhile and drink from the cup direct, or with the help of a spoon.

When eating meat, hold it down on the plate with your

fork, while cutting it; knife in the right hand, fork in the left hand. When one piece is cut off let the knife go noiselessly by the side of the plate, and taking the fork in your right— almost horizontally—bring the morsel to your mouth.

Do not cut all your meat at one and the same time, but proceed as above; a little practice will make the task easy and graceful.

The fork is to be held with the handle in the palm of the hand and be gently brought from plate to mouth; the fingers stretched along the handle in a natural position. Always remember it is a fork, *not* a pitchfork.

Do not place a provision of anything (salt or olives or almonds) next to you on the tablecloth; nor place there fruit or potato peelings.

If you do not accept of one course, wait until the others are through with it before accepting of the next.

Do not butter a whole slice of bread; butter fragment after fragment.

Never encourage a dog or cat to play with you at the table

Do not get up from the table before the others do; your home is not a restaurant; the home you are invited to, still less.

Never take any food in your hands, except fruit. Mutton chops and fowls' legs and wings are not to be held in the fingers while being eaten. Civilized beings do not *devour*, they *eat*.

Do not clean your plate, with your bread or otherwise; it would look as if you were famished or miserly, which let us hope you are not.

When peeling fruit or potatoes hold them at the end of your fork—in the left hand—and peel them with your knife —in the right.

It is awful to have to say this, but do not, keep, or bring a cuspidor in the dining room.

When eating grapes or cherries, hold your right hand close to your mouth, and discreetly dispose—upon your plate- of the stones and skins.

Never carry fruit, confectionery or anything else from the table, except for a sick person and by special permission of the hostess.

Never wear gloves at the table.

Be careful not to drop or break or spill anything. If some such accident happens to you, take it calmly, excusing yourself to the hostess.

When sneezing or coughing, turn your face aside, or better hide it behind your handkerchief.

Avoid stretching your hand over other people's plates to reach anything. Rather ask for it, or do without.

Don't ask for a second service of soup or fish.

Never leave the spoon in your cup when bringing it to your lips.

When sending your plate for a second service of meat, or vegetables, or sweets, take away your fork and knife, and lay them on your right, side by side, and perpendicular to the table's edge.

If you are the host (or hostess) do not press any dish upon your guests. Out of misjudged courtesy they might eat more of it than they care to.

If finger bowls are brought upon the table at the close of a meal, only wet the tip of your fingers, passing them slightly over your lips. Remember this little glass vessel is not intended as a wash basin.

In a dinner by invitation, the host leads the way from the drawing room to the dining room, having on his arm the lady he wishes particularly to honor. Each gentleman then follows escorting the lady the hostess has requested him to "take in." The hostess comes last with the gentleman who is entitled to most consideration on this special occasion.

If the gentlemen do not stay in the dining room after the ladies' withdrawal—according to the English custom—the party returns to the drawing room in couples, as before, the hostess this time leading the way, and the host closing the march.

If the gentlemen are to stay in the dining room, they all rise when the hostess gives the signal for the ladies to withdraw, and the gentleman nearest to the exit opens the door with a bow, closing it after all the ladies have filed out.

After the lapse of about half an hour the butler, or waitress, announces that coffee is served in the drawing room, and the gentlemen join the ladies.

The half hour before dinner has always been considered as the great ordeal through which the mistress, in giving a dinner party, will either pass with flying colors, or lose many of her laurels. The mistress, however, must display no kind of agitation, but show her tact in suggesting light and cheerful subjects of conversation, which will be much aided by the introduction of any particularly new book, curiosity of art, or article of vertu, which may pleasantly engage the attention of the company. "Waiting for Dinner," however, is a trying time, and there are few who have not felt—

> "How sad it is to sit and pine,
> The long *half hour* before we dine,
> Upon our watches oft to look,
> Then wonder at the clock and cook,
> *   *   *   *   *   *   *
> And strive to laugh in spite of Fate,
> But laughter forced soon quits the room,
> And leaves it in its former gloom.
> But lo ! the dinner now appears—
> The object of our hopes and fears,
>   The end of all our pain !"

ARTISTIC COOKERY

There are many occasions—such as gala dinners, banquets, marriage luncheons, silver weddings, etc.,—when the mistress of the house is desirous of displaying some extra talent and introducing to her delighted guests some dish of unusual size or merit, surrounded by those beautiful little conceits which have made the reputation of French cooks.

We should have failed in one of our clearest duties in not giving a place in TREASURES OLD AND NEW, to a select number of those ornamental and exquisite specimens of what ought to be called

ARTISTIC COOKERY;

and, although it is going somewhat out of our original plan of treating only of simple and home-made dishes, we insert in this volume *forty-seven* descriptions (with steel plate illustrations), of some of the best examples of foreign cookery, such as is daily presented upon the tables of Europe's grandees.

We may add that both descriptions and designs are the work of the famous Chef of the court of Germany, Monsieur Urbain Dubois.

In these descriptions will be found a few, a very few technical words, but any hotel cook of average experience knows their meaning, and may be easily consulted concerning it.

Our purpose, we may add, is to furnish, in this department, some first class information for professional cooks, always in quest of something new and unique.

FISH

See Plate No. 1

Blue Fish. In form the blue fish resembles the salmon, or rather the houchen of Bavaria. Its lower jaw protrudes like that of the *bécar*. The head is very big, its skin bluish, and to this tint it owes its name. It is one of the prettiest fish in the New World. Its flesh, when cooked, assumes a slightly dull blue color, and remains soft. This fish usually weighs as much as ten pounds; from its size it therefore constitutes a remove, which can be served at a large dinner. If cooked whole, the blue fish is usually served broiled; if cooked in a *court bouillon*, it ought to be divided into slices. Filets of the blue fish are often served, cut, *sautés* with butter, and garnished either à la *Normande* or à la *Joinville*.

Artistic Cookery—Plate No. 1

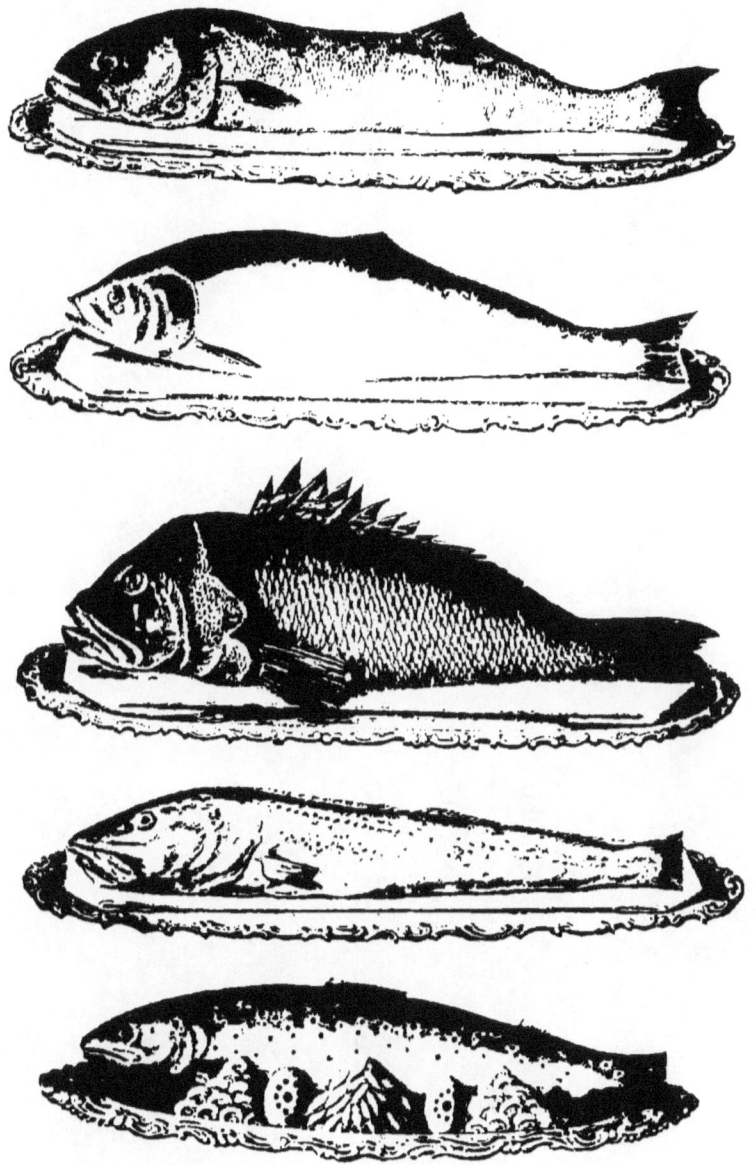

Blue Fish.   Shad, maître d' hôtel.   Black Fish.
Cod Fish with Oyster Sauce.   Salmon Trout, a la Chambord.

The Shad is very good, broiled "à la maître-d'hôtel;" but is also excellent, braised in wine, with little liquid, dished up with a "matelote" or a "génoise"-sauce; if the shad is to be broiled, it ought previously to be crimped. With broiled shad, butter "à la maître-d'hôtel," and a garnish of sorrel, are usually served; the latter ought to be served separately. If braised, it may be surrounded with any garnish applicable to removes of fish.

Black Fish. The physiognomy of the black fish is indeed remarkable. If in the drawing, the body of the fish be covered, as far as the lateral fin, with a piece of paper, it will be found, that the expression of the head is somewhat similar to that of the tiger. Its jaws are very strong, furnished inside with large teeth, and the surfaces of the palate are provided with very hard asperities; which confirms the opinion that this fish feeds more particularly on crustacea. The skin of the black fish is black, and very much like that of the tench. Its cooked flesh is white and firm, and much esteemed by epicures. It possesses a gelatinous principle, which renders it suitable to concentrated cooking, that is braising.

This fish attains a weight of from five to six pounds; if served whole, it may be surrounded with a fine garnish, and accompanied with a brown sauce, *Matelote*, *Bordelaise*, or *Génoise*.

The Cod is generally cooked in salted water, and plunged in while boiling; but if the fish is entire, it is only necessary to plunge it into lukewarm water well salted. An entire cod takes very long boiling, for it must be cooked without ebullition; that is to say, that at the first boiling of the liquid, the kettle must be placed on the side of the fire, so that the liquid may simmer only, without the ebullition making itself evident. With boiled cod nothing but a good sauce and boiled potatoes, ought to be served; other garnishes do not harmonize well with this sort of fish. Oyster sauce is most in use; but in Holland it is served simply with good melted butter. This dish, so delicate, if the fish is quite fresh and properly cooked, is far from possessing the same merit, if stale and negligently cooked; these two obstacles are easily removed, if the cook is intelligent, and is aware of the responsibility attached to his or her office.

The Trout represented in the drawing is stuffed, and trussed, then fixed on the drainer of a fish-kettle, taking care to place it on its belly; it is covered with a good "court-bouillon," and cooked in it; the liquor must be poured out cold on the fish; it is afterward brought to ebullition, but immediately removed from the fire. A salmon-trout of about ten pounds must remain an hour and a quarter in its liquor kept at the same degree of heat, but without any visible ebullition.

The trout is dished immediately, resting on its belly; but, for more safety, it must be kept in equilibrium by means of fried bread crusts put on the dish, so as to keep the fish upright; this bread must be masked with raw force-meat, and poached in the oven.

The garnish which surrounds the fish, is composed on one side of mushroom-heads, whole truffles, small quenelles, shaped with a tea-spoon, as well as ornamented quenelles; on the other side it is composed of carp-milts, crayfish tails, or a whole crayfish with the tails trimmed, and lastly with quenelles. All these garnishes are slightly masked with "génévoise" or "matelote"-sauce; the remainder is served up in a sauce-boat.

REMOVES, ENTREES AND ROASTS

See Plates Nos. 2, 3 *and* 4.

Lobster Cutlets a la Victoria. This entrée is dished up on a croustade, made of fried bread, composed of two pieces. When the top of the croustade is fried, the upper surface is slightly hollowed out, the empty space masked with a coating of force-meat, which afterward is poached in the oven, or in the hot closet. The cutlets are composed of cooked lobster flesh, cut in small dice, and mixed with an equal quantity of blanched oysters, and as many truffles as lobsters, cut in the same manner. This salpicon is mixed with a *Béchamel*-sauce well reduced, finished with crayfish-butter; it is afterward spread on a baking-sheet, the coating being about three-quarters of an inch; let it cool there; then it is divided into the shape of cutlets, which are immediately masked with a thin coat of raw quenelle force-meat, dipped in beaten eggs, crumbed, and fried in a sauté-pan with clarified butter. When well drained, each gets a small frill, and they are dressed in a circle, the cavity of which is garnished with crayfish tails. A *matelote* or *Normande*-sauce is served separately.

Sheeps' Tongues, a la Dominicaine. This entrée suits better for a supper, or rather for a ball-*buffet*, than for a dinner; however, it can always be admitted in a dinner, if preceded or followed by cold entrées of another kind.

The sheeps' tongues must be salted *à l'écarlate*, cooked, well trimmed, and well glazed; they are dished on a jelly-border. The tongues do not rest on the border, the latter having its cavity filled with a circle of wood, on the center of which is fixed a support, that is masked with butter, or paper. The round, and the support, are covered over with salad, composed of vegetables, cut into the form of small dice, and mixed with some mayonnaise, prepared with aspic-jelly. On the top of the support is fixed a small cup of fat, the base of which is sunk into a thick string of chopped aspic-jelly. A sauce-boatful of egg-mayonnaise, is sent up with this entrée.

Ham "Historie." The sucking-pig represented in the plate, which in reality is not a sucking-pig, but only has the form of one, is in modeled butter; it is only on the back, that the ham is placed. To shape the latter neatly, it should first be entirely boned, wrapped round with a napkin, and so cooked; when done, it is taken out of the napkin to be wrapped up again, and left to cool in the required form; when trimmed and neatly carved, the small animal, which must bear it, should be carved. The piece is surrounded with pretty plaited paper-cases, garnished with glazed truffles; the base of the "pain-vert" is surrounded with bold *croûtons* of aspic-jelly, an indispensable garnish to cold pieces.

Salmis of Woodcocks. This entrée is dished up, on a border of game force-meat, on the center of which is fixed a pyramidal croustade of fried bread. It is against this, that the entrée is placed; for without this support it would be impossible to give it the required height and regularity. The legs of the woodcock form the base of the pyramid, the filets are placed on the center; the breast-pieces are set upright, with a few truffles at their base; and on the top of the croustade is inserted a skewer, garnished with a truffle. The woodcocks, and the border, are slightly masked with a *salmis* sauce, reduced with an extract of game, and with the raw trimmings of truffles; the remainder of the sauce is sent up in a sauce-boat. This entrée is edged with *nouille*-paste. *Salmis* sauce is prepared from some Espagnole, well drained, thickened on a brisk fire, and stirred continually. A few tablespoonfuls of extract of game, a little good cooked Madeira sauce, are introduced gradually.

Artistic Cookery—Plate No. 2

Lobster Cutlets.   Sheep's Tongues.
Ham historié.
Salmis of Woodcocks.   Mayonnaise of Chicken.
Patties à la Financière.   Filets of Snipes in Cases.

Mayonnaise of Chickens with Jelly. To prepare this entrée, two good chickens must be trussed, wrapped up in slices of bacon, cooked in a good *mirepoix*, but kept lightly cooked. When the chickens have cooled, each of them is divided into five parts; these are carefully trimmed, the skin, as well as the superfluous bones removed; particularly of the pinions, and fat of the thighs. The parts of the chickens are put into an earthen basin, marinated for an hour, then masked with a layer of mayonnaise sauce with jelly, and arranged on a baking sheet. As soon as the sauce has set, the pieces are trimmed again, and covered with a layer of half-set aspic jelly. They are removed with the aid of a fork, but must be touched as little as possible, and dished in a pyramid shape, in the hollow of an aspic-jelly border, and turned out on a cold dish. Care must be taken, that this border be previously filled with a support of bread, masked with butter, lest the filling up should injure the aspic-jelly. A sauce-boatful of mayonnaise of eggs, is sent up with this entrée.

Patties a la Financiere. To render these hot patties acceptable to an epicure, they ought to be prepared with a good short paste, melting in the mouth, and well baked. The outside of the patties ought to be of a nice brown, and the inside be filled with a well chosen garnish, mixed with a good sauce. These patties are dished in a pyramid on a napkin; but in order that this pyramid may be firm, a foundation of bread should be gummed to the dish. The space where the circle of patties rests immediately on the napkin, ought to be filled up with a bouquet of fried parsley. Patties, that is to say, cases of paste, may be cooked filled with flour, or with common force-meat. A moment before serving, they are emptied and filled anew with a ragoût composed of fat liver, cocks'-kernels, cocks'-combs, and truffles. This ragoût is thickened with a good "sauce Espagnole" reduced with port-wine or madeira. The patties are dished up on a folded napkin.

Filets of Snipes in Cases. Small cases of folded paper may be purchased everywhere, either of round or oval shape. Paper cases must be oiled previously to being garnished; if their garnish consists of moist materials, the cases can be double. To prepare this dish, the filets of seven or eight snipes must be removed, trimmed, and placed in a "sauté"-pan to be cooked with clarified butter. A purée is prepared with cooked legs of snipes, a few poultry-livers, a small part of the giblets of game, some boiled rice, a little sauce, and a piece of butter. The filets are cooked just before sending to table; the purée is warmed without ebullition, and the cases filled up with the latter. On the purée, a filet of a snipe is placed, then masked immediately with a little good brown sauce, reduced with the perfume of game. The cases are ranged on a baking-sheet, to be kept a few minutes at the mouth of the oven, in order to give brilliance to the sauce covering the filets. The cases are afterward dished up on a folded napkin.

Loin of Veal a La Montglas. A fine loin of veal, white and fat, is a remove of the first order, which can be admitted in all dinners. The loin must be cut rather long, trimmed, then trussed, roasted or baked in the oven; if baked, care must be taken that no liquid be added; it must be cooked in butter and its own fat, without any other liquid, but with moderate heat; if roasted on the spit, it must be wrapped up in buttered paper, and allowed to remain for two hours in front of the fire, not forgetting to unfasten it in time to give it a nice color; it is better to cook the kidney by itself.

When the loin is done, the lower and the upper filet must be taken out, the latter cut through and put back in its place; then the loin is dished on a thick layer of thin mashed pota

Artistic Cookery—Plate No. 3

Loin of Veal. Beef à la Jardinière. Filet of Beef.
Sweetbreads à la Colbert. Lambs' Brains.

toes, or anything else put on the dish, to keep in the same place; on one of the extremities of a dish, or even upon both, there is fixed a pretty *croustade* of rice, or bread, or a large white turnip, cut in three parts. The loin is surrounded with two bunches of sweetbread *croquettes*, between these some small patties are dished up, garnished with a montglas of sweetbread and truffles. On the other side of the dish are two heaps of potatoes á la duchesse, divided by the kidney cut in slices. The two cups are garnished with a montglas prepared with the under filet and truffles, mixed with a cream sauce. There must not be any sauce at the bottom of the dish; but the loin may be accompanied with a half *Espagnole*, or a light tomato sauce. With veal, some salt meat, ham, or tongue *à l'écarlate*, is generally served.

Piece of Beef a La Jardiniere. This piece is taken from the loin of the ox; that is to say, that part which, starting at the extremity of the sirloin, stops at the junction of the lower part of the thigh; the quarter of beef. The loin is the most delicate, savory, and agreeable part of the animal, because the fibers and flesh are rich and interlarded. Done to the exact point, in a good stock, well glazed and garnished, served very hot, the loin of beef can be admitted to the most sumptuous dinners, and will always be welcome. The loin of beef is a rich showy piece, but costly; as fine an appearance as possible must be given to it, in which case it is difficult to employ less than about 30 pounds of meat; for the most delicate part of the loin, what is called the chubb, would not be sufficient to form a remove; a sufficient quantity of meat must therefore be left on it, to give a good shape. The loin of beef, coming from a fine animal, must be covered with a thick coat of fat; after having been boned, it is rolled in its natural way lengthwise, then tied firmly with a string, put into a long stewpan, in which is laid some bacon, cut roots and vegetables; the meat is slightly salted, then moistened and covered with light broth; it must remain in the liquid from 6 to 7 hours, on a very moderate fire, with hot ashes on the lid. When three parts done, it is drained, to trim it underneath; then put back into the pan, with the stock, strained, skimmed, and mixed, with a little white wine; it must be finished thus in the good, succulent, richly colored stock. It is dished up on a piece of cooked meat; this must be cooled under a press, trimmed to the required size, warmed, and placed at the bottom of the dish. This foundation relieves the aspect of the piece, and facilitates the dishing up of the garnishes. The piece of beef is represented, carved in slices, surrounded with a garnish of fine, fresh, and tender vegetables, divided into bunches; this garnish may also be composed of green peas, French beans, cauliflowers, young carrots, glazed turnips; but too many kinds should not be used.

Then the piece is dished up, and glazed with a brush; it is ornamented with three different vegetables, and skewers; the liquid in which it has been cooked is sieved, skimmed, thinned, and mixed with a few spoonfuls of Espagnole and tomato sauce. This sauce is served in a sauce boat, hot.

Sweet Breads a La Colbert. This is a simple and good meat entrée, which can very well be served at a dinner, especially if there are several hot entrées. To prepare this entrée, some large sweetbreads, blanched or cooled under press, then cut in two; the two parts are then well trimmed, seasoned, floured, dipped in beaten eggs, bread crumbed, and fried in a saucepan with clarified butter; they must be of a nice color. Just before serving, the scollops are dished in a circular order, on a coat of forcemeat, poached on a dish, the cavity of the circle is garnished with green peas, plain boiled after the English fashion, well drained and well shaken together, off the fire, with a pat of fine butter. The sweetbreads, and the bottom of the dish, are mashed with a Colbert sauce, the remainder of which is served in a sauce boat.

Lambs' Brains a L'Italienne. This is a meat entrée which is often served in France, Italy, and England. These entrées must always be dished with a certain elegance; if not, they sink into the order of common entrées. To prepare this entrée, some large and beautiful lamb's brains must be chosen, and the skin removed without affecting their shape; when well cleaned and blanched, they are cooked in a good stock with wine.

The entrée is dished up on a pâté-chaud case, well pinched, and baked to a nice color; but its interior is filled with common force-meat; the force meat is poached in the stove, or at the entrance of the oven. The brains are dished in a circular order, on the border of the crust, placing alternately between them a pretty crouton of pickled tongue, cut in the shape of a cock's-comb; the cavity of the circle is garnished with a purée of artichoke bottoms; over this purée is poured a little melted glaze, the croutons are also glazed, the brains are mashed with a little good velouté sauce, the remainder is served in a sauce boat.

Filet of Beef a la Godard. This remove is one of the most elegant, which can be served at a sumptuous dinner; it can be placed on the table on a beautiful hot-water dish; but if carved, and the slices not too large, it can be presented to the guests. Two good small filets of beef, but not too fat, are neatly trimmed, larded, and braised in a good stock; when done, glazed, and of a nice color, they are carved in slices, that is to say, this carving stops at some distance from the extremities, and penetrates no further than three parts of the meat; the carved pieces are put back in their places.

These filets are dished up on a bottom of cooked rice, cut

in a long shape, and on an inclined plane on both sides
Between the two filets are dished three quenelles with pieces
of truffles large enough to fill the empty space; under these
quenelles, at the bottom of the dish, is ranged a beautiful
ring of slices of sweetbreads, partly crumbed with bread and
partly with truffles; they are done in clarified butter. Between the quenelles, and the chain formed by the sweetbreads, are distributed groups of mushrooms; at both ends
of the dish some fine, whole truffles surround the tops of the
filets. This garnish is similarly repeated on the other side
of the dish. Between the two filets, and in the center of the
dish, a pretty garnished cup is fixed on the foundation; this
cup may be of metal, masked with English or with nudel
paste, and ornamented; it may also be made of bread, or
even cut out of large turnips. With a little skill some very
elegant cups can be made out of these turnips. With so rich
and elegant a remove, a good light Espagnole sauce must be
served, that is, not too thick, but juicy, beaten well and
thinned with a good stock and some Madeira, as well as with
the liquor of the truffles. This sauce is sent up separately.

Saddle of Venison, Larded and Roasted. A
saddle of venison, not too high, and well roasted, always
makes a distinguished dish, even in countries abounding
with this game. Nowhere is venison finer or of a more
delicate flavor than in England; nowhere either is it more
esteemed and sought after. However, in England the haunch
of venison is more generally eaten, that is to say, the leg of
the animal to which a part of the saddle adheres; but in
Germany, in Russia, and even in France, the saddle of red
deer or of fallow deer is very often served, and it is more
often larded; for, the filets of venison are not always
covered with fat. In order to eat vension in perfection, it
must be mortified to a certain degree, for without this mortification the flesh will be found less delicate.

Artistic Cookery—Plate No. 4

Saddle of Venison.　　Veal Nut.　　Sirloin of Beef.　　Ham Printanière.

If the buck be fat, the saddle should be cooked without being larded, and without removing the fat from the filets, as this fat is generally much esteemed; but if the filets are not covered with a thick coat of fat, the skin is removed, and the flesh larded with bacon. In such conditions the saddle may either be roasted on the spit, or baked in the oven. It must be basted with butter whilst cooking. A saddle of venison may be served with a piquant sauce, with *poivrade* or venison sauce, with gravy, or currant jelly; but it is often served with gravy in the dish, and some venison sauce can be served separately. When a saddle of venison is served carved, the filets should first be removed, then cut slanting, put back into their places, and glazed with a paste-brush.

A Nice Large Noix of Veal is not one of the least estimable dishes, nor one of the least choice, if the meat is nice, fat, white, and delicate, cooked to the exact point, and well glazed. In England some salt meat is generally served with removes of veal.

The noix represented in the plate is select, voluminous, and with all the *tétine* adhering to it. The meat is larded with bacon, the piece secured in an oval shape, with a string, cooked with little liquid, and nicely glazed; it is dished up on a foundation of cooked meat, cooled under a press, and glazed at the entrance of the oven; this foundation is necessary, to heighten the form and aspect of the piece. It is surrounded with groups of vegetables, cooked in water, or glazed; cauliflowers, carrots, green peas, French beans. Two skewers of vegetables are inserted in the meat on each side. The bottom of the dish is masked with good gravy, the dish itself placed on a hot-water dish. With this remove is served a brown sauce, slightly thickened, and worked with the residue, freed of the fat, of the noix of veal.

A Fine Sirloin of Beef, the produce of a young animal carefully fattened and just sufficiently developed, is a most captivating picture for a connoisseur; but the joint must have hung sufficiently long to have acquired the wished-for tenderness; and it is of the highest importance that it should be roasted on the spit, and attended to with the utmost care. Beef, even when taken from a young animal, is always tough, dry, and without aroma, if it has not hung the proper time. The most perfect beef may become dry and tasteless, by not observing the proper medium between its being too much over, or underdone. The sirloin represented in the plate, is served on the *filet mignon*—optical exigencies alone have induced me to present it thus —but I have no intention of giving it as a rule. Every practitioner knows, that in England sirloins of beef intended for great dinners, are always served with the large filet underneath.

Ham a la Printaniere. A fine ham, properly cured, boiled with care, prettily ornamented, and trimmed with a nice sauce, is certainly a most excellent remove. If a ham is not sufficiently dissalted, it is placed in a kettle, and covered with cold water: the kettle is set over the fire, where it remains till the water boils. When this takes place, the ham is drained, then placed back into the kettle, moistened with wine and water, set on the fire, and garnished with a few big vegetables. At the first boiling of the liquid the kettle is removed to the side of the fire thus letting the liquid only simmer gently for three hours, and even longer, if the ham is large; the kettle must be taken away from the fire; half an hour afterward the ham is drained, and trimmed.

The ham shown in the drawing is placed on a hot-water-dish: it is cut flat underneath, so that it lies well on the dish; it is then surrounded with small timbales of spinach and potatoes, poached in a "bainmarie;" the bottom of the dish is masked with a little "Espagnole" sauce, worked with Madeira wine, and kept light. The ham is glazed with a paste-brush; the remainder of the sauce is sent up in a sauce boat, and served at the same time with a dish of green peas.

POULTRY

See Plate No. 6

Turkey "a l' Imperiale." A nice, fat white hen turkey is trussed, singed, its breast and legs larded. It is then placed in a *braisière* pan, cooked with a good stock, and glazed to a pretty color. When about to be served, the turkey is drained, divested of the string, and placed on a long dish, and made to lean against a foundation of force meat. Two small *croustades* of bread, or rice, carved with a knife, are stuck on each end of the dish, garnished with "montglas" of poultry, encircled with small truffles. The turkey is then surrounded, on both sides, with a garnish composed of cocks' combs and button-mushrooms, piled up in groups. These mushrooms and cocks' combs may be masked with a little "Allemande" sauce, and the truffles glazed with a paste brush. Two boatfuls of "Espagnole" sauce, worked with the gravy of the turkey, are served at the same time. This piece is dressed, to appear on the table, on a hot-water-dish; if the turkey has been previously carved, the dish may be handed round to the guests.

Roasted Capons, with Water Cresses. A nice, fat, tender capon constitutes a roast so highly distinguished, as to be neither common nor easy to be found everywhere. Capons should above all be young: it would be of little use to have them well fattened, if they were tough.

Roasted capons are never larded: they are covered with bacon, or wrapped in buttered paper, until three parts roasted. The spit is the only method applicable to the cooking of roasted capons: if the flesh be basted with good butter, it becomes unctuous and succulent.

The carving of capons is very simple. The legs are first slipped off, and divided into two parts. Two small filets, with the pinion of the wing adhering, are taken off the breast; a nice slice is then cut on each side of the breast, and this is divided either lengthwise or transversely. Some nice gravy and bread sauce must be served with roasted capons. If the gravy is sent up separately, the capons when dished up may be garnished with water cresses. The capons may be filled with truffles.

Larded and Roasted Turkey, with Truffles. A fat and very tender turkey is an excellent roast; larded, or covered with bacon, it is always welcomed; the best way to roast a turkey is on the spit. It should be previously wrapped in buttered paper, and basted with butter while cooking. One hour and a half, to two hours, is required to roast a turkey on the spit; the fire should be moderate and continual.

When it is three parts done, the paper is taken off, so as to facilitate the coloring of the surface. There are two ways of serving roasted turkey, with truffles; the first one consists in filling the turkey with peeled and seasoned truffles; these may be whole or cut up, they are mixed up with rasped bacon. The second consists in filling the turkey simply with rasped bacon mixed with the raw peel of the truffles; previously chopped up; in this case the peeled truffles are cooked at the time in a little good wine, then the liquor is reduced with good gravy. At the moment the roast is dished, the truffles are piled round the turkey, and the gravy sent up in a boat. The leg bones of a roasted turkey should be cut up short, and a truffle put thereto. The carving of the turkey is very simple; it suffices to slip off entirely the two filets of the breast, to cut them in slices and to put them back in

Artistic Cookery—Plate No. 6

Roasted Partridges.   Larded Turkey with Truffles.

Roasted Capons with Water Cresses.   Turkey à l' Impèriale.

their places. At a select dinner, the legs of a roasted turkey should never be carved or served at all.

Roasted Partridges. Partridges for roasting should be young, this is the first point. They do not require to be kept long before cooking; they may be stuffed with raw, peeled, and seasoned truffles; truffled partridges constitute a very distinguished roast. They should be trussed with two strings, and may be larded or covered with bacon; they should, in preference, be roasted on the spit; twelve minutes suffice to roast tender partridges, if the fire is kept alive. While they are being cooked, they should be frequently basted with butter. Partridges, like nearly all game roasts, should be kept underdone.

When the partidges are taken off the spit, and freed of the strings, they are either dished up whole, or carved, according as they are served on the table, or handed round to the guests. The carving of the partridges is done in several ways. The most elegant consists in slipping off the breast from the back part, to cut it up in three parts, and put it in form and in its place again. The partridges may also be divided into three parts, by cutting off at once a filet and a leg, so as to leave the breast part adhering to the backbone; this is afterward done away with, and the partridge is formed again. With roasted partridges, some good gravy, bread sauce, water cresses, or simply some lemons in quarters, may be served. If the partridges are garnished with water cresses the gravy must be sent up in a boat: with game roasts, only a little gravy is required, but this should be limpid and succulent.

VEGETABLES

See Plate No. 5

Boiled Asparagus. White or violet asparagus is one of the most distinguished and delicate of vegetables. Large sized asparagus is certainly the most highly valued, but only of a good sort, freshly gathered, and properly cooked.

Previous to cooking asparagus, they must be plucked, scraped, and cut to equal lengths; then selected and arranged according to their different sizes taking the middle-sized, small, and large ones separately. Then they are tied closely together with thread, or narrow strips of ribbon, plunged into boiling water at a few minutes' interval, the largest first, in order that the bundles all may be done at the same time. The water, in which the asparagus are boiled, must be highly salted.

The right moment for the cooking of asparagus is a consideration on no account to be overlooked; as, if asparagus is too hard, it becomes unpalatable; and if too soft, it loses all its good qualities. In short, it is not well done, if when held by the thick end in a horizontal position between the fingers, it does not bend lightly, but falls heavily down. If the flavor of asparagus is to be well appreciated, it must be eaten immediately when boiled. As soon as the asparagus are well drained they are dished in a pyramid on a folded napkin. Boiled asparagus are generally served with Dutch sauce, cream sauce or sauce with bread crumbs fried in butter.

Fried Salsify, or Oyster-Plant. Although a very common vegetable, yet it is to be served at every family dinner. Previous to frying the salsify, they must be scraped and boiled in white stock. When drained and cooled, they are cut to equal lengths (about 2 inches), placed in a dish, and left to macerate; that is, seasoned with salt and pepper, moistened with oil and lemon juice. A few minutes previous to serving, the salsifies are drained, slightly floured, dipped into a light frying paste, and immediately plunged into very hot fat. But a small quantity must be cooked at a time, lest they should not all of them get a nice color. As soon as removed from the fat, and well drained, they are sprinkled with a little salt, and dished in two parallel groups on a neatly folded napkin, thus to be served without delay.

Artichokes, with Dutch Sauce. The artichokes, intended to be boiled, must be selected from the largest sort; the young ones being not so well adapted for this method of cooking. Previous to being boiled, the artichoke bottoms must be trimmed, and rubbed with lemon juice; the leaves shortened by cutting them straight on the side opposite the bottom. They are plunged, one by one, into cold water, slightly acidulated, either with citric acid, or with lemon juice. Then the artichokes are plunged into acidulous boiling water, and left thus to boil on a moderate fire, while the stewpan is kept covered. They are taken out of their cooking stock, by the aid of a skimmer, as soon as the hay (the center part of the artichoke) falls off, when touched and pushed with the fingers. When emptied, and well cleaned, they are put back into their own cooking-stock, and kept thus a few minutes, previous to being served. They are then well drained, and dished in a pyramid on a folded napkin. Artichokes generally are accompanied by Dutch sauce or melted butter; in either case, this sauce must be served separately.

Farced Mushrooms. Mushrooms of *couche*, or *comestible* mushrooms, and the *cèpes*, can be served farced, if they are large, and of an equal shape. Of whatever sort the mushrooms intended to be farced may be, they must always be chosen fresh, trimmed, but not turned, emptied and seasoned. The force meat which the mushrooms are farced with, is generally composed of minced mushrooms, and sweet herbs reduced with butter or oil, mixed up with bread crumbs, and thickened with raw eggs; this mince, however, may be replaced by a quenelle force meat mixed with cooked sweet herbs. As soon as the mushrooms are farced, they are bread crumbed, placed in a stewpan, or on a baking sheet, then moistened with melted butter or oil, and baked in the oven. This done, they are dished in a pyramid on a folded napkin.

Green Peas, with "Croutons." Green peas, and asparagus, these are the vegetables preferred by the *gourmets* of all countries. To green peas of truly fine quality all kinds of preparation may be applied; all of them will succeed. The French species, those sweet, fine, slightly perfumed green peas, are spread all over the world. In the middle of Russia, in Moskau, at Kiev, at Odessa; as well as in Algiers, Spain, Germany, Italy, and all over America, everywhere we have found green peas.

For the preparation of green peas *à la Francaise*, they must be selected very fine, young, tender, and freshly gathered. In summer, green peas are soon affected by heat, and thus sometimes lose their best qualities in the lapse of but a few hours, if kept in a place shut up from the contact of the air. They are mixed with a little good butter and cold water boiled, with a sprig of parsley, a whole little onion, a little salt, a pinch of sugar; and are thickened, at the last moment, with butter mixed with flour. But, to make them delicate and savory, they must be cooked with moderation, and at the last moment be copiously enriched with good butter. The only garnish agreeing with green peas, is of course the most simple one, bread *croûtons* fried in butter and glazed.

Spinach, with Eggs Boiled Soft. Spinach, although a vegetable common to all countries, is nevertheless highly appreciated, and well deserves to be so. The spinach, represented by the drawing, is prepared with butter, thickened and garnished alternately with eggs boiled soft, and bread *croûtons*, cut in a crescent shape, fried in butter, and glazed with the paste-brush. But few cooks prepare spinach well; and yet there is nothing simpler than the cooking of this vegetable. If prepared with cream or gravy, the spinach previously must be blanched, but in plenty of liquid, and on a very brisk fire; thus it preserves its nice color without

Artistic Cookery—Plate No. 5

Boiled Asparagus.

Artichokes, Dutch Sauce.

Green Peas with croûtons.

Cauliflower, Dutch Sauce.

Truffles in Napkin.

Fried Oyster Plant

Farced Mushrooms.

Spinach with Eggs.

Asparagus Heads.

Cardoons with Marrow.

however boiling too long. When well drained, the water carefully pressed out, it is chopped, and plunged into hot melted butter, cooked *à la noisette;* which means, giving it a fine hazel, light brown color. The dampness of the vegetable having dispersed, it is seasoned, and thickened with reduced good *Béchamel* sauce. The sauce may be short, and yet the spinach be reduced again, for a few minutes only, with the sauce. Then the spinach is removed from the fire, and finished with a piece of good butter.

If the spinach is prepared with gravy, it is slightly floured, after being well warmed in the hazel butter; or else it is thickened with a brown sauce well reduced, and is boiled for a few minutes more, to take consistence by being mixed with a little succulent gravy, or rather some good half-glaze; at the last moment, it is finished with a piece of good butter.

Cauliflower, with Dutch Sauce. Previous to cooking cauliflowers, they are divided, trimmed if large; then they are boiled, either in salt water or steam, well drained and arranged in a dome-like fashion on a folded napkin. To give this dome a more regular shape, the cauliflowers can be placed beforehand in a dome-mould, and then turned out on the napkin.

Cauliflowers generally are accompanied with either Dutch sauce, or butter sauce, or even with a good cream sauce. In Germany cauliflower is served with the same sauce that is applied to asparagus; some bread crumbs fried in butter. For the preparation of this sauce, half a pound of good butter is melted; when warm, two handfuls of grated white bread crumbs are added to it, and a little salt. The preparation is boiled, and for three minutes stirred continually; then the stewpan is removed onto a moderate fire. Five minutes afterward, the sauce may be served.

Asparagus Heads, a La Duchesse. In this case, the asparagus are selected of equal length, scraped at the lower ends; then from the tender part, pieces one to one and one-half inches long are cut off. The asparagus is boiled in salt water or steam on a brisk fire, and done to the moment. When well drained, they are placed in a flat stewpan, with good butter, then seasoned, and moistened with a little good sauce, such as Béchamel. Then they are taken off the fire, and bound with a preparation of a few yolks of eggs, finished with a piece of butter. When dished up, they are surrounded with a garnish of Brussels sprouts, baked without sugar; which, when taken out of the oven, have to be sprinkled with a little Parmesan.

Truffles in Napkin (a La Serviette). This is a dish, simple as well as rich, one of those producing the highest effect imaginable. However indifferent a man may be to the charms of gastronomy; yet the beautiful appearance, as well as the fine perfume, of a dish of truffles, will always rouse his imagination.

Truffles must be selected fresh, perfumed and aromatic, but above all of good origin. Those of *Perigord* are the most valuable, as no other part of the world produces finer or better. It is a pity, they are so very scarce; and that not everybody is able to distinguish the genuine species from those that are brought to market; which for the most part are gathered very far indeed from that land so richly favored.

If truffles are to be served whole, it is a matter of course, that the finest, and largest must be chosen. When well brushed, well cleaned (not peeled), they are placed in a stewpan, moistened to half their height with good stock with white wine, Madeira, or Champagne; the choice of one of these sorts being merely a matter of taste. The great point is to cook the truffles at the moment of serving; the stewpan must be kept covered, and shut hermetically, so that they be cooked judiciously; that is, they must have time enough to be just penetrated, without getting dry. The inner pulp of the truffle must be tender, soft, and aromatic; if cooked too long, all these fine qualities are lost. The largest truffles will take eight or nine minutes; for middle-sized, seven minutes will do. Truffles cooked to excess not only lose their good qualities, but are apt to shrivel up, and get out of shape.

The truffles represented in the drawing are dished in the hollow of a folded napkin. The following is the mode of proceeding:

A fine damask napkin is spread entirely unfolded over a large table, thus forming an exact square. The four corners are taken up, folded over, and brought together in the middle; this proceeding is repeated three times more; then the left hand first is laid on the center of the napkin, and with the right hand the edges are folded over, and kept straight upright; the napkin is placed on a dish, and its hollow filled with any mould at hand; which later is filled with the truffles.

Cardoons with Marrow. Cardoons are a vegetable not produced in the Northern climates, not even in Germany. The best cardoons are those produced in Spain; those cultivated in the South of France, however, and in Italy, are also superior qualities. They are also grown in the United States.

Nowadays fresh as well as preserved cardoons are almost common, everywhere; *i. e.* in all gastronomic countries; they are the subjects of a large trade. If exported fresh in winter time, they may be preserved in the best condition for several days. If exported in boxes, preserved according to the methods applied to other preserved victuals, they will keep for years, without their qualities being injured in the least.

The great point in the preparation of cardoons, the point never to be forgotten is, keeping them as white as possible **in cooking, and cooking them without excess; as cardoons** having cooked too long, lose a great deal of their fine flavor, yet neither dare they be kept too firm, because this would render them disagreeable to be eaten.

Cardoons can be served, either with brown or yellow sauce; in either case this sauce must be succulent, well clarified, and not too liquid.

If the cardoons are fresh, they ought to be divided into pieces of equal length, then blanched in water moderately acid, to get off the outer fibres. They must moderately soak in cold water, then be boiled in a white stock, mixed with some white wine, and some white broth from which the fat has not been skimmed; they are covered over with slices of bacon, so as to get very white indeed. When they are boiled and drained, they are cut into equal lengths, well sponged, dished in a pyramid on a silver vegetable dish, with a good espagnole sauce poured over them. The vegetable dish is placed on a flat dish, and surrounded with a chain of very small patties garnished with small bits of cooked marrow.

FRUITS, ICES, SWEET ENTREMETS, Etc.

See Plates Nos. 7 and 8

Crusts with Cherries. These crusts are made with brioche paste, which has been prepared the day before; it is then cut into slices of an equal shape and thickness, sprinkled with pounded almonds and sugar, and glazed in the oven. The centerpiece may be either of punch cake, or simply of bread. If required, it may also be of tin, masked with office paste (raw paste). If of eatable paste, it must be coated with a layer of reduced apricot marmalade, with the aid of a pastebrush; if of bread, it is fried; if masked with raw paste, it is sufficient to give it a nice golden color, and let it dry in the air, previous to setting it on the dish. When about to be served, the cup is garnished

Artistic Cookery—Plate No. 7

Crusts with Cherries.

Bombe à la Napolitaine. Plum Pudding.

Basket of Fruit.

Ices in Fruit Shapes. Pine Apple à la Creole.

Apricots à la Condé.

with either fresh or preserved cooked cherries; its base is surrounded with the crusts, being very hot and dished up in pyramids. The bottom of the dish is then slightly masked with a little good Madeira sauce, smoothed with some apricot marmalade. The remainder of this sauce is sent up in a sauceboat, after having introduced into it some preserved cooked cherries.

Bombe, a La Napolitaine. This bombe is moulded in a spherical tin mould, opening in three pieces, and closing with hinges, but having on the top-center an aperture. The mould is previously spun and cooled, open, on salted ice; then the sides are masked with a layer, half an inch thick, of well-set chocolate ice; as soon as the mould is shut up, the hollow is filled, through the top aperture, with a preparation of whipped cream *à la vanille*. The topmost opening is then closed hermetically, the mould wrapped in paper, sprinkled with salt and saltpetre, and covered again with a thick layer of ice, also salted. The mould should remain in the ice for two hours and a half. Some fresh ice must then be put over it, and the mould must be kept in the same state one hour and a half longer.

When ready to serve, the mould is washed in cold water, and the bombe is dished up on a folded napkin; it is then surrounded at the base with a wreath of small cakes. The bombe is ornamented on the top with a tuft in white spun-sugar, pricked in the opening, in imitation of a flame.

Plum Pudding, with Punch. This is an *entremets* of English origin, but known and served in all countries; the receipt I am about to give here, although not usually adopted in England, is nevertheless one producing the best results. The English plum pudding is generally too heavy and massive; the one I am about to describe, which is often served up even at the most sumptuous dinners, is lighter and of a fine flavor.

The composition of plum pudding is: One pound or chopped beef kidney-suet, a pound and a quarter of grated fresh bread crumb, one pound of mixed dried raisins, half a pound of orange peel and citronate, a pound of moist sugar, a tablespoonful of powdered ginger, eight whole eggs, three-quarters of a glass of brandy, and half a glassful of good raw cream.

The different ingredients are mixed and well worked, then put into a buttered and floured dome mould, covered with a napkin, likewise buttered and floured; this napkin is tied together on the other side of the mould, which is then plunged into boiling water.

The pudding requires to be cooked for four hours, the kettle being closed, and without letting the water cease to boil. As soon as the pudding is drained, it is turned out of the cloth upon a hot dish, then a little cavity is formed on its center, to pour into it a few tablespoonfuls of very good brandy, previously mixed with a little sugar, then warmed and ignited. Plum pudding must be served and eaten while very hot.

Basket of Fruit for Center-Piece. In the center of a table laid for dinner, it is usual to place some ornamental piece, such as a surtout or a dormant, a candelabrum, or some stand in silver, bronze, or china. This centerpiece however, is nothing more than an accessory, which may easily be replaced by a simple vase of flowers, or a "corbeille" of fruit. The more handsome the dinner-service, the more elegant and rich, both in material and workmanship, must be the centerpiece.

A "corbeille" of fruit, rich, abundant, and varied in its selection, is in fact only a centerpiece, when placed in the middle of the table. The "corbeille" itself may be in rustic work, osier, china, or metal. To prevent any chance of the fruit falling from its position, a piece of cardboard, in the form of a pyramid, surrounded and garnished with moss, should be made for the fruit to lean against.

When arranging a "corbeille" of fruit for a dinner table, only the freshest, the rarest, and the most beautiful kinds should be selected. The sort and color to be chosen, must of course depend on the season; but as great a variety, and as diversified in tint, as is possible. If the fruit be large, as pears, apples, or pineapples, they must be removed from the "corbeille," to be cut up and handed round in plates. Pineapples are peeled and sliced, large pears are quartered without being peeled.

Pewter Fruit-Moulds, Imitating Pineapples, Small Melons, Pears, Peaches, Etc., are known to everybody; it is necessary that each species of mould should be filled with ices varied in their nature and color. When the moulds are filled up, they are well closed, wrapped each in a piece of paper, set afterward on a thick layer of pounded ice, strongly salted and saltpetered; they are sprinkled with salt, and covered over with a thick layer of salted and saltpetred ice. One hour later, the moulds must be sufficiently frozen; they are freed of the paper, dipped in cold water, then the fruit ices are taken out of the mould, piled up symmetrically on the stand, round a small pyramid, in plain ice, either moulded or cut out, on which is placed the pineapple. The fruits are intermingled with natural green leaves. The tuft of the pineapple is imitated with angelica.

Pineapple "a La Creole." Although in itself very simple, this dish is nevertheless very elegant and attractive; if the fruit be well imitated, the slices of pineapple fine, this dish is sure to meet with applause. It is necessary to have a pineapple mould, in which good rice *à la crême*, finished with a few yolks of eggs, is moulded. As soon as the rice is cooked and firm in the requisite condition, it is turned out on a foundation of bread of the same dimension (having about two inches of thickness), and fried in butter. If no mould be handy, the rice can be raised with the hands on the fried foundation, which in this case, is set on a dish. The surfaces of the rice are smoothed, then modeled by the aid of a little knife, so as to imitate the asperities of the pineapple. In each of the protruding parts is stuck a little bit of angelica. The rice is then masked with a paste-brush, with a coating of hot, reduced apricot marmalade, to give it a higher degree of brilliancy. The crown of the pineapple is imitated with cut up angelica; its base is surrounded with nice slices of fresh pineapple in *compôte*, cut regularly, but not too thin. Above these slices a crown of pointed triangles of angelica is stuck into the rice. The bottom of the dish is slightly masked with apricot or marasquin sauce, the remainder of which is sent up in a sauceboat.

Apricots, a "la Conde." The apricots being cut in two, they are peeled, and cooked with a little butter and sugar, or simply in some light syrup; they are kept firm. Then they are placed in a sauce pan, thickened with a little apricot marmalade, and dished in a dome on a layer of rice, spread so as to form a cavity on the bottom of a dish.

The apricots are sprinkled with some chopped almonds, mixed with sugar and a little white of eggs, glazed with salamander, and at last surrounded with little rice croquettes, in the shape of a pear, fried, and rolled in powdered sugar, flavored with vanilla. A bit of angelica is stuck to the most pointed end of each of the croquettes; halves of apricot almonds are placed on the fruit. Some apricot syrup with maraschino is served in a sauce boat.

Sultan Cake. This is composed of two cakes with vanilla, one baked in a dome-shaped mould, the other baked in a square tin, and then cut in the shape of a cushion, iced over with a rose-colored tint, decorated with white icing,

Artistic Cookery—Plate No. 8

Blancmanger rubané. Charlotte Russe with Pistachios.
Sultan Cake. The King's Meringues.
Muscovite Jelly. Suédoise of Fruits.

with the aid of a cornet. It is placed on a dish, surrounded with sweet jelly, minced; the tassels are imitated in spun-sugar. The second cake is glazed, emptied, filled with a *bavaroise* preparation with pistachios or strawberries; the center of the cushion is surrounded with a turban, imitated in fine white spun-sugar, garnished with small red beads. The two tufts (pompons) on the top and center, are also imitated in spun-sugar. This *entremets* well executed, has always a beautiful effect.

The King's Meringues. These *méringues* are the traditional and indispensable *entremets* of the family dinners of the Prussian court. For this reason they are called the king's méringues. They are made with a very fine méringue-paste, according to a process specially observed in the royal kitchens.

The preparation for méringue is composed in the proportions of a pound of sugar to eight whites of eggs, and a pinch of salt. The king's méringues are small in size; each shell has on the central point a hollow, very difficult to produce, but which characterizes them in a peculiar manner. They are moulded with the spoon. The mode of proceeding deserves to be studied with care. The preparation is taken, in equal portions, with a tablespoon; it is then rolled up against the sides of the basin. When the preparation is quite smooth, it is dropped onto a sheet of paper, while holding the spoon perpendicularly, and turning it from left to right, as soon as the preparation touches the paper; it is by so doing, that it falls in a round form, leaving a hollow on the central part. When the shells are all laid on the paper, they are sprinkled with icing sugar powder, and sifted through a piece of wool. The méringues are baked in the usual way, that is, on damp boards in a very moderate oven; then they are allowed to dry completely in a hot closet, and then cooled.

A quarter of an hour before serving them, the méringues are garnished with whipped cream, flavored with sugar and vanilla. They are then piled up on a sugar or gum-paste stand, light and low in shape, ornamented on the friese with a nice wreath of oak leaves, imitated in gum-paste.

Muscovite Jelly. It is composed of sweet jelly prepared with isinglass, juice of fresh pineapple mixed with lemon juice, filtered and mixed with a little champagne; the jelly is set in an entremets mould, embedded in common ice; it must be set, layer by layer; each of which layers is intermingled with slices of raw pineapple. The jelly having set, the mould is *frappé* with salt, with its lid shut; it must be *frappé* for twenty-five or thirty minutes. At serving time, it is washed with cold water, then dipped into water not too warm, wiped, and turned out on a bordered bottom, masked with gum paste, or white paper. This Muscovite preparation must be slightly glued (that is, with but half the usual quantity); for if too much glued, the jelly would not be eatable, because the action of the salt hardens the glue. This entremets must be served, shortly after being turned out of the mould; because, when coming out of the mould, it bears quite a particular physiognomy.

Charlotte Russe, with Pistachios. This charlotte is formed with biscuit; half of which is glazed white, half light green with pistachios. The biscuit is cut in a slanting direction, rising to the same height, and the same length, as the charlotte mould; against the sides of which, the pieces of biscuit must be leaned, placing them one beside the other, and alternating the shades. The bottom of the mould is masked, first with a flat of paper, then with a round of plain biscuit. This mould is embedded in ice, an hour previous to serving; ten minutes afterward, it is filled with some bavaroise preparation; this preparation is composed with a purée of pistachios, diluted with plain syrup, perfumed with orange flowers, and glued, slightly thickened on ice, by stirring it, then mixed with good whipped-cream— three glasses full; the cream must be mixed with the preparation by degrees only. The preparation having got firm, the charlotte is turned out on a bottom of gum paste, the top of which is simply bordered with a circle of white beads of icing sugar, squeezed through a cornet. The basis of the bottom may be garnished with jelly croûtons, or chopped jelly. The top of the charlotte is masked with a layer of marmalade. The rim is surrounded with little glazed biscuit; the center of this circle being garnished with whipped cream, or chopped jelly.

Suedoise of Fruits, with Jelly. This dish is formed in a high shaped charlotte mould; this mould is first embedded in ice, then garnished along its sides, with little balls of white apples and reddened pears, which must be moderately boiled in light syrup. First they are left to cool well on ice, then they are pricked with a larding needle, and dipped in white, half-set jelly; then they are set against the sides of the mould, alternating the shades by two and two, thus forming diagonal stripes.

As soon as the fruits are raised, they are supported by a coating of orange jelly, one-eighth of an inch thick, applied on the bottom, and all round; the hollow is then filled by a pineapple bavaroise preparation with pistachios or strawberries, mixed up with a salpicon of preserved fruits. The preparation must be kept on ice for an hour. At serving time, the mould is quickly dipped in warm water, and the entremets turned out on a bordered bottom of gum paste. The top of the suédoise is then decorated with a fine rosace of preserved fruits or of jelly, the center of which is garnished with a fine green gage. The bottom of the dish may be also garnished with chopped jelly, or with **jelly croûtons.**

Blancmanger Rubane. For this dish, first of all, there must be prepared some almond milk, with enough of extract, and sufficient in itself to fill a mould with cylinder and channelings; it must be well glued and sweetened, passed through a sieve, and divided into three parts; one of which, having some pounded almonds mixed with a little spinach green infused, is then passed through a tammy; the second part into which is infused the peel of a good orange, is then slightly colored with vegetable red, and likewise passed; whilst the third and last part, with a stock of vanilla infused, is kept in its natural shade and passed likewise. An oiled channeled mould is embedded in ice; a layer of the green preparation, one centimeter and a half thick, is poured on the bottom of it; as soon as this layer has got firm, another layer of the same thickness of white preparation, is poured on; when it has set, it is covered with a third layer, always of the same thickness, of red preparation, which is left to get firm; then the same operation is begun anew. Optical motives have induced me to take only two colors.

An hour afterward, that is to say at serving time, the mould is dipped in hot water, wiped, and turned out on a bottom of bordered gum paste, bearing a little stem on its center. The base of the bottom of gum paste may be surrounded with croûtons of sweet jelly; the top of the stem is decorated with a pompon of spun sugar.

NOTE: A few of the cooking utensils mentioned in this Chapter although in constant use in Europe have become obsolete in this country, in most households; but are still in use in America, in hotels and the kitchens of the very rich.

HOW TO KEEP PERSONS AND THINGS NEAT AND FRESH

I.—THE CARE OF THE PERSON.

II.—THE CARE OF THE CLOTHES.

III.—THE CARE OF THE HOUSE, FURNITURE, AND BRIC-A-BRAC.

IV.—THE CARE OF THE PANTRY.

I

THE CARE OF THE PERSON

The employment of baths goes back to the highest antiquity, and was indulged in almost to excess by the Greeks and Romans. So important are baths in warm countries, that the Jewish and Oriental religions enjoin frequent ablutions as necessary part of the ceremonials of their creeds, thus no doubt largely contributing to the health and well-being of their devout disciples.

The Toilet Case.

In order to understand the value of bathing, we must glance briefly at the anatomy and physiology of the skin. In the first place we have on the entire outer surface of the body, a layer of membrane, like thin leather, called the epidermis; this stratum is not supplied with nerves, is therefore insensible, and constitutes the portion which rises up when the hands are blistered by rowing, for example, or when a fly blister is applied.

Just beneath the epidermis lies the true skin, or corium as it is called, a tough, strong membrane, richly supplied with bloodvessels and nerves. Hence it bleeds and feels pain at the slightest cut or puncture, since even the finest needle cannot be thrust into it without wounding some little artery or vein, and some tiny filament of nerve. Under the true skin again lies the subcutaneous cellular tissue, which generally contains a good deal of fat.

The most important constituents of the skin to our present inquiry, however, are: 1st, the sweat glands; 2d, the oil glands; 3d, the hair and nails, usually spoken of as appendages to the skin.

The sweat glands are twisted and coiled-up tubes, occupying the true skin and the layer of tissue beneath. They open upon the outside of the epidermis by an immense number of minute openings called *pores*, almost invisible to the naked eye. When we are at rest, the flow of the perspiration though constant, is seldom so free that it does not evaporate almost as rapidly as it exudes, so that the skin is only kept pleasantly moist; but during exercise, especially in warm weather, the cutaneous surface becomes covered with drops of fluid.

When the pores of the skin are partly choked up, so that they cannot do their work properly, some of this duty of purifying and regulating the volume of the blood is thrown upon certain internal organs, such as the kidneys or intestines; and should these happen to be weak, diseased, or already overtasked, serious disturbance may be quickly brought on throughout the whole system.

Warm Baths. For purposes of cleanliness, the baths par excellence are those of warm water, this term being applied to those in which water of a temperature from 70° to 80° is employed.

Liquids of this degree of heat usually give a sensation of warmth when placed in contact with the human skin, and therefore avoid the disadvantage of the shock to our systems produced by a cold bath (that is, below 60°), and the excessive stimulation resulting from a hot bath, *i. e.*, one of 85° and upward. Soap, or alkali in some form, is necessary to remove the fatty matter poured out by the oil glands already described, and for most people there is nothing better than the old-fashioned white castile. Many persons are apt to remain too long in a warm bath, and care should be taken to avoid this mistake, which has a very debilitating effect if often indulged in.

The frequency with which a bath should be repeated varies somewhat with different individuals. A safe rule, to which of course there are sundry exceptions, would be to bathe the body twice a week in winter and every other day in summer, gradually increasing the frequency to a tri-weekly washing in winter and a daily one in summer, if experience proves that better health is secured by such a habit. It is very important to avoid being exposed to cool air after immersion in a warm bath.

A Good Bath for Persons Suffering from Debility. Take a quart of cheap whiskey and put into it a teacupful of rock salt; dip a crash towel in this and let it dry; then wet the body all over with the salt and whiskey, and rub dry with the towel. The rubbing should be done with short, light strokes, and *toward the heart;* that is, the limbs should be rubbed *up* and the face, neck and upper part of the chest down. This bath relieves congestion and facilitates circulation by bringing the blood to the surface of the body. Add to the mixture 1 tablespoonful camphor and ½ tablespoonful ammonia.

Alcohol Sweat Bath. Procure a small alcohol lamp and after filling it with alcohol, light and place under an ordinary cane-seated chair on which several thicknesses of paper have been placed. Divest the person of all clothing and after being seated in the chair, wrap one or two large blankets around the person, chair and all. Be very careful to have the blankets reach well to the floor and to have no openings for the heat to escape. To facilitate perspiration wring a thick towel out of hot water and place on the head, and over that put a light woolen covering. After perspiring freely take a plunge bath in a tub of clear warm water. No soap should be used. After bathing, rub the surface of the body thoroughly dry with a crash towel and retire for at least an hour or two. The best time to take this bath is at night, when one can remain undisturbed until morning. This bath will be found most beneficial when suffering from colds, or exhaustion caused by excessive mental or physical labor.

Baths for Children should be given according to age and constitution. Some require warm baths, and cannot stand the effect of cold water, while with other children it agrees perfectly. A tepid bath is the one most generally suitable. Young children should have their bath in the morning, and if they are under two years may take it after their first meal. A child should never be given a hot bath in a very cold room, and thorough drying after bathing is of great importance.

The Face. So much that is ill-advised has been written about the means of acquiring a beautiful complexion that it seems charitable to warn women against the numerous so-called skin beautifiers advertised by perfumers and druggists. In most cases these preparations are downright dangerous and bring on pimples, wrinkles and even serious troubles of the dermal tissues. The bleaching fluids destroy the epiderm and absorb the oily matter necessary for a healthy function of the skin, which soon becomes as dry and hard as parchment. The pomades fill up the pores and produce blackheads. Of a truth, many of the cosmetics, especially those prepared by conscientious chemists, are absolutely harmless; that is all that can be said of them, however, for in no way do they improve a complexion which is bad or indifferent by nature.

Circassian women, who are noted for their velvety skins and hedge-rose bloom, never use ointments of any kind. They apply to their faces half an hour before their daily bath, a thorough coating of white of egg. When this has completely dried they wash it off with tepid water, and then proceed to bathe as usual in soap and water. A spoonful of tincture of benzoin is added to the bath, pervading it with sweet and invigorating perfume. The white of egg cleanses the skin perfectly, freeing it from all impurities and obstructions, and leaves it smooth and soft like that of a baby.

Black Spots on the Face. The black spots on the face are not always what are called fleshworms. What are mistaken for them are produced in this way: The skin may be coarse, and the ducts, being large, collect the perspiration, which hardens and blackens, and hence the common supposition of their being grubs or maggots in the skin. The remedy is simple. Clean the part affected by squeezing out the substance that is lodged, and then use a lotion of diluted spirits of wine several times a day, until the blotches have disappeared. If they are really fleshworms, take something to purify your blood—sulphur or sarsaparilla.

To Remove Sunburn and to Prevent the Skin from Cracking. Melt two ounces of spermaceti in a pipkin, and add two ounces of oil of almonds. When they are well mixed and have begun to cool, stir in a tablespoonful of fine honey and continue to stir briskly until cool. Put in small jars. Apply it on going to bed, after washing the face, and allow it to remain on all night.

It is said that strawberries rubbed over the face at night will remove freckles and sunburn.

Pearl Water for the Complexion. Take castile soap, one pound; water, one gallon; dissolve. Then add alcohol, one quart; oil of rosemary and oil of lavender, of each, two drachms; mix well.

Freckles No. 1. Take grated horseradish and put in very sour milk. Let it stand four hours, then wash the face night and morning.

Freckles No. 2. Rectified spirits of wine, one ounce: water, eight ounces; half an ounce of orange-flower water, or one ounce of rosewater; diluted muriatic acid, one teaspoonful; mix. To be used after washing.

Freckles No. 3. Take one ounce lemon juice, one-fourth drachm of powdered borax, half drachm sugar. Mix and let them stand in a glass bottle for a few days. Then rub it on the face and hands night and morning. Two teaspoonfuls of lemon juice equal an ounce.

Freckles No. 4. Take of sulpho carbolate of zinc, 2 drachms; glycerine, 3 fluid ounces; alcohol, half a fluid oz.; rose water, enough to make 8 fluid ounces. Apply locally.

Wash for the Face. Wash the face at night with either sour milk or buttermilk, and in the morning with weak bran tea and a little eau de cologne. This will soften the skin and remove the redness, and will also make it less liable to burn again with exposure to the sun. Bathing the face several times in the day with elder flower water and a few drops of eau de cologne is very efficacious.

Calamine Lotion. Take of levigated calamine (white) ten grains; oxide of zinc, twenty grains; glycerine, twenty drops; rose water, one ounce. Apply to face. (A favorite prescription with ladies who have flushed faces.)

Cure for Chapped Lips. Dissolve a lump of beeswax in a small quantity of sweet oil—over a candle—let it cool, and it will be ready for use. Rubbing it warm on the lips two or three times will effect a cure.

Lip Salve. Melt a lump of sugar in one and a half tablespoonfuls of rosewater; mix it with two tablespoonfuls of sweet oil, a piece of spermaceti half as large as an English walnut; simmer the whole and turn it into boxes.

The Hands. Soap is an indispensable article for cleansing hands, but it often leaves the skin rough; cracks on the hands come, and soap is often unpleasant. Use honey, rub it on when the skin is dry; moisten a little, rub harder, use a little more water; finally wash thoroughly and your hands will be as clean as though the strongest soap were used, and no cracks or roughness will annoy you.

To Soften the Hands. To soften the hands, fill a wash-basin half full of fine white sand and soapsuds as hot as can be borne. Wash the hands in this, five minutes at a time, washing and rubbing them in the sand. The best is the flint sand, or the white, powdered quartz sold for filters. It may be used repeatedly by pouring the water away after each washing, and adding fresh to keep it from blowing about. Rinse in warm lather of fine soap; and, after drying, rub them with dry bran or cornmeal. Dust them, and finish with rubbing cold cream well into the skin. This effectually removes the roughness caused by housework, and should be used every day, first removing ink or vegetable stains with acid.

To Soften the Hands, No. 2. Keep a dish of Indian meal on the toilet stand near the soap, and rub the meal freely on the hands after soaping them for washing. It will surprise you, if you have not tried it, to find how it will cleanse and soften the skin, and prevent chapping.

To Soften the Hands, No. 3. Before retiring take a large pair of gloves and spread mutton tallow inside, also all over the hands. Wear the gloves all night, and wash the hands with olive oil and white castile soap the next morning.

After cleansing the hands with soap, rub them well with oatmeal while still wet. Honey is also very good, used in the same way as lemon juice, well rubbed in at night.

To Whiten the Hands. (1) Keep some oatmeal on the washstand, and, as often as the hands are washed, rub a little oatmeal over them; then rinse it off, and when dry, put on a little bit of pomade, made as follows: Take about five cents' worth each of white wax, spermaceti and powdered camphor and olive oil enough to make it the thickness of soap; put it in a gallipot, and let it stand in an oven to melt; mix it up, and when cold, it will be found very good for the hands. Gloves, worn either in the day or night, will help to keep the hands white.

(2) Half an ounce of white wax, half an ounce of spermaceti, quarter of an ounce of powdered camphor. Mix them with as much olive oil as will form them into a very stiff paste, and use as often as you wash your hands.

(3) Mixtures of two parts of glycerine, one part ammonia, and a little rosewater, whiten and soften the hands.

Almond Paste To Keep the Hands White and Soft. Beat four ounces of bitter almonds. Add to them three ounces of lemon juice, three ounces of almond oil, and enough of weak spirits of wine and ether to make a paste. Apply when retiring.

The Nails. Great attention should be paid to keeping the nails in good order. They should be brushed at least twice a day, and the skin round the lower part should be kept down by rubbing with a soft towel. The sides of the nails need clipping about once a week. If they become stained, wash them well with soap; and after rinsing off the soap well, brush them with lemon juice.

Cold Cream. This is a simple and cooling ointment, exceedingly serviceable for rough or chapped hands, or for keeping the skin soft. It is very easily made: Half an ounce of white wax, put into a small basin, with two ounces of almond oil; when quite melted add two ounces rosewater. This must be done very slowly, little by little; and as you pour it in, beat the mixture smartly with a fork to make the water incorporate. When all is incorporated the cold cream is complete, and you may pour it into jars for future use.

The Teeth need brushing at least before going to bed every night, and are better for being cleansed after each meal. Tartar can be removed by using pumice stone reduced to powder, rubbing it on the teeth with a bit of soft wood made into a brush. Where the gums are sensitive, there is nothing better than the chalk and myrrh dentifrice. Where the top of a tooth is very sensitive, wet a bit of chalk and lay it on under the lip. Where the breath is offensive, the mouth should be rinsed with water in which an atom of permanganate of potash has been dissolved; just enough should be used to make the water pink. Take care not to swallow any, as it is a poison. Crooked teeth in children can often be straightened, without applying to a dentist, if the parents watch the teeth when coming through, and several times a day press the crooked one into position. Of course, where the arch of the mouth is defective, the upper teeth protruding over the under lip, or the under jaw projects, the services of a skillful dentist will be required. It is only after the permanent teeth arrive that such operations are performed.

Tooth Powder. (1) Dissolve two ounces of borax in three pints of boiling water, and before it is cold, add one teaspoonful of the spirits of camphor, and bottle for use. A tablespoonful of this mixture, mixed with an equal quantity of tepid water, and applied daily with a soft brush, preserves and beautifies the teeth, extirpates all tartarous adhesion, arrests decay, induces healthy action of the gums, makes the teeth pearly white.

(2) Ten cents' worth ground chalk, five cents' worth orris root, five cents' worth myrrh, one teaspoonful powdered castile soap. Mix all well together.

(3) Prepared chalk, one pound; camphor, one or two drachms. The camphor must be finely powdered by moistening it with a little spirit of wine, and then intimately mixed with the chalk.

(4) Ingredients: Powdered charcoal, four ounces; powdered yellow bark, two ounces; powdered myrrh, one ounce; orris root, half an ounce.

(5) A mixture of honey with the purest charcoal will prove an admirable cleanser.

(6) A good way to clean teeth is to dip the brush in water, rub it over genuine white castile soap, then dip it in prepared chalk. A lady says: "I have been complimented upon the whiteness of my teeth, which were originally anything but white. I have used the soap constantly for two or three years, and the chalk for the last year. There is no danger of scratching the teeth, as the chalk is prepared, but with a good stiff brush and the soap is as effectual as soap and sand on a floor."

Violet Mouth Wash. Tincture of orris, half pint; esprit de rose, half pint; spirit, half pint; otto of almonds, five drops. Shake thoroughly and rinse the mouth after eating.

To Sweeten the Breath. From six to ten drops of the concentrated solution of chloride of soda in a wineglassful of spring water, taken immediately after the ablutions of the morning are completed, will sweeten the breath by disinfecting the stomach, which, far from being injured, will be benefited by the medicine. If necessary this may be repeated in the middle of the day. In some cases the odor from carious teeth is combined with that of the stomach. If the mouth is well rinsed with a teaspoonful of the chloride in a tumbler of water, the bad odor of the teeth will be removed.

Care of the Hair. To keep the hair healthy, keep the head clean. Brush the scalp well with a stiff brush while dry. Then wash with castile soap, and rub into the roots bay rum, brandy, or camphor-water. If this is done twice a month, it will prove beneficial. Brush the scalp thoroughly twice a week. Dampen the hair with soft water at the toilet, and do not use oil.

Hair Wash. Take one ounce of borax, half ounce of camphor-powder—these ingredients fine—and dissolve them in one quart of boiling water. When cool, the solution will be ready for use; damp the hair frequently. This wash is said not only to cleanse and beautify, but to strengthen the hair, preserve the color and prevent baldness.

Hair Wash No. 2. The best wash we know for cleansing and softening the hair is an egg beaten up, and rubbed well into the hair, and afterward washed out with several washes of warm water.

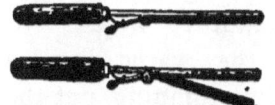

Hair Curler.

To Curl the Hair. There is no preparation which will make naturally straight hair assume a permanent curl. The following will keep the hair in curl for a short time. Take borax, two ounces; gum arabic, one drachm; and hot water, not boiling, one quart; stir, and, as soon as the ingredients are dissolved, add three tablespoonfuls of strong spirits of camphor. On retiring to rest, wet the hair with the above liquid, and roll in twists of paper as usual. Do not disturb the hair until morning, when untwist and form into ringlets.

Crimping the Hair. To make the hair stay in crimp, take five cents' worth of gum arabic, and add to it just enough boiling water to dissolve it. When dissolved, add enough alcohol to make it rather thin. Let this stand all night and then bottle it to prevent the alcohol from evaporating. This put on the hair at night after it is done up in papers or pins, will make it stay in crimp the hottest day, and is perfectly harmless.

Walnut Hair Dye. The simplest form is the pressed juice of the bark or shell of green walnut. To preserve this juice, little rectified spirit may be added to it, with a few bruised cloves, and the whole digested together, with occasional agitation, for a week or fortnight, when the clear portion is decanted, and, if necessary, filtered. Sometimes only a little common salt is added to preserve the juice. It should be kept in a cool place.

Hair Restorative. A good hair restorative may be made of boxwood leaves, of which take a handful and put into one pint of boiling water; digest for an hour, simmer ten minutes, and then strain. In applying it to the hair, rub it well into the roots.

To Wash Brushes.  Dissolve a piece of soda in some hot water, allowing a piece the size of a walnut to a quart of water. Put the water into a basin, and after combing out the hair from the brushes, dip them, bristles downward, into the water and out again, keeping the backs and handles as free from the water as possible. Repeat this until the bristles look clean; then rinse the brushes in a little cold water; shake them well, and wipe the handles and backs with a towel, *but not the bristles*, and set the brushes to dry in the sun, or near the fire; but take care not to put them too close to it. Wiping the bristles of a brush makes them soft, as does also the use of soap.

To Clean Combs. If it can be avoided, never wash combs, as the water often makes the teeth split, and the tortoise shell or horn of which they are made, rough. Small brushes, manufactured purposely for cleaning combs, may be purchased at a trifling cost; with this the comb should be well brushed, and afterward wiped with a cloth or towel.

To Clean Sponges. The following is a very simple and certain way of cleaning sponges from grease or any other impurities: Take some soda and break it up. Measure about three tablespoonfuls; put it—as much as you can—into the holes of the sponge, and keep the rest. Then fill a large jug with boiling water and immediately put in your sponge and all your soda. Cover over and leave it standing for about twelve hours. After you rinse it well you will see the sponge look almost like a new one.

HOME-MADE PERFUMERY

Perfume for Handkerchiefs. Oil of lavender, three fluid drachms; oil of bergamot, three fluid drachms; extract of ambergris, six minims; camphor, one grain; spirits of wine, one pint. To be well shaken every day for a fortnight, and then filtered.

Essence from Flowers. Procure a quantity of the petals of any flowers which have an agreeable fragrance; card thin layers of cotton, which dip into the finest Florence or Lucca oil; sprinkle a small quantity of fine salt on the flowers alternately until an earthen vessel or wide-mouthed glass bottle is full. Tie the top close with a bladder, then lay the vessel in a south aspect to the heat of the sun, and in fifteen days, when uncovered, a fragrant oil may be squeezed away, leaving a whole mass quite equal to the high-priced essences.

Otto of Roses. Fill a large glazed earthen jar with rose leaves, carefully separated from the cups; pour upon them spring water, just sufficient to cover them, and set the jar with its contents in the sun for two or three days, taking it under cover at night. At the end of the third or fourth day, small particles of yellow oil will be seen floating on the surface of the water, and which, in the course of a week, will have increased to a thin scum. The scum is the otto of roses; take it up with a little cotton tied to the end of a stick, and squeeze it into a phial.

Violet Powder. Wheat starch, six parts by weight; orris root powder, two. Having reduced the starch to an impalpable powder, mix thoroughly with the orris root, and then perfume with otto of lemon, otto of bergamot and otto of cloves, using twice as much of the lemon as either of the other ottoes.

Scent Powder. A good recipe for scent powder to be used for wardrobes, boxes, etc., far finer than any mixture sold at the shops, is the following: Coriander, orris root, rose leaves and aromatic calamus, each one ounce; lavender flowers, ten ounces; rhodium, one-quarter drachm; musk, five grains. These are to be mixed and reduced to a coarse powder. This scents clothes as if fragrant flowers had been pressed in their folds.

Almond Paste. Take of bleached almonds four ounces, add the white of one egg. Beat the almonds to a smooth paste in a mortar, then add the white of an egg and enough rosewater, mixed with its weight of spirits of wine, to give the proper consistence. This paste is used as a cosmetic to beautify the complexion, and is also a remedy for chapped hands, etc.

Shampooing Liquid. An excellent shampoo is made of salts of tartar, white castile soap, bay rum and lukewarm water. The salts will remove all dandruff; the soap will soften the hair and clean it thoroughly, and the bay rum will prevent taking cold.

Toilet Soap. Take two pounds of pure beef tallow, two pounds of sal soda, one pound of salt, one ounce of gum camphor, one ounce of oil of bergamot, one ounce of borax. Boil slowly an hour, stir often, let it stand till cold. Then warm it over so it will run easily, and turn into cups or moulds dipped in cold water. This is very nice for all toilet purposes, and is greatly improved by age.

II

THE CARE OF THE CLOTHES

Hints for the Laundry. The laundress will find it useful to "paste this in her hat." Thirty yards of cotton cloth may be bleached in fifteen minutes by one large spoonful of sal soda and one pound of the chloride of lime dissolved in soft water; after taking out the cloth rinse it in soft cold water so that it may not rot.

Wringer.

The color of French linen may be preserved by a bath of strong tea of common hay. Calicoes with pink or green colors will be brightened if vinegar is put in the rinsing water, while soda is used for purple and blue. If it is desired to set colors previous to washing, put a spoonful of ox gall to a gallon of water and soak the fabrics in the liquid. Colored napkins are put in lye before washing, to set the color. The color of black cloth is freshened if it is put in a pail of water containing a teacupful of lye.

Washing Fluid. One pound of concentrated lye dissolved in two gallons of hot soft water, and when nearly cold, add one ounce of sal ammonia and one ounce of tartar.

Washing Fluid No. 2. Take one pound of sal soda, one-half pound of lime, and one gallon of water; boil one-half hour, skim, then set off to settle; pour off the clear fluid, put on more water and boil again, and so continue until you have a gallon of fluid.

Hard Soap. Three pounds of grease, one pound of Babbit's potash, ten quarts of water, one-half pound of borax;

boil four or five hours, pour into a square wooden box, and when cold cut into blocks and set away to dry.

Hard Soap No. 2. Five pounds of grease, one pound of concentrated potash and two quarts of water; put the potash into the water and when dissolved heat the grease and add to it; let it stand over night and in the morning add four quarts of water, and boil; turn into moulds and when cold turn out and set aside to dry.

Good Blueing. One ounce of Prussian blue, one-half ounce of oxalic acid; put in a quart jar and fill with boiling soft water. Let stand two or three days before using.

To Glaze Linen. The gloss, or enamel, as it is sometimes called, is produced mainly by friction with a warm iron, and may be put on linen by almost any person. The linen to be glazed receives as much strong starch as it is possible to charge it with, then it is dried. To each pound of starch a piece of sperm or white wax, about the size of a walnut, is usually added. When ready to be ironed, the linen is laid upon the table and moistened very lightly on the surface with a clean wet cloth. It is then ironed in the usual way with a flat-iron, and is ready for the glossing operation. For this purpose a peculiar heavy flat-iron, rounded at the bottom, as bright as a mirror, is used. It is pressed firmly upon the linen and rubbed with much force, and this frictional action puts on the gloss. "Elbow grease" is the principal secret connected with the art of glossing linen.

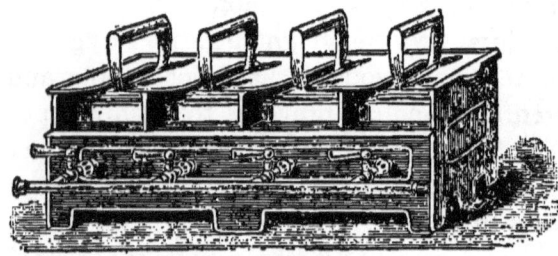

Irons.

To Remove Grease from Cloth. Take soap and Fuller's earth, of each half a pound; beat them well together in a mortar, and form into cakes. The spot, first moistened with water, is rubbed with a cake and allowed to dry, when it is well rubbed with a little warm water and afterward rinsed or rubbed off clear.

Wax Stains on Cloth. An old-fashioned way of removing wax stains from cloth is the following: Lay over the stains two thicknesses of blotting paper, and apply for a moment the pressure of a moderately hot iron. The wax becoming melted will be absorbed by the two layers of paper, and the stains will be instantaneously and entirely removed.

Holes in Stockings. To mend large holes in stockings or merino underwear, tack a piece of net over the rent and darn through it.

To Take out Spots and Stains from Dresses. To remove grease spots from cotton or woolen materials, absorbent pastes, purified bullock's blood, and even common soap, are used, applied to the spot when dry. When the colors are not fast, use fullers' earth or pulverized potter's clay, laid in a layer over the spot, and press it with a very hot iron. For silks, moires, and plain or brocaded satins, begin by pouring over the spot two drops of rectified spirits of wine; cover it over with a linen cloth instantly. The spot will look tarnished, for a portion of the grease still remains; this will be removed entirely by a little sulphuric ether dropped on the spot, and a very little rubbing. If neatly done, no perceptible mark or circle will remain; nor will the luster of the richest silk be changed, the union of the two liquids operating with no injurious effects from rubbing. Eau de Cologne will also remove grease from cloth and silk. Fruit-spots are removed from white and fast-colored cottons by

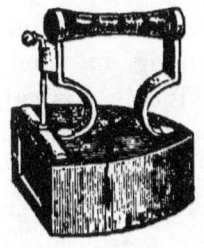
Box Iron.

the use of chloride of soda. Commence by cold-soaping the article, then touch the spot with a hair pencil or feather dipped in the chloride, dipping it immediately into cold water, to prevent the texture of the article being injured. Ink spots are removed, when fresh applied to the spot, by a few drops of hot water being poured on immediately afterward. By the same process, iron mold in linen or calico may be removed, dipping immediately in cold water to prevent injury to the fabric. Wax dropped on a shawl, table-cover, or cloth dress, is easily discharged by applying spirits of wine. Syrups or preserved fruits, by washing in lukewarm water with a dry cloth, and pressing the spot between two folds of clean linen. Essence of lemon will remove grease, but will make a spot itself in a few days.

To Wash Silk. The idea of washing silk dresses, and other articles of wearing apparel or furniture made of silk, will be novel to most of our readers. For a dress to be washed, the seams of a skirt do not require to be ripped apart, though it must be removed from the band at the waist, and the lining taken from the bottom. Trimmings or drapings, where there are deep folds, the bottom of which is very difficult to reach, should be undone so as to remain flat. A black silk dress, without being previously washed, may be refreshed by being soaked during twenty-four hours in soft, clear water; clearness in the water being indispensable. If dirty, the black dress may be previously washed. When very old and rusty, a pint of gin or whisky should be mixed with each gallon of water. This addition is an improvement under any circumstances, whether the silk be previously washed or not. After soaking, the dress should be hung up to drain dry without being wrung. The mode of washing silk is this: The article should be laid upon a clean, smooth table. A flannel should be well soaped, just made wet with lukewarm water, and the surface of the silk rubbed one way with it, care being taken that this rubbing is quite even. When the dirt has disappeared, the soap must be washed off with a sponge and plenty of cold water, of which the sponge must be made to imbibe as much as possible. As soon as one side is finished, the other must be washed precisely in the same manner. Let it be understood that not more of either surface must be done at a time than can be spread perfectly flat upon the table, and the hand can conveniently reach; likewise the soap must be quite sponged off one portion before the soaped flannel is applied to another portion. Silks, when washed, should always be dried in the shade, on a linen horse, and alone. If black or dark blue, they will be improved if, when dry, they are placed on a table and well sponged with gin or whisky, and again dried. Either of these spirits alone will remove, without washing, the dirt and grease from a black necktie or handkerchief of the same color, which will be so renovated by the application as to appear almost new.

To Clean Ribbons. INGREDIENTS.—½ pint of gin, ½ lb. of honey, ½ lb. soft soap, 1-8 pint of water.

MODE.—Mix the above ingredients together; then lay each breadth of silk upon a clean kitchen table or dresser, and scrub it well on the soiled side with the mixture. Have ready three vessels of cold water; take each piece of silk at two corners, and dip it up and down in each vessel, but do not wring it; and take care that each breadth has one vessel of quite clean water for the last dip. Hang it up dripping for a minute or two, then dab it in a cloth, and iron it quickly with a very hot iron.

The Lady's Maid.

Cleaning Cream. One-half pound of white castile soap, one-half pound of lump ammonia, two ounces of spirits of wine, two ounces of ether, cut the soap up fine and dissolve in one quart of hot water, then take off the fire and add four quarts of cold water and the other ingredients. Bottle at once and cork tightly. This is for cleaning wearing apparel, taking out grease spots, etc.

To Renovate Silk. Sponge faded silks with warm water and soap; then rub them with a dry cloth on a flat board; afterward iron them on the *inside* with a smoothing iron Old black silks may be improved by sponging with spirits. In this case, the ironing may be done on the right side, thin paper being spread over to prevent glazing.

To Renew Velvet. Hold the velvet, pile downward, over boiling water, in which two pennyworth of stone ammonia is dissolved, double the velvet (pile inward) and fold it lightly together.

To Clean Feathers. Cover the feathers with a paste made of pipe clay and water, rubbing them one way only. When quite dry, shake off all the powder, and curl with a knife. Grebe feathers may be washed with white soap in soft water.

Feather Cleaning.

To Clean Cloth. You need dry fullers' earth moistened with lemon juice, and a small quantity of pulverized pearlash. Mix the fullers' earth and pearlash into balls with sufficient lemon juice to moisten. Scour the cloth with the balls.

To Make Old Crape Look Nearly Equal to New. Place a little water in a tea kettle and let it boil until there is plenty of steam from the spout; then, holding the crape with both hands, pass it to and fro several times through the steam, and it will be clean and look nearly equal to new.

Cleaning Lace. To wash or clean fine linen or cotton lace, make a suds with warm water and some good white soap and add a few drops of ammonia or a little powdered borax. Put the lace in this and let stand for half an hour, then spat with the hand until the dirt is all removed. Be very careful not to rub as it destroys the texture. If very much soiled use two waters. When clean rinse twice, and in the last water put a little clear boiled starch, about a tablespoonful to two quarts of water. Then squeeze dry. Cover a round glass bottle with clean white cloth and over this wind the lace, using small pins to keep points or scallops in position, set away and when thoroughly dry unwind, taking out the pins carefully. If these instructions have been carefully followed, the lace will look as good as new.

How to Brush Clothes. Brushing clothes is a very simple but very necessary operation. Fine clothes require to be brushed lightly, and with rather a soft brush, except where mud is to be removed, when a hard one is necessary, being previously beaten lightly to dislodge the dirt. Lay the garment on a table, and brush it in the direction of the nap. Having brushed it properly turn the sleeves back to the collar, so that the folds may come at the elbow joints; next turn the lapels or sides back over the folded sleeves; then lay the skirts over level with the collar, so that the crease may fall about the center, and double one half over the other, so that the fold comes in the center of the back.

How to Wash Flannels. There are many conflicting theories in regard to the proper way to wash flannels, but I am convinced, from careful observation, that the true way is to wash them in water in which you can comfortably bear your hand. Make suds before putting the flannels in, and do not rub soap on the flannel. I make it a rule to have only one piece of flannel put in the tub at a time. Wash in two suds if much soiled; then rinse thoroughly in clean, weak suds, wring, and hang up; but do not take flannels out of warm water and hang out in a freezing air, as that certainly tends to shrink them. It is better to dry them in the house, unless the sun shines. In washing worsted goods, such as men's pantaloons, pursue the same course, only do not wring them, but hang them up, and let them drain; while a little damp bring in and press smoothly with as hot an iron as you can use without scorching the goods. The reason for not wringing them is to prevent wrinkles.

How to Clean Corsets. Take out the steels at front and sides, then scrub thoroughly with tepid or cold lather of white castile soap, using a very small scrubbing brush. Do not lay them in water. When quite clean let cold water run on them freely from the spigot to rinse out the soap thoroughly. Dry without ironing (after pulling lengthwise until they are straight and shapely) in a cool place.

Boot Cleaning. Three good brushes and good blacking must be provided; one of the brushes hard, to brush off the mud; the other soft, to lay on the blacking; the third of a medium hardness, for polishing. The blacking should be kept corked up, except when in use, and applied to the brush with a sponge tied to a stick. When boots come in very muddy, wash off the mud, and wipe them dry with a sponge; then leave them to dry gradually on their sides, taking care they are not placed near the fire.

To Clean Patent Leather Boots. They require to be wiped with a wet sponge, and afterward with a soft dry cloth, and occasionally with a soft cloth and sweet oil, blacking and polishing the edge of the soles in the usual way, but so as not to cover the patent polish with blacking. A little milk may also be used with very good effect for patent leather boots.

III

THE CARE OF THE HOUSE, FURNITURE AND BRIC-A-BRAC.

To Remove Stains from Boards. Take ¼ lb. of fullers' earth and ¼ lb. of pearlash; make them into a paste with about a quart of boiling water; spread a thick coating of this over the grease stains and leave it for ten or twelve hours; then wash it off with clean water, using sand if necessary. If the grease stains are very numerous and the floor very dirty, a coating may be spread all over the floor, and left for 24 hours before it is washed off. In washing boards never rub crossways, but always up and down with the grain.

To Clean Floor Cloth. Shred half an ounce of good beeswax into a saucer, cover it entirely with turpentine, and place it in the oven until melted. After washing the floor cloth thoroughly with a flannel, rub the whole surface lightly with a flannel dipped in the wax and turpentine, then rub with a dry cloth. Beside the polish produced, the surface is lightly coated with the wax, which is washed off together with any dust or dirt it may have contracted, while the floor cloth is preserved. Milk is also very useful for cleaning floor cloth, applied after the usual washing with a damp cloth, and it should then be rubbed over with a dry one.

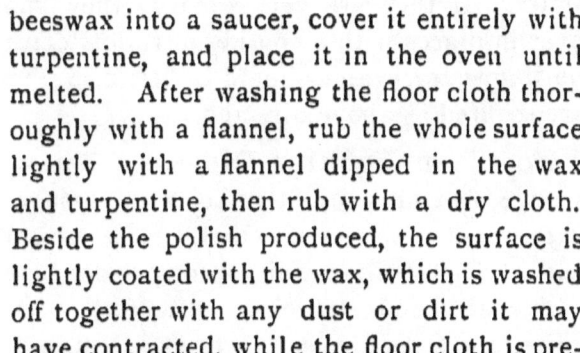

The House Maid

To Clean Marble. Take two parts of soda, one of pumice stone, and one of finely powdered chalk. Sift these through a fine sieve, and mix them into a paste with water. Rub this well all over the marble, and the stains will be removed: then wash it with soap and water, and a beautiful bright polish will be produced.

To Whiten Stones. Wash the surface with clean water, and let it dry; then rub it lightly over with a flannel dipped in a mixture of the following materials: Boil 2 cakes of pipe clay, 2 tablespoonfuls of carbonate of lime, ½ pint of size, ½ pint of stone blue water, in 2 quarts of water. When the stones are dry, after this mixture has been applied, rub them with a dry flannel till they look well.

To Scour Boards. Mix in a saucer three parts of fine sand and one part of lime; dip the scrubbing brush into this and use it instead of soap. This will remove grease and whiten the boards, while at the same time it will destroy all insects. The boards should be well rinsed with clean water. If they are very greasy, they should be covered over in places with a coating of fullers'earth moistened with boiling water, which should be left on 24 hours before they are scoured as above directed.

To Clean Looking Glasses. Remove, with a damp sponge, fly stains and other soils (the sponge may be damped with water or spirits of wine). After this, dust the surface with the finest sifted whiting or powder-blue and polish it with a silk handkerchief or soft cloth. Snuff of candle, if quite free from grease, is an excellent polish for looking glasses.

To Clean Brass. Dissolve 1 oz. of oxalic acid in one pint of soft water. Rub it on the brass with a piece of flannel, and polish with another dry piece. This solution should be kept in a bottle labeled "poison," and the bottle well shaken before it is used, which should be only occasionally; for in a general way the brass should be cleaned with pulverized rottenstone, mixed into a liquid state with oil of turpentine. Rub this on with a piece of soft leather, leave it for a few minutes, and then wipe it off with a soft cloth. Brass treated generally with the latter, and occasionally with the former mode of cleaning, will look most beautiful; or a very good general polish for brass may be made of ½ lb. of rottenstone and 1 oz. of oxalic acid, with as much water as will make it into a stiff paste. Set this paste on a plate in a cool oven to dry, pound it very fine, and apply a little of the powder, moistened with sweet oil, to the brass with a piece of leather, polishing with another leather or an old silk handkerchief. This powder should also be labeled "poison."

To Clean and Polish Old Furniture. Make a mixture of a quart of old beer or vinegar, with a handful of common salt and a tablespoonful of muriatic acid, and boil it for fifteen minutes; put it in a bottle and warm it when wanted for use. Wash the furniture you wish to clean with soft hot water, so as to remove all the dirt, then afterward wash it with the mixture in the bottle; then polish with a soft flannel rag.

Glue Paint for Kitchen Floors. To three pounds of spruce yellow add one pound, or two pounds if desired, of dry white lead, and mix well together. Dissolve two ounces of glue in one quart of water, stirring often until smooth and nearly boiling. Thicken the glue water after the manner of mush, until it will spread smoothly upon the floor. Use a common paint brush and apply hot. This will fill all crevices of a rough floor. It will dry soon, and when dry apply boiled linseed oil with a clean brush. In a few hours it will be found dry enough to use by laying papers or mats to step on for a few days. When it needs cleaning, use hot suds.

Treasury Department Whitewash. This receipt for whitewashing is sent out by the Lighthouse Board of the Treasury Department, and will answer on wood, brick, or stone nearly as well as oil paint, and is quite cheap:

Slack one-half bushel of unslacked lime with *boiling* water keeping it covered during the process; strain it and add a peck of salt dissolved in warm water; three pounds ground rice, put in boiling water and boiled to a thin paste; one-half pound powdered Spanish whiting and a pound of clear glue dissolved in hot water; mix these well together and let the mixture stand for several days. Keep the wash thus prepared in a kettle or portable furnace, and when used put it on as hot as possible with painter's or whitewash brushes.

To Paper Whitewashed Walls. Make a flour starch as you would for starching calico clothes, and with a whitewash brush wet with the starch the wall you wish to paper. Let it dry; then, when it is wanted to apply the paper wet both the wall and paper with the starch, and apply the paper in the ordinary way.

To Clean Wall Paper. The following is a most excellent and simple method of cleaning wall paper and can be used with confidence in every house: Take one quart of flour and stir in five cents' worth of ammonia and enough water to make a stiff dough; work and knead until smooth, then wipe the paper with this batch of dough, working it so that a clean surface will be presented with every stroke. Go over the paper in this way and your wall paper will be clean.

A Wash for Carpets. Mix together 30 cents' worth of ground soap-tree bark (which can be purchased at any drugstore), 5 cents' worth of ammonia, one cup of vinegar, one and a half pails of water. Boil this mixture one hour in a boiler, and use it on the carpet with a sponge.

To Destroy Carpet Bugs. Make a solution of one tablespoonful of corrosive sublimate in a quart of hot water and saturate the floors and cracks of walls or closets. A weaker solution can be used to sponge the carpets. It is a sure cure.

To Destroy Cockroaches. Mix together thoroughly one pound of powdered sugar, one pound of powdered borax and ten cents' worth of Paris green. Put in all places where they are seen, with a small bellows or puffer.

How to Sweep a Carpet. It is an easy matter to sweep well, at any rate, if we may judge by experience; for when a broom is put into the hands of the uninitiated, more harm than good generally results from the use of it. Without the greatest care and some little knowledge, furniture and paint, by being knocked about with the broom, may soon receive an irreparable amount of damage. Before sweeping rooms, the floors should be strewed with a good amount of dry tea leaves, which should be saved for the purpose; these will attract the dust and save much harm to other furniture, which, as far as possible, should be covered up during the process. Tea leaves also may be used with advantage upon drugget and short-piled carpets. Light sweeping and soft brooms are here desirable. Many a carpet is prematurely worn out by injudicious sweeping. Stiff carpet brooms and the stout arms of inexperienced servants are their destruction. In sweeping thick-piled carpets, such as Axminster and Turkey carpets, the servant should be instructed to brush always the way of the pile; by so doing they may be kept clean for years; but if the broom is used in a different way, all the dust will enter the carpet and soon spoil it.

Furniture Polish. One pint of boiled oil, four ounces of vinegar, two ounces of spirits of camphor, one ounce of ammonia, one half ounce of antimony. Shake and let stand two or three days before using.

Spots on Furniture. Spirits of camphor or ammonia will remove white spots from furniture.

To Take out Marks from Mahogany. The whitish stain left on a mahogany table by a jug of boiling water, or a very hot dish, may be removed by rubbing in oil, and afterward pouring a little spirits of wine on the spot and rubbing it dry with a soft cloth.

To Brighten Gilt Frames. Take sufficient flour of sulphur to give a golden tinge to about one and one-half pint of water, and in this boil four or five bruised onions, or garlic, which will answer the same purpose. Strain off the liquid, and with it, when cold, wash, with a soft brush, any gilding which requires restoring, and when dry it will come out as bright as new work. They may also be brightened in the following manner: Beat up the white of eggs with chloride of potass or soda, in the proportion of 3 oz. of eggs to 1 oz. of chloride of potass or soda. Blow off as much dust as possible from the frames, and paint them over with a soft brush dipped in the above mixture. They will immediately come out fresh and bright.

To Preserve Cut Flowers. A bouquet of freshly cut flowers may be preserved alive for a long time by placing them in a glass or vase with fresh water, in which a little charcoal has been steeped, or a small piece of camphor dissolved. The vase should be set upon a plate or dish, and covered with a bell glass, around the edges of which, when it comes in contact with the plate, a little water should be poured to exclude the air.

To Revive Cut Flowers after Packing. Plunge the stems into boiling water, and by the time the water is cold, the flowers will have revived. Then cut afresh the ends of the stems, and keep them in fresh cold water.

To Clean Ivory. To clean and preserve the color of ivory ornaments, brooches, card cases, bracelets, chains, etc., place the articles to be cleansed in a basin of cold water and allow them to remain in it twenty-four hours. Take them out of the water and lay them on a clean, soft towel, but do not wipe them, they must dry by the air, and any water that remains in the carving of the ivory should be blown out; if allowed to settle on the ivory it would destroy the color.

To Polish Tortoise Shell. When by wear tortoise shell articles have lost their luster, the polished surface may be restored to its original condition by carefully rubbing with powdered rottenstone and oil. The rottenstone should be very carefully sifted through the finest muslin. When all scratches on the surface of the tortoise shell are thus removed, a brilliant polish may be given to it by applying gentle friction with a piece of soft leather, to which some jeweler's rouge has been applied.

To Clean Lamp Chimneys. Rub lamp chimneys with newspaper on which has been poured a little kerosene. This will make them much clearer than if soap is used; they will also be less liable to crack.

Stains on Leather. A piece of cloth dipped in spirits of wine and rubbed upon soiled leather will remove every spot on it.

Polish for Black Grates. One pound of common asphaltum, one-half pint of linseed oil, one quart of oil of turpentine. Melt the asphaltum, and add gradually to it the other two ingredients. Apply this with a small painter's brush, and leave it to become perfectly dry. The grate will need no other cleaning, but will merely require dusting every day, and occasionally brushing with a dry black lead brush. This is, of course, when no fires are used. When they are required, the bars, cheeks and back of grate will need black-leading in the usual manner.

How to Dust a Room. Soft cloths make the best of dusters. In dusting any piece of furniture begin at the top and dust down, wiping carefully with the cloth, which can be frequently shaken. A good many people seem to have no idea what dusting is intended to accomplish, and instead of wiping off and removing the dust it is simply flirted off into the air and soon settles down upon the articles dusted again. If carefully taken up by the cloth it can be shaken off out of the window into the open air. If the furniture will permit the use of a damp cloth, it will more easily take up the dust, and it can be washed out in a pail of soapsuds. It is far easier to save work by covering up nice furniture while sweeping, than to clean the dust out, besides leaving the furniture looking far better in the long run.

The routine of a general servant's duties depends upon the kind of situation she occupies; but a systematic servant should so contrive to divide her work, that every day in the week may have its proper share. By this means she is able to keep the house clean with less fatigue to herself than if she left all the cleaning to do at the end of the week. Supposing there are five bedrooms in the house, two sitting rooms, kitchen, laundry, and the usual domestic offices; on Monday she might thoroughly clean two of the bedrooms; on Tuesday, two more bedrooms; on Wednesday, the other bedroom and stairs; on Thursday, the drawing room; on Friday morning she should sweep the dining room very thoroughly, clean the hall, and in the afternoon her kitchen tins and bright utensils. By arranging her work in this manner, no undue proportion will fall to Saturday's share, and she will then have this day for cleaning plate, cleaning her kitchen, and arranging everything in nice order. The regular work must, of course, be performed in the usual manner, as we have endeavored to describe. Before retiring to bed, she will do well to clean up plate, glasses, etc., which have been used for the evening meal, and prepare for her morning's work by placing her wood in the range, ready to light, taking care there is no danger of its igniting, before she leaves the kitchen for the night. Before retiring, she will have to lock and bolt the doors, unless her employer undertakes this office himself.

IV

THE CARE OF THE PANTRY

Washing of Glass. Glass is a beautiful and most fragile article; hence it requires great care in washing. A perfectly clean wooden bowl is best for this operation, one for moderately hot, and another for cold water. Wash the glasses well in the first and rinse them in the second, and turn them down on a linen cloth folded two or three times, to drain for a few minutes. When sufficiently drained, wipe them with a cloth and polish with a finer one, doing so tenderly and carefully. Accidents will happen; but nothing discredits a servant in the drawing room more than continual reports of breakages, which, of course, must reach that region.

The Waitress.

Decanters and water jugs require still more tender treatment in cleaning, inasmuch as they are more costly to replace. Fill them about two-thirds with hot but not boiling water, and put in a few pieces of well soaped brown paper; leave them thus for two or three hours; then shake the water up and down in the decanters; empty this out, rinse them well with clean cold water, and put them in a rack to drain. When dry, polish them outside and inside, as far as possible, with a fine cloth. To remove the crust of port or other wines, add a little muriatic acid to the water and let it remain for some time. Fine pieces of coal placed in a decanter with warm water, and shaken for some time, will also remove stains left by wine, etc.

To Cleanse Bottles. Make a lye by boiling equal quantities of soda and quicklime. When cold, put this in the bottles with some small pebbles, and shake well. Set the bottles to drain thoroughly, then warm them, and blow inside with a pair of bellows to absorb all moisture.

To Clean Plate. Mix to a paste ¼ lb. of prepared chalk with 2 dr. of spirits of camphor, 1 dr. of ammonia, 1 oz. of turpentine, and a dessertspoonful of spirits. When the silver is clean and dry, dab on the paste with a sponge and leave it to dry before brushing off.

Plate Rags for Daily Use. Boil soft rags (nothing is better for the purpose than the tops of old cotton stockings) in a mixture of new milk and hartshorn powder, in the proportion of 1 oz. of powder to a pint of milk; boil them for 5 minutes; wring them, as soon as they are taken out, for a moment in cold water, and dry them before the fire. With these rags rub the plate briskly as soon as it has been well washed and dried after daily use. A most beautiful deep polish will be produced, and the plate will require nothing more than merely to be dusted with a feather or a dry, soft cloth before it is again put on the table.

Plate Basket.

Washing of Knives. The handles of knives should never be immersed in water, as, after a time, if treated in this way, the blades will loosen and the handles discolor. The blades should be put in a jug or vessel kept for this purpose, filled with hot soda water. This should be done as soon after they are used as possible, as stain and rust so quickly sink into steel.

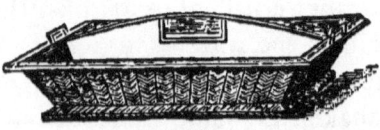
Knife Basket.

OUR

MEDICAL ADVISER

PART I.—WHAT TO DO IN CASE OF ACCIDENT OR SUDDEN ILLNESS.—BANDAGING TAUGHT BY PICTURES.

PART II.—IN THE SICK ROOM.

PART III.—THE FAMILY DOCTOR—ALLOPATHIC AND HOMEO-PATHIC METHODS.

WHAT TO DO IN CASE OF ACCIDENT OR SUDDEN ILLNESS.

Apoplexy. *Treatment.*—When a person is in an apoplectic fit, prevent all unnecessary movement; raise the head and remove everything tight from the neck, then apply ice or cold water cloths to the head; put the feet in mustard and water or apply mustard leaves or poultices to the calves of the legs.

Bruises. These are caused by blows, the skin remaining unbroken. *Treatment.*—Apply tincture of arnica, spirit and water, vinegar or sal-ammoniac and water. The following is a useful combination: Chloride of ammonium (sal-ammoniac), one ounce; rectified spirit, lavender water, or eau de cologne, two ounces; vinegar, three ounces; water to make sixteen ounces. Rags dipped in this should be laid over the bruise and kept constantly wet.

Choking. *Treatment.*—If the substance causing choking be at the upper part of the throat thrust the finger and thumb into the mouth and endeavor to seize it. If this cannot be done, take a penholder, a quill, or piece of whalebone—anything, in fact, that will do, and endeavor to push it down the gullet. A smart blow on the back will sometimes dislodge a foreign body from the throat.

Concussion of the Brain. *Treatment.*—Move the patient as little as possible; remove all tight articles from the neck. Apply hot bottles to the feet and sides, or hot bricks wrapped in flannel and a mustard poultice or mustard leaf over the stomach.

Dislocations. *Treatment.*—If medical assistance is at

hand do not touch a dislocation: in any case do not use or submit to rough handing. If skilled assistance cannot be had, get some one to seize the part of the limb nearest the body, and then apply gentle, steady traction upon that furthest removed. (*See Bandaging taught by pictures.*)

Drowning. *Treatment.*—Place the patient on the floor or ground with the face downward, and one of the arms under the forehead. If there be only slight breathing, or no breathing, or if the breathing fail, then turn the patient instantly on the side, supporting the head, and excite the nostrils with snuff, hartshorn and smelling salts, or tickle the throat with a feather. Rub the chest and face warm, and dash cold water or cold and hot water alternately on them. If there be no success, imitate breathing, and in

Artificial Respiration. First Position.

order to do this, place the patient on his back, supporting the head and shoulders on a small, firm cushion or folded article of dress. Draw the tongue forward and slip an elastic band over it and under the chin, or tie a piece of string or tape in the same way. Grasp the arms just above the elbows and draw them gently and steadily upward above the head, and keep them stretched upward for two seconds; (*First Position.*)

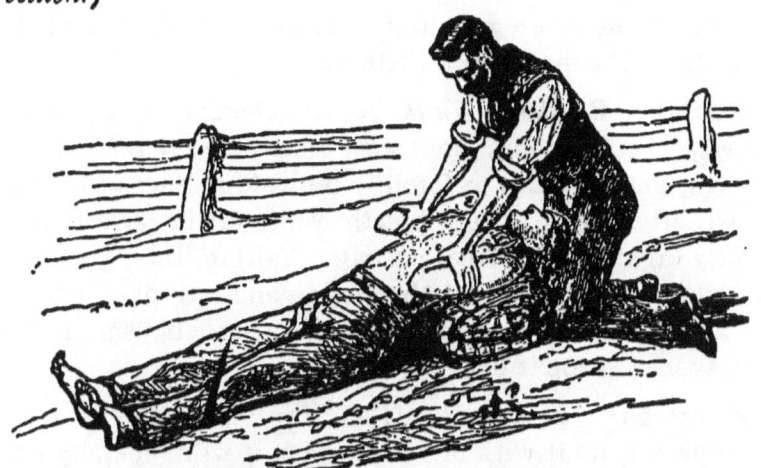

Artificial Respiration. Second Position.

then turn them down and force them gently and firmly for two seconds against the sides of the chest; (*Second Position.*)

Repeat these measures about fifteen times in a minute. When breathing is restored, rub the limbs upward with firm, grasping pressure and energy, using handkerchiefs, flannels, etc. Apply hot flannels or bottles, bladders of hot water or heated bricks to the pit of the stomach, the armpits, between the thighs, and to the soles of the feet. On the restoration of life a teaspoonful of warm water should be given, and then small quantities of warm coffee.

Epilepsy. *Treatment.*—At the onset of a fit the patient should be caught in the arms of a bystander and laid gently down upon his back, with something under his head for a pillow, and everything tight should be removed from his neck. Insert a cork between the teeth to prevent the tongue being bitten, then wait patiently till the fit it is over.

Fainting. In this affection there is pallor of the face, coldness, perspiration, feeble, shallow and irregular breathing, noises in the ears, indistinctness of vision, and giddiness.

Treatment.—Lay the patient at once upon the back; remove all constricting articles of clothing from about the neck, and apply strong smelling salts to the nostrils. Sprinkle cold water over the face; give half a teaspoonful of spirit of sal volatile by the mouth in a little water.

Foreign Bodies. *In the Nose.* These are peas, beads, sweets, cherry stones and such like. *Treatment.*—If old enough, get the child to forcibly blow down the obstructed nostril after taking a deep breath, while the finger is pressed tightly against the free nostril. Failing this, grasp the nostril behind the seat of obstruction and introduce a small flat article such as the handle of a salt spoon beyond it and endeavor to scoop it out.

In the Ear. Treatment.—If an insect has found its way into the ear, fill it with olive oil, when it will generally float on the top. If a pea, bead or cherry stone, use the head of a hair pin as a snare and *with the utmost gentleness* endeavor to insinuate it beyond the object it is intended to remove.

In the Eye. Treatment.—If the offending substance is not embedded in the globe of the eye it will generally be easily removed, either with or without everting the lid, by using the corner of a soft pocket handkerchief, or a camel's hair pencil moistened with water or olive oil. If the substance is embedded in the globe of the eye, a camel's hair pencil dipped in water or oil may be passed over it and an effort made to dislodge it. Should this fail, and medical assistance is not at hand, a blunt-pointed instrument may be carefully passed across the surface. Should quicklime get into the eye, wash it out as thoroughly as possible with water, then bathe with a lotion consisting of a teaspoonful of vinegar to a wineglassful of water, or drop a little sweet oil into the eye. In case of injury by acid, bathe with milk or one part of limewater to three of water.

Fractures. *Treatment.*—When a fracture has taken place

the object is to bring the ends of the bone that has been broken as nearly as possible to the condition they were in previous to the accident. In order to do this, the part nearest the body must be steadied by some one, while that furthest removed is gently stretched out, the sound limb being uncovered and acting as guide. Having got the limb into good position splints must be applied to fix it in the position in which it has been placed. (*See Bandaging, etc.*)

Hemorrhage or Bleeding. Bleeding from an artery is distinguished from that of a vein by being brighter in color, and by its coming out of the wound in a saltatory or jumping way. *Treatment.*—If from a vein make a compress by folding a piece of lint or a small handkerchief up, and apply it to the wound with a bandage over it. This treatment also generally answers in bleeding from small arteries, although the pressure requires to be greater.

From Varicose Veins. Treatment.—Place the patient on his back, and apply a compress and bandage, or put a fifty cent piece in a handkerchief, place it over the wound, and tie it.

From the Nose. Treatment.—Apply cold water cloths or ice to the forehead; raise the arms above the head; seize the nose between the fingers, and squeeze the sides together; syringe the nostrils with vinegar or hot water and salt. One or other of these methods may be tried, or they may all be tried in turn if the bleeding is difficult to check.

From Leech Bites. Treatment.—Lay a crystal of iron alum upon the wound. Dried alum and tannic acid may be used in a similar manner. Two strong needles run through the skin cross-wise, passing beneath the wound, and a piece of linen thread tied round them, frequently answer when the simpler means fail.

After Tooth Extraction. Treatment.—Press a small crystal of iron alum into the cavity left by the removal of the tooth, and bleeding will generally be checked.

After Confinement. Treatment.—Keep the patient at absolute rest on her back, and remove the pillows so as to keep her head low; cover very lightly with bedclothes. Place the hands on the lower part of the belly, and press deeply down with a kind of kneading motion. If the womb is felt contracting into a hard lump under the hands, grasp it and keep it tight till the arrival of the doctor. Give a little tepid milk and water.

From the Umbilical Cord. When bleeding takes place from the umbilical cord, the child generally becomes restless, and blood may saturate its clothing. *Treatment.*—Undress the child immediately, and tie a ligature of three or four thicknesses of worsted or linen thread behind the other.

Internal Bleeding. Instances of this form of bleeding are seen in hemorrhage from the lungs and stomach. That from the lungs is generally bright scarlet in color and frothy in appearance, owing to the admixture of air; that from the stomach is dark in color, and is not frothy. *Treatment.*—Keep the apartment cool and the patient quiet in the recumbent posture. Ice may be given, or cold water when ice cannot be had. Five to ten grains of gallic acid may be given along with ten or fifteen drops of aromatic sulphuric acid every three or four hours.

Hysteria. This may manifest itself by intense sobbing or immoderate laughter, or these may alternate with one another. There is frequently wild tossing about of the arms, the hair is disheveled, the face is generally pale and complaint is made of a suffocating feeling in the throat. *Treatment.*—The patient must be spoken to kindly, yet firmly, and be told to stop any eccentricities. Loosen the dress and remove anything tight from the neck. Give a teaspoonful of spirit of sal volatile in water. If no heed is taken in regard to what is said, dash cold water upon the face.

Intoxication. *Treatment.*—When loss of consciousness has occurred from this cause, give an emetic of mustard and water (a tablespoonful in tepid water) or twenty grains of sulphate of zinc or powdered ipecacuanha. Remove to a warm atmosphere and give strong tea or coffee.

Poisons. *Treatment.*—Many of these give rise to vomiting and are thus got rid of. In such cases the vomiting should be encouraged by giving draughts of tepid water. An instrument that may be used with much benefit, if it is at hand, is the stomach syphon—easier to use a good deal than the stomach pump—by which the poison may be got rid of. Care must be taken to pass the tube along the *back* of the throat, as otherwise harm may result. If the poison has not given rise to vomiting, a handful of salt in lukewarm water may be given and draughts of tepid water afterward. Mustard is a good emetic when the poison taken is not irritant in character. Twenty grains of powdered ipecacuanha or the same quantity of sulphate of zinc may be used in the same way.

General Directions. When an *alkali* is the poison, give weak vinegar, chalk and water, whiting, plaster from the walls. When an *acid*, give white of egg or milk; if a *narcotic*, give strong coffee and do everything to keep the patient awake.

Particular Poisons. *Aconite*, *Monkshood or Blue Rocket*. *Treatment.*—Give a tablespoonful of mustard in water or twenty grains of sulphate of zinc in water; then a dose of castor oil. Hot bottles should be applied to the feet, and a teaspoonful of spirit of sal volatile in water or strong coffee, be given.

Alkalies, such as potash, soda, ammonia, met with as pearl ashes, soap lees, common washing soda and ammonia in vapor, solution and solid form. *Treatment.*—Give drinks containing vinegar, or lemon juice or olive oil.

Arsenic. Treatment.—Give large quantities of sugar and water or linseed tea.

Barytes. Treatment.—Give two teaspoonfuls of Epsom or Glauber's salts every two hours until the bowels act.

Belladonna. Treatment.—Give twenty grains of sulphate of zinc or a tablespoonful of mustard in water; then drinks of tepid water. Afterward give strong coffee.

Carbolic Acid. Treatment.—Use the stomach syphon if at hand, otherwise give large quantities of olive oil or melted butter.

Copper. Treatment.—Give white of egg, afterward, enemata to act upon the bowels.

Corrosive Sublimate. Treatment.—Give white of egg beaten up with water. Milk or sugar and water may be given if eggs are not at hand.

Foxglove. Treatment.—Give an emetic of mustard and water or twenty grains of sulphate of zinc in water, then give a dose of castor oil and a cup of strong tea.

Fungi. Treatment.—Give an emetic of mustard and water, afterward a dose of castor oil.

Hemlock. Treatment.—Give a tablespoonful of mustard and water or twenty grains of sulphate of zinc; afterwards a dose of castor oil and strong tea.

Henbane, Thorn Apple and Tobacco. Treatment.—The same as for belladonna.

Hydrochloric Acid. Treatment.—The same as for sulphuric acid poisoning.

Laburnum. Treatment.—Give a tablespoonful of mustard in water; then ten or fifteen drops of spirit of sal volatile in a little water.

Laudanum. Treatment.—Give twenty grains of sulphate of zinc or a tablespoonful of mustard in water, then drinks of tepid water. Afterward give strong coffee and keep the patient constantly in motion till the drowsy feeling wears off.

Lead. Treatment.—Give an emetic in the first place; then two teaspoonfuls of Epsom or Glauber's salts every two hours till the bowels act. When this has been accomplished continue the salts in smaller doses, after which large doses of iodide of potassium may be given.

Nitric Acid or Aquafortis. Treatment.—Give bicarbonate or carbonate of soda or potash; in other respects the treatment is the same as for poisoning by sulphuric acid.

Oxalic Acid or Acid of Sugar. Treatment.—Give magnesia or chalk mixed with water.

Phosphorus. Treatment.—Give twenty grains of sulphate of zinc in water; then give lime water, barley water, linseed tea or white of egg and water.

Prussic Acid. Treatment.—Dash cold water from a height upon the head; apply smelling salts, and employ artificial respiration.

Shell Fish. Treatment.—Give an emetic, then a purgative, afterward twenty or thirty drops of spirit of sulphuric ether on a lump of sugar.

Sulphuric Acid or Oil of Vitriol. Treatment.—Give bicarbonate or carbonate of soda or potash. If these are not at hand, chalk or magnesia will do instead. Olive or almond oil may also be given.

Scalds or Burns. *Treatment.*—When a part has been scalded, immerse it in cold water or pour cold water over it, or dust bicarbonate of soda over it and apply a wet cloth above this. When blisters have formed, prick them with a needle or pair of scissors, and press the cuticle carefully down, after which apply the bicarbonate of soda as before, or chlorate of potassium ointment (5 grains to the ounce of lard) or carron oil; thymol or carbolic oil (1 part to 100 parts of olive oil) answers well.

Sprains. *Treatment.*—Foment the part well with warm water, then brush tincture of arnica over it several times a day. When the more acute symptoms have passed, wrap the part in cotton wool and apply a good firm bandage, India-rubber if it can be had, so as to diminish the swelling and give a feeling of security when the patient comes to move about. Later on, if not quite right, use the cold douche and friction with a rough towel.

Suffocation. *Treatment.*—If the person is found hanged he should be at once cut down, and artificial respiration employed. If the suffocation results from articles of food blocking up the throat, the treatment recommended in choking must be had recourse to. If the suffocation is the result of breathing coal gas or sewer gas, or by being in a room in which charcoal has been burnt, the first thing to do is to get the patient out as speedily as possible.

Sunstroke. *Treatment.*—Dash cold water over the face and head; apply ice or ice cloths, or cold water to the head, and give a teaspoonful of spirit of sal volatile in water. Tea or coffee may be given afterward.

Wounds. The simplest are those in which the tissues are clean cut through, and where the edges, when brought together, fit accurately the one to the other. *Treatment.*— Remove all dust or dirt, and bring the edges carefully together by means of a bandage or strips of plaster. Keep at rest a few days.

Contused or lacerated wounds should be treated by cleansing the parts with sanitas and water, carbolic acid and water (a teaspoonful to eight or ten ounces of water), or Pond's Extract and water, then place a piece of lint, or rag soaked in carbolic oil (one part to twenty of olive oil), or boro-glyceride over the wound, and keep the edges as nearly as possible together.

Perforating wounds are dangerous because of their depth. *Treatment.*—Keep the part at rest, and apply ice-bags or cloths soaked in cold water, to which some sanitas or carbolic acid has been added, to the wound.

Gunshot Wounds.   *Treatment.*—If a stimulant is necessary, give a teaspoonful of spirit of sal volatile in water. Remove pieces of clothing, wadding, or bits of paper that may be found in the wound, then bathe it with sanitas and water, carbolic acid and water, or Pond's Extract and water, then soak a piece of lint in carbolic oil or sanitas vaseline, and lay it into the wound.

Poisoned wounds may result from a number of causes, such as stings of insects, snake bites, the bites of rabid animals, etc.

Dog Bites.   When any one is bitten by an animal supposed to be mad, unless the actual fact of the animal's madness is known, it should be kept and carefully watched, and if it is found not to be suffering from rabies, no harm will result to the patient. This will soon make itself apparent, for, if mad, it will be seen snapping at imaginary objects, with a copious flow of saliva from the mouth, and a convulsive closing of the jaws.   *Treatment.*—The wound should be at once sucked, and a red-hot wire or a cinder laid upon it as a cautery, and then some soothing alkaline lotion, as ammonia water or lead and opium, applied. Stimulants, such as the spirits of sal volatile in teaspoonful doses, may be given. The Pasteur treatment is the only sure cure.

Snake Bites.   Bites from venomous serpents are exceedingly formidable injuries, and may be followed by death within a few hours, so that prompt action is necessary. *Treatment.*—The part should be at once sucked. A tight bandage should be applied above the wound, either by means of an elastic band, a leather strap, or a handkerchief twisted tightly by means of a stick. The wound should then be freely cauterized by means of a red-hot wire, or a red-hot cinder; or the part may be cut out with a knife, or a caustic, such as nitrate of silver, may be applied to the wound; a red-hot wire is, however, the best. Stimulants, especially preparations of ammonia, must be freely given. A teaspoonful may be put into a wineglassful of water, and the patient given a tablespoonful every quarter of an hour. If those present are afraid to suck the wound, a wineglass, into which a piece of burning paper has been put to exhaust the air, should be inverted over it.

Stings. If the sting still remains in the wound, it must of course be removed; then some alkaline lotion should be applied to the part, such as a little ammonia water or liquor potassæ and water, or bicarbonate of soda and water.

NOTE: A number of the above cases are also mentioned and treated more fully in THE FAMILY DOCTOR. The Editor thought, however, that the grouping under one heading of all these cases which are generally called "Emergencies," would be well received features of TREASURES OLD AND NEW.

BANDAGING TAUGHT BY PICTURES

Small Sling for Arm.

Comfortable Arm Sling.

Hand Bandage.

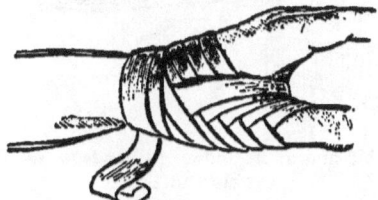

Thumb Bandage.

Head Bandage.

Splint for a Fracture of the Radius.

Form of Splint used in the Treatment of Fracture
of Bones in the Leg.

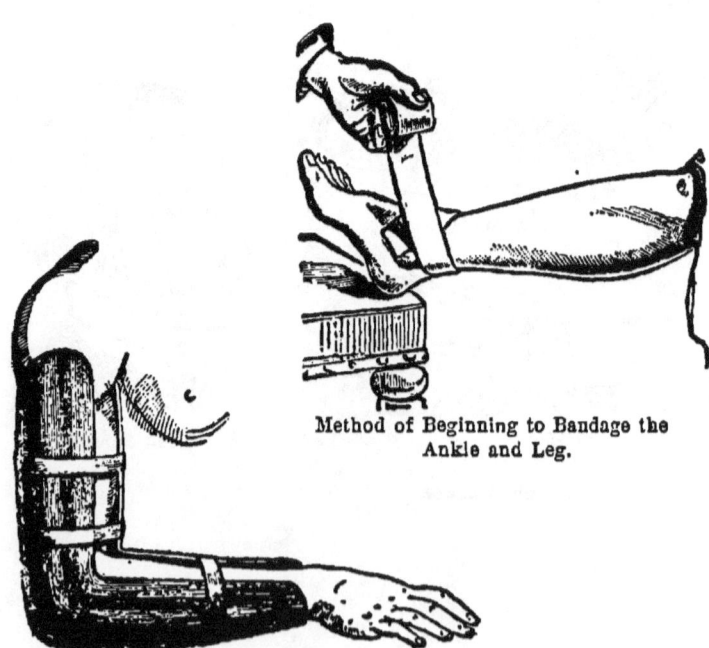

Method of Beginning to Bandage the
Ankle and Leg.

Fracture of the Arm.

II

IN THE SICK ROOM

Furnishing of the Sick Room. No unnecessary article of furniture should be found in the sick room. If there is space to accommodate two beds so much the better, as the day can be passed in one and the night in the other. An iron bedstead is the most convenient, the mattress should be of hair, and the pillow the same. All curtains should be removed. Light blankets only should be used as a covering for the sick. In addition to the bed or beds there should be two tables, a wash stand, a chest of drawers, one or two chairs and a sofa. The wash stand, should be provided with one or two basins and a plentiful supply of water. The room is perhaps better uncarpeted; if carpeted, the carpet must be removed in cases of infectious disease. If there is a mirror in the room it had better be taken away. Flowers may be placed about the room, and the walls should be hung with pictures.

Ventilation. One of the foremost subjects to be treated of in a chapter on sick nursing is that of ventilation. It is impossible to deal successfully with disease if fresh air is debarred from entering the sick room; because impure air not only depresses those already weakened by disease, but the poison in the case of infectious disease becomes concentrated, and in consequence more injurious both to patient and nurse. In order to ventilate in the true sense of the word, fresh air must be admitted without giving rise to draughts, and impure air must be got rid of. Perhaps the most efficient means capable of general employment is by means of a window and open fire. The lower sash of the window may be raised an inch or two, and boarded up; the fresh air will then enter at the center, and be diffused without causing draught.

Light. An abundant supply of light may, with one or two exceptions, be regarded as essential in the sick room. The exceptions are cases of eye disease and affections of the brain, when it becomes necessary to moderate the light admitted to the sick chamber. In most other instances the sun's rays must be looked upon as beneficial; they exert a great oxidizing power upon organic matters, and render them innocuous. The patient's bed should be so placed that he can easily see out of window. All lights employed for purposes of artificial illumination should be so placed that the eye does not suffer.

Temperature. A good fire in the sick room kept burning equally will suffice to maintain a uniform temperature, but care must be taken to see that the chimney is acting well. The temperature which answers best in the sick room in most cases is one about 60° Fahrenheit. It is well to regulate it by means of a thermometer. Should it be necessary to increase this, it can be done by permitting steam to pass into the room from a kettle: or if it is necessary to cool the air of the apartment, this can be readily accomplished by placing a shallow dish containing pieces of ice in the room or by suspending a piece of cloth that has been previously moistened with water.

Food. Food must be properly cooked and given at regular intervals to be determined by the nature of the case. Everything intended for the invalid's use should be made ready out of his sight and be brought on scrupulously clean dishes, and not too much at a time. Punctuality must be attended to, and strict quiet enjoined at meal times. (See special chapter on the subject).

Cleanliness. In the treatment of disease attention to cleanliness is of the utmost importance. If the sick room is carpeted it should be swept with a soft hair broom; if without carpet it can be gone over with sponges wrung out of hot water and dried by means of the floor brush. Damp cloths may be used instead of sponges. The articles of furniture may be dusted by means of damp cloths. The walls should be painted or whitewashed with lime. The body linen ought to be frequently changed and the hands and face washed daily. The hair should also be combed out at the same time. The body should also be frequently washed with a sponge or flannel and tepid water, only small portions being exposed at one time. It should be rapidly dried with a heated towel.

Tranquility. This is most essential to speedy recovery. Whispering is objectionable in the sick room; so also is talking outside the patient's door. All slamming of doors should be avoided. The room immediately over the sick room should, if possible, remain unoccupied. The admission of too many people into the sick room is another fruitful source of harm to a patient.

Influence of Mind on Body. Anything that weighs upon a patient's mind producing care or anxiety, exerts a depressing influence upon the nervous system and retards recovery. Everything of this kind should, therefore, be carefully guarded against. It is a part of the duties of those who wait upon the sick to cheer them and instil hope into their minds; otherwise fear may take possession of them and add to their danger.

Convalescence. This is that condition in which the period of active disease being at an end, the powers of nature are exerted toward repairing the waste of structure that has occurred during disease. During convalescence the greatest care is necessary, as relapses may occur and the disease end fatally, or it may assume a chronic form. It is now that the injudiciousness of friends begins to manifest itself, and unless firmness be exercised on the part of those in attendance, the patient may suffer through their mistaken kindness. One of the most frequent signs of returning health is the return of the patient's appetite, but it must be remembered that his desire for food should never be fully satisfied. The time which the patient must remain in bed varies in individual cases, and can only be satisfactorily determined by the medical attendant. When a person gets out of bed for the first time after a severe illness he is generally only allowed up for a short time, and the effect produced upon him must be carefully watched. The clothing of the patient should be warm and comfortable. A change to the seaside will often work wonders. During convalescence, if the patient is at all intellectually inclined, much pleasure may be given him by reading to him or by supplying him with literature of an interesting nature. A little more caution during convalescence than is usually found, and the chances of relapse occurring would be greatly lessened, an otherwise precarious time rendered comparatively safe, and the patient's recovery be made more permanent and complete.

Sick Nursing. All women are likely, at some period of their lives, to be called on to perform the duties of a sick nurse, and should prepare themselves as much as possible, by observation and reading, for the occasion when they may be required to fulfil the office. The main requirements are good temper, compassion for suffering, sympathy with sufferers, which most women worthy of the name possess, neat handedness, quiet manners, love of order, and cleanliness. With these qualifications there will be very little to be wished for; the desire to relieve suffering will inspire a thousand little attentions, and surmount the disgust which some of the offices attending the sick room are apt to create.

In the Sick Room

Where serious illness visits a household, and protracted nursing is likely to become necessary, a professional nurse will probably be engaged who has been trained to its duties; but in some families, and those not a few, let us hope, the ladies of the family would oppose such an arrangement as a failure of duty on their part. There is, besides, even when a professional nurse is ultimately called in, a period of doubt and hesitation, while disease has not yet developed itself, when the patient must be attended to; and, in these cases, some of the female servants of the establishment must give their attendance in the sick room. There are, also, slight attacks of cold, influenza, and accidents in a thousand forms, to which all are subject, where domestic nursing becomes a necessity; where disease, though unattended with danger, is nevertheless accompanied by the nervous irritation incident to illness, and when all the attention of the domestic nurse becomes necessary.

Doctor's Orders are never disregarded by a nurse worthy of the name. Should she by watching the case think any other treatment or diet would be beneficial to the patient, she should not act upon her own opinion, but state it to the doctor. She should always report to him any change she observes in the patient, which she should be watchful to detect. The hearty co-operation of a nurse is of incalculable help to a doctor.

Administering Medicine. Although this is given by medical advice, and at the time the doctor orders it as a rule, it sometimes happens that a bottle sent has only the indefinite directions such as "A dessertspoonful twice daily" or "A wineglassful every four hours," and in the case of an amateur being the nurse it may not be given at the best times.

When medicines have to be taken at intervals during the day, it is best to give it at first at 10 o'clock in the morning; if only once during the day, then at nine in the morning, or at bedtime; if twice, at 10 and 4 o'clock.

It is always safest to have a medicine glass marked with the different measures, for the size of the spoons may considerably vary in different households; and it cannot be too firmly impressed upon the nurse, whether professional or amateur, that regularity and exactitude in the administration of medicine are absolutely essential, the only deviation from the time fixed for it being made when the patient happens to be asleep at the specified hour.

Professional Nurses need not only the qualifications already named in addition to their training, they should be physically strong, have good health, nerves well under control, and be sure that nursing to them is a congenial occupation. What a friend or relative can do for one she holds dear in the time of sickness, the taxing of strength, the loss of sleep that she makes light of in such a case, is no proof that she is fitted for the post of a professional nurse. The very self-sacrifice is against this, for a nurse must do what she does in a business like way; she must not over-fatigue herself, should eat, drink and sleep well, and take regular exercise; while it should not be (as it is so often to the amateur) actual suffering to see pain inflicted when it is necessary that any operation be performed. She should be like the surgeon, able to think of the future good instead of the present suffering.

To some nervous, highly organized persons this would be impossible, and they are therefore unsuited for nursing as a business, although they may be the most devoted and patient attendants upon those they love.

In the First Stage of Sickness, while doubt and a little perplexity hang over the household as to the nature of the sickness, there are some things about which no doubts exist; the patient's room must be kept in a perfectly pure state, and arrangements made for proper attendance; for the first canon of nursing, according to Florence Nightingale, its apostle, is to "keep the air the patient breathes as pure as the external air, without chilling him." This can be done without any preparation which might alarm the patient; with proper windows, open fireplaces, and a supply of fuel, the room may be as fresh as it is outside, and kept at a temperature suitable for the patient's state.

Fomentations. Sometimes these are medicated and rendered more soothing by the addition of opiates, as in the well-known decoction of chamomile flowers and poppy heads, but the principal object for which they are employed is to convey warmth to a part. The best application of this kind is made by wringing flannel—by means of two sticks turned in opposite directions—out of boiling water, and then, shaking it up, apply it lightly to the part. In this way the heat may be retained for a considerable time. In order to do this thoroughly, two pieces of flannel should be made use of, each of the pieces being about three yards long, and having the ends sewn together so as to admit of the boiling water being wrung *out* of them. One of these should always be getting ready while the other is being applied. The coarser the flannel the more efficiently does it act; owing to its diminished power of conducting heat, warmth is longer retained.

Poultices. There are few applications more constantly in demand in sickness than poultices, and yet few people make them well. Poultices, when made well, should be sufficiently thick to retain their humidity, but not too thick, as they may then press injuriously upon the part to which they are applied. They should be of uniform consistence throughout, and ought to be applied at a proper temperature. This last can generally be ascertained by applying the poultice to the back of the hand or to the face before putting it to the part.

Linseed Meal Poultices. That which is of most frequent use is a poultice of linseed meal. It should be boiled till it is of the consistence of a thick pap when it will retain heat and moisture longer. Instead of using water alone a decoction of mallows may be employed, by which the emollient properties will be increased. The surface may be smeared with olive oil or lard. A piece of gauze may be applied over the surface of the poultice, if it is considered necessary to interpose anything between it and the skin.

Besides poultices made from linseed meal, there are others in frequent use, such as those made from bread and water, oatmeal, arrowroot, bran; and others, which are much less often employed, made from carrots, potatoes, onions, etc. In addition to these there are poultices more strictly medicated, such as those made of foxglove or hemlock. As these may prove dangerous if carelessly employed, they ought only to be made use of when ordered by the medical attendant.

Mustard Poultice. This is ordinarily made by sprinkling the surface of a linseed meal poultice with mustard, and covering it with muslin to retain the mustard in its place.

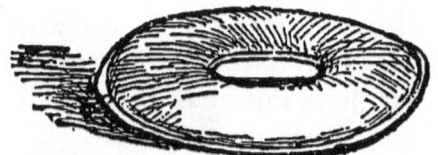

The Invalid's Air-cushion.

III

THE FAMILY DOCTOR

Prescriptions are herein found which apply to some of the cases mentioned in a preceding chapter, "What to Do in Case of Accident or Sudden Illness." They have been preserved, however, as they are more especially applicable to HOME TREATMENT *in general.*

Asthma. The attack most frequently comes on between one and three o'clock in the morning. The sufferer sits or stands up, leaning forward, and labors to breathe. The countenance is anxious, with pallor, coldness, and in severe cases, lividness of the face and hands. The attack may pass over in a few minutes, or may last for hours; or, with some remission, days or weeks. Death almost never occurs during the fit of asthma. Those subject to it often live to old age. But dilation of the pulmonary air-cells, and enlargement of the heart, may follow in protracted cases, breaking down the health. Asthma is hereditary in a majority of cases. Males have it more often than females. Smoke, fog, fumes of various things, ipecac, mustard, new hay may cause it. During the attack take the following: Take of wine of ipecac and tincture of lobelia, each a half a fluid ounce. Mix, and take one-half teaspoonful every half hour until expectoration or nausea occurs. Smoking tobacco relieves in some instances; smoking cigarettes of stramonium leaves in others, as also the inhalation of burning nitre paper.

As an adjuvant, the warm mustard foot bath may be employed, as well as mustard plaster or dry cupping applied between the shoulders. Take of nitre, half a drachm, powdered anise seed, half an ounce, powdered stramonium leaves, one ounce; mix, place a thimbleful in a plate, light it, and inhale the fumes. Between the attacks, take five grains of iodide of potassium three times a day. No disease is more curiously capricious in its causation than asthma. Some always have an attack if they visit the seashore; others are more secure there than elsewhere. Each must learn his own peculiarities, and be governed thereby. The climate of Colorado is said to possess a remarkable influence in promoting the amelioration and cure of asthma.

Biliousness. Take of ipecac, 3 grains; blue mass, 8 grains; compound extract of colocynth, 16 grains; mix, and divide into eight pills. Take one at night and morning. Generally in mild cases, two or three grains of blue mass at bedtime, followed in the morning by citrate of magnesia, or a seidlitz powder will give relief. The diet should be light, and fifteen grain doses of bicarbonate of soda should be taken twice a day for several days.

Bronchitis. It is an inflammation of the membrane lining the bronchial tubes. It may be acute or chronic, and affect the larger or smaller tubes, or both; or one or both lungs throughout, or only a portion of them. The causes are usually cold, damp, wet, exposure to vicissitudes of weather, inhalation of irritants, etc. Acute bronchitis may be dangerous in old persons and young children; seldom fatal in vigorous middle life. Chronic bronchitis is not often fatal, even by exhaustion, but it may last an indefinite time, even many months. Abortive treatment of a "cold on the chest" may sometimes be effected within the first twenty-four hours by taking at bedtime, a glass of hot lemonade, six grains of quinine, or ten grains of dover powder, after a warm mustard footbath. Should this treatment fail, and there be a dry imperspirable skin, a febrile state, cough and difficulty in breathing, and breast sore, frequent draughts of flaxseed tea should be taken, also a brisk saline purgative of epsom salt or Rochelle salts, or citrate of magnesia. A large mustard plaster should be applied to the chest, or frictions made with oil of turpentine. The following prescriptions will also give prompt relief: Take of tartar emetic, one grain; morphine sulphate, one grain; syrup of wild cherry two ounces; mix, take a teaspoonful every two or three hours. Syrup of ipecac ¼ or ½ teaspoonful doses every two or three hours, will also act well, and it should be continued until the cough softens, and the breathing becomes easier. When the expectoration is free, use the following cough mixture: Take of muriate of ammonia, 2 drachms; Brown's mixture, 4 ounces; mix; take a teaspoonful four times a day. Or any of the following cough mixtures: Take of syrup of squills, 5 ounces; paregoric, one ounce; mix; take a teaspoonful three or four times a day. Or the following domestic mixture: Take of molasses, ½ pint; rum, ½ pint; vinegar of squills, ½ gill; laudanum, 40 drops. Mix and take a dessertspoonful three times a day, half hour before meal. Or, carbonate of ammonia, 60 grains; spirits of chloroform 2 drachms; syrup of snakeroot, 2 ounces; water enough to make 6 ounces; mix, take a tablespoonful four times a day. If there be a history of gout or rheumatism, iodide of potassium and balsamic remedies should be taken. If there be debility and impoverishment of the blood, iron will assist the cure. In many cases, change to a warm climate may be distinctly indicated, as cold air is found to keep up and aggravate the lingering mischief. When bronchitis remains in a chronic form from sheer debility in the patient, the cod liver oil, syrup hypophosphites compound, and good food, are the measures which will be found most satisfactory.

Bruises. A bruise or contusion is an injury caused by a fall, a wrench, or a blow from a blunt instrument, without rupture of the skin. It is to be treated by keeping the part at rest, and cold or iced water, or a bladder containing ice should be applied at once. Hamamelis is also a good application. Should there be an inflammatory pain and swelling, apply leeches. To produce absorption of the effused fluids and restore the use of the parts, use friction with a stimulating liniment, and lastly apply a bandage. After tenderness has subsided, take of oil of turpentine, spirit of camphor, water of ammonia and olive oil, each two tablespoonfuls; mix well together, and rub externally.

Burns and Scalds. Collapse comes on from the terrible shock to the nervous system through the impression on the widely distributed cutaneous nerves. The pulse is then very low, the body cold, commonly thirst is great. The treatment for this prostrated condition must be stimulant as well as quieting. Whiskey or wine should be given as freely as in any other condition of positive debility or exhaustion. The patient's clothes should be gently and carefully removed, being cut wherever they are adherent to the body. If blisters have formed, they should be pricked and the serum let out, but the cuticle should on no account be detached. For a local application nothing is better than limewater and linseed oil, equal parts, well shaken, on cotton wadding, and covered with oil silk. When once the dressing has been applied, it should be changed as seldom as possible—indeed, only where the discharges render such change absolutely necessary. In this way, the repair goes on most favorably, and the patient is saved from much pain and distress. If the burn is deep, this treatment should be followed for a few days, and then poultices should be applied. When the sloughs have separated, the wound should be treated with a weak solution of carbolic acid until cicatrization is complete.

Catarrh. An inflammation of a mucous membrane, especially of the air passages of the head and throat, with an exudation on its free surface.

Treatment.—Simple but effective. Take one ounce each of fine salt, pulverized borax and baking soda, mix thoroughly together and dissolve in one-half pint of water. To use take one tablespoonful of the solution to two or three of warm water, and snuff up the head at bedtime. The salt stimulates, the borax cleanses and heals, and the soda soothes; use soft water.

Cholera. (Asiatic or Epidemic Cholera.) This last disease seems to have been known in India for centuries, and to have its natural home or headquarters in the Delta of the Ganges. In this country the disease has almost always prevailed in its worst form, in poor, crowded dwellings, among those whose food supply was bad and whose hygienic conditions were otherwise unfavorable; but especially among those who had a tainted supply of water. Very frequently when cholera prevails, diarrhœa also does.

In a case of ordinary intensity, the disease is ushered in by an attack of diarrhœa. This may last a longer or shorter period, but speedily the matters passed by the bowel assume a flocculent or rice-water character. Vomiting, too, comes on, the fluid being thin and colorless. Then follow severe cramps, especially of the abdominal muscles and legs. The flow of urine ceases, the body becomes icy cold on the surface, the tongue is cold, and so even is the breath. The lips are blue and shriveled, the face pinched, the voice is hardly audible. This is called the cold or algid state of the disease. The condition may go on getting worse till the heart stops the patient being quite conscious to the end. Frequently it is impossible to tell whether the patient is to live or die, when suddenly the sickness lessens, the body begins to get warm, the face flushes, and restlessness subsides. The patient seems on the very verge of getting well. But sometimes the urine does not flow, or there may be congestion of the lungs or brain, and so, though reaction has set in, the man may yet perish. Thus, in an ordinary mild case of cholera, a man will pass through three stages: Firstly, that of premonitory diarrhœa; secondly, that of collapse; and thirdly, that of reaction, probably in about forty-eight hours.

The disease is produced by some particular poison, which may be transmitted through the air, by water, or communicated by one individual to another. There can be no doubt that the discharges are one main source of this poison, and hence should be most carefully disinfected.

He who would avoid cholera during a cholera season ought to live by rule and method. First, see that his water closets are in good order, and that every precaution is taken in cleansing and disinfecting them. Any good carbolic acid powder answers very well for this purpose. See that the house is clean, sweet and airy; let no foul and decaying matters remain upon the premises. See that the water supply is pure. Let no stale meat or vegetables, no sausage, game or substances likely to create digestive disturbance be used; avoid unripe fruit, prolonged abstinence from food, and excessive fatigue. Avoid strong aperient medicines of every kind. The astringents to be used should not be powerful; chalk mixture, sulphuric acid, lemonade, or these with a little opium added, are best.

No Diarrhœa in Cholera time is to be Neglected. Try to keep up the bodily heat in every way that will not disturb or fatigue the patient. The patient is consumed with thirst and there is no reason for refusing him drink if it is of a wholesome kind. Should reaction occur he must be kept quiet. If his head troubles him, and his face is flushed, apply cold water to it. If there is much sickness, let him have a little ice or ice water. If his lungs get gorged, warm poultices or turpentine stupes will be best. But the great anxiety is the kidneys. If they do not act, warmth must be tried, perhaps as a warm bath, but this requires caution. If they are acting well and the patient requires a stimulant, let him have some sal volatile. The food given is of especial importance; broths, soups and jellies may be given, but certainly not meat. Small quantities must be given at a time, and repeated as frequently as necessary.

One of the greatest dangers in the disease is the collapse produced by the extraction of the water from the system. To counteract this, salt water is sometimes injected into the veins. This, of course, should not be done except by a physician or surgeon. Almost equally efficient, however, are methods which can be used by any one in safety.

As a result of the extraction of the water the blood flows less freely, the hands and feet and ears first begin to get cold and purple, the temperature of the body falls, sometimes alarmingly. If now the patient is put in a bath tub, and kept there with only his head out of the water, and the water is kept at a temperature of 100 degrees to 102 degrees Fahrenheit, further loss of heat will be prevented, and the system will absorb some water from the bath. The temperature of the patient must be kept up as near normal as possible. Perhaps a bath like this is not obtainable. If so, the use of a hot pack may be a good substitute, wrapping the patient in sheets wrung out of hot water and covering him thoroughly with woolen blankets. An old way of using the hot pack consisted in boiling a lot of corn on the ear, and packing the hot corn all around the patient. Hot bottles and water bags are better than nothing, but in this case moist heat is better than dry heat.

The blood must not be allowed to stagnate. To prevent this the extremities should be rubbed firmly *toward the body*. Don't simply chafe the skin, but grasp the hand or foot firmly and press the blood along toward the heart.

Asphyxia is often found in the disease, the lungs being collapsed and emptied of air. To counteract this condition prompt and intelligent action, as if to resuscitate a drowning person. Place the patient upon his back, with a small pillow under the small of the back. Place yourself at his head, and grasping both his elbows, raise the arms alongside the patient's head. This expands the chest. Then force the elbows against the chest and express the air. This should be done about fifteen times a minute. The action should be strong, regular, and not sudden or jerking. At the same time the bodily heat must be preserved.

The judicious use of alcohol internally is of great assistance in the collapsed stage, but it is often abused.

There is relatively little danger of the spread of the disease from the exhaled breath or from the urine. The danger is great from the discharges from the bowels. It is found that the bacteria are less strong and less prolific when first discharged. After standing a little time they are very prolific and hard to kill.

Discharges should therefore be passed into a solution of corrosive sublimate (proportion 1 to 1,000) or into a 4 per cent. solution of carbolic acid, to which has been added a little sulphuric acid. Even with these precautions they should not be allowed to remain in the room. They should, if possible, be burned. Under no condition should they be cast into the sewers without previous disinfection. Neither should a surface or dry closet be used.

Absolute rest is demanded to preserve the strength of the patient, and prevent the rapid exhaustion. In fact, fatigue is one of the strong, predisposing causes of the disease. When exhausted by work or worry, and especially when the nervous system is exhausted, a person otherwise proof against the disease will quickly fall under exposure.

Cholera. (Asiatica.) Sir Edwin Arnold, who has spent much time in India and other countries where cholera is more or less prevalent at all times, has this to say of that dread disease: "No well or prudent man should fear the disease. Just go about as usual, and don't think of it. Why, I have seen so much of it, and been so close to it, that I have not the slightest fear of it. I'll tell you my own preventive, which I have used in India with the very best results. The cholera bacillus does not like acid. He can't stand it at all. So every other morning, when the cholera actually appears, I would take, if I were you, five drops of hydrochloric acid in a cup of tea. You will find it excellent as a preventive, if you are also careful in your habits of life. I don't believe in quarantine."

Here is another effective cure for cholera, dysentery, flux in its worst stages. Some years ago 50,000 people died in Constantinople in fifty days. The following receipt is taken from the report of our missionaries, who had 200 cases under their care, and did not lose a single case: One-quarter of an ounce of tincture of laudanum, one-quarter of an ounce of tincture of camphor, one-quarter of an ounce of tincture of capsicum, one-quarter of an ounce of tincture of cardamom, one-quarter of an ounce of tincture of ginger, one-eighth of an ounce of peppermint. Dose, fifteen drops in half tumbler of water; a swallow of this every fifteen or twenty minutes until relieved. And now, we add:

A Few More Words of General Advice. Do not unnecessarily visit cholera patients or cholera houses; receive no visitors from cholera regions. It is best to avoid large gatherings or even schools during cholera times.

Do not handle or use any food coming from a house where cholera exists; in case of any possible doubt whether the food comes from where the disease exists, it should be boiled or cooked. This applies particularly to milk. As milk can but rarely be traced to its source, all milk should be boiled. Ten minutes' actual boiling kills the cholera germs without **fail.**

Cholera Morbus. It generally occurs during warm weather. The direct causes are indigestible articles of food, as unripe fruit, etc., sudden change of temperature, checking perspiration, excess of ordinary food. A large mustard plaster should be applied over the stomach, and followed by a spice poultice, of ginger, cloves, and cinnamon, each a full teaspoonful, with a tablespoonful of flour moistened with whiskey. Ice is good to relieve thirst. Internally give: Take of aromatic spirit of ammonia, one drachm; calcined magnesia, one drachm; peppermint water, four ounces. Mix; take a teaspoonful every twenty minutes until relieved. Should there be much diarrhœa, add to the above two drachms of paregoric, and omit the magnesia. Give brandy or whiskey if there should be much prostration.

Cholera Infantum, popularly known as "summer complaint" is very destructive to children during the hot weather. The period of dentition is particularly liable to this disorder; it seldom occurs after two or three years of age. In the early stage, these powders will be found quite useful: Take of calomel, two grains; bicarbonate of sodium, one scruple; powder of ginger, twelve grains; mix, and divide into twelve powders, and give one three of four times a day. Or take of mercury with chalk and powder of cinnamon each twelve grains; mix, and divide into twelve powders. Give one three times a day. To check diarrhœa, give this: Take of tincture of krameria, paregoric, each a fluid drachm; sugar and gum arabic, each ½ drachm; cinnamon water enough to make two fluid ounces; mix, and give a teaspoonful every two, three or four hours. The food should be limewater and fresh milk, arrowroot, farina, chicken water, and beef tea. So long as vomiting continues, keep over the stomach a spice poultice wet with brandy. Ice may be given to quench thirst.

Chronic Rheumatism is most common in those advanced in age, although any one may have this affection. It is a sort of slow inflammation of the fibrous tissues, investing the joints and muscles, following exposure to cold and wet. The thighs especially exposed to the rain during a stormy ride are the common seats of chronic rheumatic pains. If the pains are restricted to the collar-bone, humerus, and the shin, they suggest the probability of a syphilitic factor. One thing pretty certain in cases of chronic rheumatism is that they are almost invariably accompanied by an inactive condition of the skin. Consequently, a distinct part in the treatment is to make use of those remedies which act on the skin, and known in medical term as diaphoretics. Guaiac is perhaps the most typical of these. Muriate of ammonia is another They form an excellent combination in the rheumatism of young men and women: Take of muriate of ammonia, two drachms; guaiacum mixture, eight ounces; mix, and take a tablespoonful three or four times a day. Whenever there is a history of exposure in elderly persons, especially associated with florid complexion, the following prescription forms a capital remedy: Take of bicarbonate of potash, two and one-half drachms; iodide of potassium, four scruples; guaiacum mixture, eight ounces. Mix, and take a tablespoonful three or four times a day. At the same time, the skin must be kept warm and covered with flannel. Warm drinks are always indicated, and should largely take the place of solid food. Another prescription which is often useful is the following: Take of nitrate of potassium, an ounce and one-half; sulphur an ounce; guaiacum half an ounce; add two nutmegs, and a half pint of molasses; mix. Take a teaspoonful or two at night. In addition to the general measures, it is customary to use local applications; they generally do more good than medicine. They consist of hot irons, plasters and liniments. Take of oil of sassafras two fluid drachms; water of ammonia, a tablespoonful; camphorated soap liniment, three fluid ounces; mix, use as liniment. Should the pain be considerable, chloroform or aconite liniment may be applied. Blisters are sometimes advisable in bad cases.

Chronic Ulcers. The treatment should consist in taking internally a tonic mixture, as this: Take of iodide of potassium, three drachms; Fowler solution, one drachm, compound syrup of sarsaparilla, four ounces; water enough to make eight ounces. Mix; take a teaspoonful three times a day. The ulcer should be treated locally with this ointment: Iodoform, one drachm; vaseline, one ounce. Mix; use in a thin layer every night. A light woolen bandage should be applied over it, and the parts cleansed with tar-soap, and the sore dressed every night.

Cold in the Head. Use the following snuff: Muriate of morphine, two grains; powdered gum arabic, two drachms; subnitrate of bismuth, six drachms; mix.

Colic. There are several varieties of colic. The flatulent, the bilious, the spasmodic, gouty or rheumatic, the lead colic. The flatulent colic is usually caused by indigestion. If the stomach is overloaded, an emetic will be proper; a teaspoonful of mustard, or a tablespoonful of salt in a teacupful of warm water, repeated in ten minutes if necessary; then give a teaspoonful of magnesia with twenty drops of essence of ginger. Should the stomach be much unsettled and the pain violent, warm fomentations should be applied over the bowels, a mustard plaster over the pit of the stomach, and the following given: Take of bicarbonate of sodium, 1 drachm; aromatic spirit of ammonia, 1 drachm; paregoric, 4 drachms; peppermint water, 3½ ounces; mix, take a teaspoonful every twenty minutes until relieved. Infants are especially liable to crapulent colic. Very simple treatment will often suffice for these. Peppermint water or infusion of fennel seed will frequently be enough, with the application of a warm flannel over the stomach; wetting it with essence of ginger will make it more efficient. The following will not fail to give prompt relief in worse cases: Take of bicarbonate of sodium, ½ drachm; aromatic spirit of ammonia, ½ drachm, syrup of ginger, ½ fluid ounce; camphor water, enough to make two fluid ounces, mix. Dose, a teaspoonful, repeated if necessary. Keeping the bowels regular, never allowing a day to pass without an evacuation is most important in young children. For this purpose, the simple syrup of rhubarb, manna, are the best medicines. Overfeeding an infant is a very common cause of colic. In bilious colic, the bowels shoud be opened; if the stomach will bear it, castor oil is the most effectual cathartic. Magnesia is also good. The same line of treatment may be pursued as the one given above for flatulent colic. If there is reason to believe that the passage of a gall stone is the cause of the severe pain, the warm bath will be useful to promote relaxation. Phosphate of sodium is a good solvent of biliary stones. It can be taken in drachm doses three times a day. In gouty, or rather cramps of the stomach, Warner's cordial is good, taken in teaspoonful to tablespoonful doses in hot water. Essence of ginger, 10 drops, or oil of cajuput, 5 or 6 drops, on a lump of sugar often gives immediate relief.

Lead colic must be treated with epsom salts. Castor oil as a purgative, the warm bath to relax spasm, and 10 to 20 drops of laudanum to relieve pain and spasm. A milk diet is recommended in this affection.

Constipation. There is no more frequent source of bodily discomfort than constipation of the bowels. The principal causes are neglect of timely attendance upon the calls of nature, want of exercise, excess of mental strain, and all the causes of dyspepsia, of which it is an almost constant part. Fresh and stewed fruits are the best natural laxatives. Prunes are especially opening. The following prescriptions will be found quite useful. In mild forms: **Take of rhubarb**

root and Castile soap each, half a drachm; oil of anise, four drops; mix, and divide into twenty pills. Take one or two as required. Or, take of rhubarb, Castile soap and compound extract of colocynth, each half a drachm; mix and divide into twenty pills. Take one or two as required. In obstinate constipation, take of rhubarb two scruples, aloes, one scruple, extract of nux vomica, four grains; mix, and divide into twenty pills. Take one as needed. Habitual constipation occasions great distress, and produces grave morbid changes in the organs of assimilation, lungs, heart and nerves. Take of rhubarb and aloes each, one-half drachm; extract of belladonna, three grains; oil of cloves, three drops; mix, and make twenty pills. Take one twice daily. Or, take of aloes and sulphate of iron, of each, one scruple; make twenty pills, and take one twice a day. Cascara Sagrada lozenges, two at bedtime, are also most effectual. Or, take of Epsom salt, four ounces, dilute sulphuric acid, four drachms, sulphate of iron, sixty grains, water, two pints; mix, and take a tablespoonful before breakfast. A most useful prescription for women habitually constipated. Oxgall sometimes is invaluable, as follows: Oxgall, thirty grains, willow charcoal, pulverized, sixty grains, solid extract nux vomica, five grains; mix, make thirty-six pills. One at bedtime. But better than to take medicines every day or two will be the use of an injection of warm water, white soap, salt and molasses; sweet or castor oil, or glycerine may be added. A suppository of soap is less disagreeable to some persons, and will generally act well. It is made by cutting a piece of good yellow soap to the shape, and rather less than the size of the last joint of the little finger. Dip it in castor oil, or olive oil, or lard, and introduce it within the rectum. But after all, rational attention should be paid to diet, exercise, bathing, massage, accompanied by regularity in going to stool to solicit movements.

Consumption. Consumption may begin after a severe acute bronchitis or broncho-pneumonia, or more gradually, with an apparently slight hacking cough, or with a hemorrhage, or with dyspepsia and general debility. Increasing, in most cases slowly, the pectoral and constitutional disorder becomes developed. We have, then, pains in the chest, frequent and severe cough, hemorrhage occasionally, and pallor, hectic fever with bright flush of cheek, emaciation, arrest of menstruation in the female, night sweats and diarrhœa, lastly death, mostly by exhaustion, but sometimes by suffocation. The spirits of the patients are apt to be cheerful, even hopeful of life almost to the last. In advanced consumption, the cheeks are hollow, the bones prominent, the skin arid, the nose sharpened and drawn, the eyes sunken, there is a most afflicting cough, sore throat, difficult deglutition, and feeble, whispering voice, or entire extinction of the voice. Consumption is certainly one of the most destructive of diseases. About one-fourth of all deaths occurring in the human family during adult life is caused by it, and nearly one-half of the entire population at some time in life acquires it. It has been proven beyond a doubt that a living germ, called the tubercle bacillus, is the cause and the only cause of consumption. It does not seem necessary to state the facts upon which this assertion is based, for the observation first made by Robert Koch in 1882 has been confirmed so often and so completely, that it now constitutes one of the most absolutely demonstrated facts in medicine. When the living germs find their way into the lungs, they multiply there, if favorable conditions for their growth exist, and produce small new growths or nodules (tubercles) which tend to soften. The discharge from these softened tubercles, containing the living germs, are thrown off from the body. These discharges constitute, in part, the expectoration. The germs thus thrown off do not grow outside the living body, except under artificial conditions, although they may retain their vitality and virulence for long periods of time, even when thoroughly dried. As tuberculosis (or consumption) can only result from the action of these germs, it follows that when the disease is acquired, it must result from receiving into the body the living germs that have come from some other human being, or animal affected with the disease. It has been abundantly established that the disease may be transmitted by meat or milk ftom the tubercular animals. The milk glands in milch cows often become affected with the disease when their lungs are involved, and the milk from such animals may contain the living germs, and is capable of producing the disease. Among stall-fed dairy cows, twenty or thirty per cent. are sometimes found to be affected with the disease. Tubercular animals are also frequently killed for food; their flesh sometimes contains the germs, and if not thoroughly cooked, is capable of transmitting the disease. Boiling the milk, or thoroughly cooking the meat destroys the germs.

Consumption is commonly **produced by** breathing air in which living germs are **suspended** as dust. The material which is coughed up, sometimes in large quantities, by persons suffering from consumption, contains these germs often in enormous numbers. This material, when expectorated, frequently lodges where it afterward dries, as on the streets, floors, carpets, clothing, handkerchiefs, etc. After drying, in one way or another, it is very apt to become pulverized and float in the air as dust. The observations made by prominent physicians have shown that where there are cases of pulmonary tuberculosis, under ordinary conditions, the dust surrounding them often contains the tubercle bacilli and persons inhaling the air in which this dust is suspended may be taking in the living germs. However, the breath of tuberculous persons, and the moist sputum, received in proper cups, are not elements of danger, but only the dried and pulverized sputum. The breath and moist sputum are free from danger, because the germs are not dislodged from moist surfaces by currents of air. If all discharges were destroyed at the time of exit from the body, the greatest danger of communication from man to man would be removed. It is a well known fact that some persons, and especially the members of certain families, are particularly liable to consumption, and this liability can be transmitted from parents to children. So marked and so frequent is this liability, and so frequent is the development of the disease in particular families, that the affection has long been considered hereditary. We now know that consumption can only be caused by the entrance of the germ into the body, and that this transmitted liability simply rendered the individual a more easy prey to the living germs when once they had gained entrance. The frequent occurrence of several cases of consumption in a family, is then to be explained, not on the supposition that the disease itself has been inherited, but that it has been produced after birth by transmission directly from some affected individual.

Hygienic management is decidedly more important to the consumptive than medicine. An eminent physician has well laid down the following precepts: "A supply of pure and fresh air for respiration is constantly required by the consumptive patient. Daily exercise in the open air is imperatively demanded by the tuberculous patient. It is important to secure for the patient a uniform, sheltered, temperate and mild climate, about 60° and a range of not more than 10° or 15°, where, also, the soil is dry and the drinking water pure and not hard. The dress of the consumptive ought to be of such a kind as to equalize and retain the temperature of the body. The hours of rest should extend from sunset to sunrise. Indoor or sedentary occupation must be suspended, but outdoor employment in the fresh air has been and may be advantageous. Cleanliness of the body is a special point to be attended to in the hygienic treatment of consumption. Marriage of consumptive females for the sake of arresting disease by pregnancy, is morally wrong and physically mischievous. If the consumption is not inherited, the question of prevention resolves itself principally, into the avoidance of tubercular meat and milk, and the destruction of the discharges, especially the sputum of consumptive individuals. Wooden or pasteboard cups with covers should always be at hand for the reception of the sputum. These cups should be thrown, at least once a day, with their contents, into the fire. Or the spittle should be caught in earthen or glass dishes containing a solution of one part of corrosive sublimate and 1,000 parts of water. No one should sleep in a room occupied by a person suspected of having consumption. The living rooms of a consumptive patient should have as little furniture as practicable. Hangings should be especially avoided. The use of carpets, rugs, etc., ought always to be avoided. Rooms in private houses that are occupied by phthisical patients should from time to time be thoroughly cleaned and disinfected, and this should always be done after they are vacated, before they are again occupied by other individuals. The eating utensils of a person suspected of having consumption should be thoroughly washed as soon after eating as possible, using boiling water for the purpose. The unwashed clothing of consumptive patients should not be mingled with similar clothing of other persons. The bowel discharges of a consumptive patient with diarrhœa should be caught in a vessel containing corrosive sublimate one part, water 1,000 parts. Mothers suspected of having consumption should not nurse their offspring. Household pets (animals or birds) are quite susceptible to tuberculosis; therefore they should not be exposed to persons afflicted with consumption. Also, all household pets suspected of having consumption should not be kept, but destroyed at once, otherwise they may give it to human beings. It is then, very important that the people should have a full knowledge of the fact that every consumptive person may be a source of actual danger to his associates, if the discharges from the lung are not immediately destroyed or rendered harmless, and also that the rooms that are occupied by phthisical persons should be thoroughly disinfected. Although no specific has as yet been discovered which will cure consumption, yet many cases are on record which have recovered, or at least, the disease has been arrested. Cod liver oil, whiskey, quinine and iron should never be omitted. They always do good.

When the expectoration is copious and fluid, and there are night sweats and general exhaustion, the following prescription should be taken: Take of beechwood creosote one drachm, syrup of hypophosphites compound, three ounces; mix, and take a teaspoonful three times a day after meals. This prescription, even when taken early, has repeatedly arrested the disease. Expectorants and cough mixtures require discretion in their use; however, should the cough be troublesome, take the following: Syrup of wild cherry, and syrup of lactucarium, each two fluid ounces; mix; take a dessertspoonful or two at night, or one or two teaspoonfuls in the daytime. Should there occur any hemorrhage *from the lungs*, the patient ought to be kept in bed, with the shoulders somewhat raised, and only iced milk and beef essence, or beef tea should be given for food. The popular remedy of holding salt in the mouth may be of some temporary use. Slowly melting and swallowing ice will probably do more good. Gallic acid in ten grain doses every two or three hours is a very effective remedy. Change of climate is often proposed for the benefit of the consumptive. In selecting this, equability and dryness are more important than warmth. That climate which allows the patient the greatest number of days out of doors will be the best. Minnesota, and other places near Lake Superior, agree extremely well with some, in the *early*, but not so well in the later stages of the disease. Of southern localities, Florida (best of all, its central pine lands) presents an especially equable, almost maritime, climate. Santa Barbara and San Diego in Southern California are also much recommended for the colder half of the year.

Diarrhœa. Diarrhœa may be a salutary process, or an ailment serious enough to endanger life. Mucous discharges occur in inflammation of the bowels and in many cases of summer diarrhœa. Bilious passages occur in cholera morbus, serous or rice water, in Asiatic cholera, bloody discharges in dysentery. In its treatment, an important point is that in many cases it should not be abruptly checked; in some cases not interfered with at all. When the motion is preceded by severe griping pain, ceasing with the evacuation of the acrid and offensive matter, take a tablespoonful of the following after each motion: Prepared chalk, two drachms, tincture of catechu, two drachms, laudanum, 40 drops, cinnamon water, four ounces. When the motions are loose and copious, take of laudanum, one drachm, dilute sulphuric acid, two drachms, infusion of logwood, four ounces; mix, take a tablespoonful four or six times a day. When it is accompanied with cramps, take a teaspoonful of the following every hour until relieved: Spirits of chloroform, half an ounce, tincture capsicum, one drachm, syrup of ginger, two ounces. When the diarrhœa is **chronic and hemorrhagic**, take of powdered **gum arabic,**

one and one-half ounces, oil of turpentine, two ounces, water, three ounces, simple syrup enough to make twelve ounces; mix, and take a teaspoonful every three hours.

Digestion of Food.

The following table shows the time required for the digestion of the more common articles of food:

Kind of Food.	Hr.	Min.	Kind of Food.	Hrs.	Min.
Rice, boiled.............	1	..	Eggs, soft boiled......	3	..
Eggs, whipped	1	30	Beefsteaks, broiled....	3	..
Trout, fresh, fried.....	1	30	Mutton, boiled........	3	..
Soup, barley, boiled...	1	30	Mutton, broiled.......	3	..
Apples, sweet, raw. ...	1	30	Soup, bean, boiled.....	3	..
Venison steak, broiled..	1	45	Chicken soup, boiled...	3	..
Sago, boiled..	1	45	Pork, salt, broiled.....	3	15
Tapioca, boiled........	2	..	Mutton, roasted........	3	15
Barley, boiled.........	2	..	Bread, corn, baked.....	3	15
Milk, boiled..........	2	..	Carrots, boiled	3	15
Liver, beef, broiled....	2	..	Sausage, broiled.......	3	20
Eggs, fresh, raw.......	2	..	Oysters, stewed........	3	30
Apples, sour, raw....	2	..	Butter................	3	30
Cabbage, raw.	2	..	Cheese, old...........	3	30
Milk..................	2	15	Bread, fresh, baked....	3	30
Eggs, roasted.........	2	15	Turnips, flat, boiled ..	3	30
Goose, roasted........	2	15	Potatoes, Irish, boiled..	3	30
Turkey, roasted.......	2	30	Eggs, hard boiled......	3	30
Cake, sponge, baked...	2	30	Green corn, boiled.....	3	45
Hash, warmed	2	30	Beans and beets, boiled.	3	45
Beans, pod, boiled...	2	30	Salmon, salted, boiled..	4	..
Parsnips, boiled.......	2	30	Veal, fresh, fried......	4	30
Potatoes, Irish, baked..	2	30	Cabbage, boiled........	4	30
Custard, baked........	2	50	Suet, beef, boiled......	5	30
Oysters, raw	2	55			

Dropsy. Take of bruised juniper berries, mustard seed, and ginger, each half an ounce, bruised horseradish and parsley root, each an ounce, sound old cider, a quart; infuse. Dose, a wineglassful three times a day.

Dysentery. Rest is important. The diet must be bland, as ricewater, arrowroot, or other farinacea; beef tea. When thirst is intense, iced ice water; infusion of slippery elm bark may be used as a drink. At the very start, a dose of castor oil with 10 or 15 drops of laudanum will do very well, and follow with these pills: Blue mass and powder of ipecac of each, 12 grains; mix, and divide into 12 pills. Take one every three hours. Or, take of camphor, 18 grains; ipecac, 6 grains; opium, 3 grains; mix, and divide into 12 pills. Take one every three or four hours. When astringents are needed, a good pill is the following: Acetate of lead, 12 grains; opium 3 grains. Mix, and make twelve pills, and take one every three hours. Or, take of Dover's powder, 1 drachm; tannin ½ drachm; mix, and divide into twelve powders. Take one every four or five hours. Five grains of bismuth may also be added to each dose. The tincture of witch-hazel in two to five drops, doses every two hours, may be taken when the discharges are bloody. Should they be bloody and slimy, use the following: Take of corrosive sublimate, 1 grain; distilled water, ½ pint. Take a teaspoonful every hour or two. Injections are very important in dysentery. Two or four ounces of flaxseed tea with one or two ounces of starch, thin enough to be drawn into a small syringe, with 20 drops of laudanum, should be injected into the bowel. For children use the following: Take of castor oil, 1 drachm; powdered gum arabic, 20 grains; laudanum, 4 drops; simple syrup, 1 drachm; orange flower water, 6 drachms; mix, and give a teaspoonful every three hours.

Dyspepsia. It is generally caused by too much food or too little food; imperfect mastication, and hurry in eating; too little exercise; too much fatigue; excessive study or emotional excitement; inordinate use of ardent spirits, opium, tobacco, coffee, or of medicine out of place. The patient feels his stomach all the time, though not always in pain. The mouth is clammy, or has a sour or bitter taste. The complexion is more or less sallow. The bowels are costive. There is heartburn, waterbrash, hypochondria, palpitation of the heart, etc.

In the treatment of this affection, correct diet is the most important. The meals should be regular, and with sufficient time allowed. Beef, mutton, chicken, turkey, stale bread, crackers. Exercise in the open air is important, as is also bathing. The medical treatment needs tonics, laxatives, and antacids. The following prescriptions will be found quite effective: Take of compound tincture of gentian, tincture of rhubarb, each 2 ounces. Mix; take two teaspoonfuls before meals.

Or, take of dilute muriatic acid 2 drachms; pepsin, 4 drachms; syrup of orange peel, 2 ounces; water 6 ounces. Mix, and take half tablespoonful with every meal.

Or, take of elixir quinine, iron and arsenic, 4 ounces; take a teaspoonful after each meal.

Or, take of subnitrate of bismuth, 320 grains; tincture of nux vomica, 3 drachms; mucilage of gum arabic, 4 ounces. Mix, and take a teaspoonful three times a day.

Where there is much nervous debility, anæmia, and particularly in cases of long standing, use the following pills: Take of pill of carbonate of iron, 2 scruples; sulphate of quinine, 1 scruple; alcoholic extract of nux vomica, 5 grains; Mix, and divide into 20 pills, and take one thrice daily.

Epilepsy. Several great men have suffered from this disease: Cæsar, Mahomet, Petrarch, Newton, Peter the Great, Napoleon, Byron. Hereditary transmission of this disease is common. Intemperance, venereal excess and self abuse, blows on the head, and fright, are among the most frequent exciting causes. During the attack, when habitual, little or nothing is to be done. Place the patient so that he cannot strike his head or limbs against anything hard, loosen the clothing about the neck to favor free respiration and circulation, and insure fresh air about the patient; that is all. The inhalation of five drops of nitrite of amyl upon a cloth is said to ward off an attack. So simple an expedient as pulling the great toe is also said to often arrest an attack. To break up the recurrence of the fits is the problem for which a vast number of remedies have been tried. The preference, however, is given to the bromide of potassium and ammonium, 10 grains of each, three times a day. The following is the prescription largely used in his practice by the celebrated Brown-Sequard: Take of iodide of potassium, 1 drachm; bromide of potassium, 1 ounce; bromide of ammonium, 2½ drachms; bicarbonate of potassium, 2 scruples; tincture of columbo, 1 fluid ounce; water, 5 fluid ounces; dissolve. Dose, a teaspoonful with little water, before each meal. If the case is very bad, three teaspoonfuls are also taken at bedtime.

Facial Neuralgia and Hysteria. Take of croton chloral hydrate, 2 drachms; glycerine, 2 ounces; water, 2 ounces. Mix; take a teaspoonful three times a day. If symptoms are urgent, take a teaspoonful every two hours until pain is relieved.

Frost Bite: Chilblain. Gangrenous destruction of part, especially of toes, not infrequently follows actual congealation. When the feet or other parts have been so chilled as to be almost frozen, gradual warming—for instance, at first rubbing them with snow—is proper as a prevention of frosting. In its treatment, cooling ointments as Goulard's cerate or lotions of lead water, may be first indicated, and then astringents, as alum water, infusion of oak bark, creosote ointment, etc. Cabbage leaves are a popular domestic remedy for chilblains.

Frost Bitten Fingers and Toes. Take of dilute nitric acid and peppermint water, equal parts. Mix; paint surface. After three or four days, the skin becomes dark, the epidermis is shed, and a healthy skin appears underneath.

Gout greatly resembles rheumatism. It is caused by

high living, with indolent habits. An excess of animal food with scanty exercise will produce it. Strong wines and malt liquors much increase the tendency. Weak wines do not seem to have the same effect. Hereditary transmission of the gouty constitution is very common. Premonition of a gouty spell is often witnessed for some days, with symptoms of indigestion, flatulence, acidity, constipation, and palpitation of the heart. Then a joint becomes very painful, swollen, red and tender; in the majority of cases, the great toe is affected. Other toes, the fingers, ankle, wrist, or knee may be attacked; the large joints least often. The suffering with the gouty inflammation is often very intense, but its duration is not commonly more than a few days at a time. In treating this affection, cold locally applied should be absolutely avoided. More than one death has occurred from this, by repulsion of the disorder to the heart, stomach or brain. Laudanum may be safely applied to the part, by wetting a piece of linen or muslin with it, laying it on the painful joint, and covering it with oil silk. Oil of horse-chestnut has also been recommended. Either of the following prescriptions will give relief: Take of wine of colchicum root, 1 fluid drachm; Husband's magnesia, 1 drachm; peppermint water, 4 fluid ounces. Mix; take a tablespoonful thrice daily. Or, take of wine of colchicum root, 1 fluid drachm; bicarbonate of potash and Rochelle salts, each 2½ drachms; peppermint water, 4 fluid ounces. Mix; take a tablespoonful thrice daily. Or, take of carbonate of potash and nitrate of potash, each 2½ drachms; water, 8 fluid ounces; dissolve. Take a tablespoonful thrice daily. Regulation of the diet is of primary importance. But it should not be too low, especially when the patient's habits have been those of a free liver. Exercise in proportion to strength should be recommended. The state of the skin, as well as of the bowels is important. Change of air, traveling, and mineral waters are generally useful during the intervals between the attacks. Alkaline springs and baths, such as those of Vichy in France, Ems in Germany, or Gettysburg in Pennsylvania, have an especial reputation as a prophylactic against gout.

Healing Ointment. Take of vaseline, citrine ointment, each one ounce, subnitrate of bismuth, one drachm; mix, apply. Useful in various ulcers, old sores, etc.

Heartburn. Calcined magnesia, or bicarbonate of sodium will give temporary relief. Steep gentian root and horseradish in good whisky enough to cover, and use in tablespoonful doses; or, take of tincture of nux vomica, two drachms, compound tincture of cinchona, two ounces; mix, and take a teaspoonful three times a day.

Heatstroke. It is almost always, in the case of heat exhaustion, those who have been fatigued by exertion in the sun or shade who are overcome. Drinking largely of cold water when thus exhausted, increases the danger. Intemperate persons are particularly liable to heatstroke. Genuine sunstroke is commonly sudden. Falling unconscious, the head is very hot, the temporal arteries distended, the breathing is apt to be snoring, the pulse full, generally rapid, but in few instances slow. In severe cases, convulsions may precede death. In heatstroke, almost equal suddenness marks the attack. Unconsciousness is less complete, and without snoring of breathing; the whole condition resembles fainting rather than apoplexy. For heat apoplexy cupping or leeching the back of the neck or behind the ears should generally be the first remedy, after the application of ice or iced water freely to the head. The head and shoulders should be kept raised. A purgative injection should also be administered, and mustard plasters applied to the lower limbs.

Heat exhaustion requires quite different treatment, in

part, at least. Cold water or ice should be applied to the head and body, and then mustard plasters to the spine, stomach and limbs, in turn. Bleeding should be avoided. If syncopal symptoms be decided, ammonia may be for a few minutes applied to the nostrils, and if the patient can swallow, aromatic spirits of ammonia may be given by the mouth, ten drops every fifteen minutes at first, gradually increasing the interval.

Hydrophobia. When individuals are bitten by animals, such as dogs, cats, wolves and foxes, which are mad, or suspected of madness, and the necessary measures are not immediately adopted, the patient usually becomes affected with that peculiar and terrible disease, known as hydrophobia. The disease, as a rule, occurs oftenest within three months after being bitten, rarely after the sixth month. The more numerous the bites, and the greater their gravity, the earlier do the symptoms appear. They manifest themselves earlier in children than in old people. When no preventive measures are adopted, at least half, perhaps two-thirds of persons bitten, escape. The immunity may be due partly to the bites being inflicted through clothes, partly to individual insusceptibility, which has been found to exist in animals as well as in man. However, the statistics prove that the bites on the face give a mortality of 80 per cent. and those in the hands of 67 per cent. These parts being uncovered, the virus is directly deposited in the tissues, and is quickly absorbed. The most cases of hydrophobia occur during the spring and fall months. When a person has been bitten by a mad animal, he should have his wounds immediately attended to. They should be made to bleed as much as possible. Forcible suction will aid in removing the poison, and ligation with any kind of bandage above the part, will retard the absorption of it. Cauterization should never be **neglected.** A red hot iron or caustic potash are the best caustics. Every portion of the wound should be cauterized, and the parts dressed with carbolic acid and iodoform ointment. Lunar caustic is too light a caustic and is ineffectual. The next thing to do is to go to the nearest Pasteur institute and take an anti-hydrophobic treatment. This treatment was discovered by L. Pasteur of Paris, after five years of study and experimentation. It consists in injecting under the skin, once or twice a day for fifteen days, a virus attenuated and prepared according to the rules and teaching of its discoverer. This treatment is only prophylactic, that is, it will prevent the patient from having hydrophobia, and is powerless when the symptoms of the disease have once made their appearance. Hence the necessity of early treatment. These institutes have been established in every part of the world. The principal one, in Paris, has already treated eight thousand cases, and all successfully. In this country, we have two of these institutes, one in New York, directed by Dr. Paul Gibier, and one in Chicago, founded and directed by Dr. A. Lagorio. Both men have had a large experience in the subject in question, and are highly qualified to treat these cases.

Influenza or "**Grippe**." It is reported as having been quite fatal in France in 1311 and 1403. In 1570 it also prevailed, and in 1557 spread over Europe, and extended to America. It occurred again in 1729, 1743, 1775, 1782, 1833, 1837, with notable violence. In the United States, one of the most remarkable epidemics for extent, was that of 1843. Another was that of 1872, following nearly the course of the epizootic among horses of the latter part of that year. The last epidemic (1890) has been a remarkable one for its extent, invading all Europe and the United States. Mild cases require housing and little more. The following prescriptions will be found excellent: Take of antipyrin, eighteen grains, Dover's powder, twelve grains, powdered extract valerian, three grains; mix, and divide into six capsules. Take one every two hours. If there be a tight cough, take the following: Take of muriate of ammonia, thirty grains, deodorized tincture of opium, one drachm, syrup of senega snakeroot, one-half ounce, distilled water, one ounce, syrup of balsam tolu enough to make three fluid ounces; mix, and take a teaspoonful every two hours. Great prostration, especially in old people, may call for support by quinine and stimulants, as hot whisky punches.

Ingrowing Nail. A very common and troublesome affection, which most usually occurs by the side of the great toe, due to constant pressure from the use of tight shoes. The objects for its treatment are to remove the irritation caused by the nail, and reduce the swelling of the soft parts. In most cases, if the nail, having been well softened by soaking in warm water, is shaved as thin as possible with a bit of glass, the pain and irritation may easily be allayed by rest for a day or two, with fomentations and poultices. A good way to remove the nail is to wedge some cotton under the free margin of the nail, placing over it a piece of adhesive plaster with a hole cut in it the size and shape of the nail to be removed, then moisten the end of a pencil of lunar caustic and apply it to the part to be removed, taking care not to touch any other portion. The next day the nail will have assumed a black or brown appearance. Upon raising the nail, it will be found to have become separated from the subjacent tissue, and all there is required to complete the cure is to clip off the dead portion.

Lumbricoid or Round Worms. These worms are from five to fifteen inches in length, tapering to a point at each end—very common in children. We infer that a child suffers from worms when we hear that it picks its nose, grinds its teeth at night, has a voracious and capricious appetite, looks pinched and thin at the bridge of the nose, and dark around the mouth, has a tumid belly, dark rings round the eyes, is often sick, and complaining of itching at the anus. Santonine is the most effectual remedy for these worms. It requires care in its use, however, producing serious vomiting, prostration, and nervous symptoms in overdoses. A child should take not more than half a grain once or twice daily; an adult about three grains. It is best given at night, and followed in the morning by a dose of castor oil. The process may be repeated for a night or two until the canal seems cleaned.

Mastitis, or commonly known as inflammation of the breast, may result from blows or other external injuries, but it most often occurs during lactation. The following is said to be a successful method of treating it: Take of carbonate of ammonia, 2 drachms; boiling water, 8 ounces; saturate in this solution a flannel bandage three inches wide and two feet long, and apply to breast, covering with oil silk. Use hot as can be borne, and renew every two or three hours. Relief will be derived from first application, and will prevent the formation of matter.

Nasal Catarrh. The chief characteristics are langour, lassitude, debility; headache with a sense of tightness across the forehead; excessive purulent discharge from the nostrils, or tickling down the throat, which creates hawking, or it may dry up and become impacted in the nostrils. Deafness may be caused and hoarseness. If it invades the bronchial tubes, there is increased hawking, cough, emaciation, and discoloration of the skin, due to imperfect oxygenation of the blood. It is a loathsome disease, and liable to give rise to many other affections, as epilepsy, consumption, etc. Predisposition to nasal obstruction appears to have, in some persons, an anatomical origin; in a symmetrical growth of the bony structure of the nasal cavities. Usually, however, chronic nasal catarrh is the result of repeated or prolonged exposure to changes of temperature, and especially cold and damp, such as abound in our American climate. In treating this affection, full information must be had about the constitutional history of the patient. If there is a syphilitic cause, iodide of potassium in five or ten grain doses three times a day, or iodide of iron pills must be taken. Scrofulous subjects will be benefited by taking the iodide of iron and cod liver oil. Local treatment, however, is not to be neglected. The parts should be cleansed and disinfected. The nasal cavities should be douched. For this purpose, many sorts of instruments have been invented, which generally can be gotten in any drugstore. For simple cleansing, a solution of common salt in warm water (a teaspoonful in a pint) will be very suitable. Other lotions are employed, containing some of the following substances: Alum, borax, boracic acid, chloride of ammonium, chlorate of potassium, tar water, corrosive sublimate, chlorinated soda, iodoform, carbolic acid, glycerine, etc. Another mode of application to the nostrils is with the atomizer. Many prefer the insufflation of powders, as tannin, bismuth. Excellent snuffs are pulverized horse chestnut, boracic acid, chlorate of potash. In obstinate cases, resort may be had to a surgeon for the removal of some of the obstructive masses. Some of the following prescriptions may be tried: Carbolic acid, one grain. borax and bicarbonate of soda each two grains; glycerine, a fluid drachm; water enough to make a fluid ounce. Mix, to be sprayed into the nostrils. Or, take of powdered gum arabic, myrrh and bloodroot, equal parts, and use as snuff. Or, take of powdered golden seal, 40 grains; camphor, 15 grains; carbolic acid, 15 grains; common salt, 1 ounce. Mix; snuff. Or, thymol, 5 grains; alcohol and glycerine, each half an ounce. Mix, and apply locally with cotton. Or, porphyrized iodoform, 1 drachm; camphor, 1 drachm, and gum arabic 2 drachms. Mix, and use locally. Inhalations of menthol will also afford relief. Take of pure iodine,

5 grains: iodide of potassium, 2 scruples; glycerine, 1½ ounces. Mix, apply locally with brush twice a day. Solutions of permanganate of potash are very efficient when the nasal secretions are fœtid. (See also *Catarrh.*)

Nervous Prostration. Take of dilute phosphoric acid, 1 ounce; elixir calisaya, 4 ounces; elixir valerianate of ammonia, 2 ounces; glycerine, 3 ounces; sherry wine, 6 ounces. Mix, and take half or one tablespoonful three or four times a day. When accompanied with dyspepsia, use the following: Saccharated pepsin, 3 drachms; bromide of sodium, 1 ounce; fluid extract of coca, 2 ounces; glycerine, 2 ounces. Take a teaspoonful three or four times a day. In overworked, anæmic and broken down persons: Take of phosphate of lime, of iron, each one scruple. Divide into twenty powders. Take one three times a day.

Nausea and Vomiting of Pregnancy. Take of spirits of chloroform, 6 drachms; deodorized tincture of opium, ½ drachm; fluid extract of ginger, one drachm; spirits of camphor, ½ drachm; tincture of cardamom comp., 1 ounce. Mix; take a teaspoonful as required.

Night Terrors. A child who has gone to bed apparently well, and who has slept soundly for a short time, awakes suddenly in great terror, and with a loud and piercing cry. It is a fruitful source of anxiety and distress to parents. Fortunately, this condition, alarming and distressing as it is, does not prove any disease of the brain. Most frequently those children are of a very nervous temperament, and suffer more or less with difficult dentition, indigestion, constipation, or irritation of the bowels. The treatment of these cases comprises in the first place, kindness and forbearance toward the little sufferer. These terrors will be but increased by harshness, while soothing and gentleness will do much to dispel them. During the attack, the child should be at once gently lifted up from the bed, and either carried for a few minutes, or laid down in a different position. Washing the face softly with a rag dipped in cool or cold water may arouse thoroughly. If any medicine be suitable, it will be a teaspoonful or two of camphor water. Care is needed to prevent the attacks. Violent exercise and mental excitement are almost apt to bring them on, also indigestion or constipation. The bowels should, however, be kept open by rhubarb or senna, etc. The compound syrup of the phosphate of iron given in teaspoonful doses three times a day will do great good. To promote tranquil sleep, some one should remain with the child, if timid, for awhile after he goes to bed; or a light should be kept burning low. A child liable to night terrors ought to be allowed to finish its morning sleep undisturbed. Abundance of sleep is a sedative to an over excited brain. Neglect of such precautions may convert a mere transitory functional disturbance into a serious attack of brain disease.

Piles. The plethoric constitution is the most liable to them, especially with sedentary habits. Long standing or sitting upon hard seats, over-stimulating diet, misuse of purgatives, and the constipation of the bowels, always predispose to piles. The bowels must be regulated, neither over purged nor allowed to be costive; a soluble state is the most desirable. Magnesia is irritant to piles, and so are the saline cathartics. Rhubarb, sulphur and senna are the laxatives most approved for hemorrhoidal cases. A teaspoonful of compound licorice powder at bedtime will gently open the bowels. On retiring to bed at night, inject the following into the rectum: Take of fluid extract of hamamelis, three drachms, fluid extract of golden seal, two drachms, sweet oil, two ounces; mix. The following will also be found useful: Powder of galls, two drachms, opium, ten grains, lard, one ounce; mix, and apply. Or, take of extract of belladonna, one drachm, spermaceti ointment, one ounce; mix, use as ointment for *painful piles*. Or, take of extract of belladonna, one drachm, iodoform, one-half drachm, sugar of lead, one scruple, vaseline, one ounce; mix, and apply to piles three or four times a day. The piles should be bathed in cold water just before each application, and the bowels kept freely open with a gentle purgative, in painful hemorrhoids. For bleeding piles, use the following: Take of tannic acid, twenty grains, water, six ounces; dissolve, and inject (cooled with ice) into the rectum. After each morning stool, the rectum should be injected with warm water, or if great debility exists, with beef tea, and permitted to remain half an hour longer. As a palliation and often curative remedy for local and internal piles, hamamelis is very superior to all other remedies.

Rheumatism. There are two forms; first, the acute articular rheumatism, or rheumatic fever; second, chronic rheumatism. The acute rheumatism is characterized by high fever with severe inflammation of several of the larger and smaller joints, which mostly, one after another, become swollen, red, hot, tender and painful. The shoulders, wrists, knees and ankles are most frequently so affected. Absolute rest in bed is necessary, and the joints gently rubbed with a liniment containing one ounce of laudanum and three ounces of camphorated oil, then covered with cotton batting. For internal use, five grain doses of salicine every three hours is a most valuable remedy. Salicylic acid is also a very effective remedy in ten grain doses every two hours until five or six doses are taken, and afterward the same amount three or four times a day. Salicylate of sodium is probably better suited in every case for its being less disagreeable and more soluble. Its doses must be about two-thirds larger than the salicylic acid. A ten grain Dover powder at night will help to give great relief. Either of the following prescriptions will be found very useful in all acute cases: Take of salicylic acid, three drachms, bicarbonate of potassium, six drachms, water, two fluid ounces; mix; dose, a teaspoonful every three hours. Or, take of salicylic acid, three drachms, glycerine and water each two fluid ounces; mix; dose, a teaspoonful every four hours. Or, take of salicylic acid and acetate of potash each 160 grains, glycerine, ten drachms, sweet spirits of nitre, ten drachms, water enough to make four ounces; mix; dose, a teaspoonful every two hours. We also recommend:

The Late Dr. Agnew's Prescription. Take a teaspoonful of common baking soda and dissolve in a tumblerful of cold water; divide into three equal doses and take a dose between meals and on retiring. Do not take immediately before or after meals, as soda interferes with digestion. In connection with this, bathe once a day in warm water in which *sal soda* has been dissolved. Begin by using a teacupful of sal soda to a tubful of water and increase the quantity of sal soda as the skin will bear it. Should the skin smart on being rubbed dry anoint the body with a little cocoanut oil. This process has been known to cure some of the most obstinate cases of rheumatism.

Sciatica Liniment. Take of camphor, chloral and oil of cajuput, equal parts. Rub externally, and cover with cotton batting.

Take of aconite liniment, belladonna liniment, each two drachms, glycerine, two ounces; mix, spread on lint and place on thigh. Cover with oil, silk, and bandage the limb.

Seat Worms. Sulphate of iron, one grain to four ounces of water injected up the bowels, removes the worms, and an occasional injection of the same will prevent their return.

Sprains. A sprain consists in the sudden and forcible stretching of the tendons or ligaments connected with a joint. The accident is followed by severe pain and rapid swelling. It is always troublesome and tedious, and may lead to serious results. The treatment should aim at preventing inflammation, promoting absorption, and restoring healthy action. The part should be kept at rest in an elevated position, and cold continuously applied. Sometimes a poultice or a fomentation will be found to give most relief, especially if there be much inflammation; leeches may also be required. As soon as the acute symptoms have subsided, absorption should be promoted by systematic rubbing with or without stimulating liniments, or by pressure of a well adjusted bandage. Gradually passive motion may be begun in order to restore the part to its proper functions, and the joint may be moderately used. If any stiffness remain, warm salt water douches or a visit to a thermal spring is often attended with benefit.

Sore Nipples. Apply a mixture of tannin and glycerine, two drachms to the ounce daily during the last month of pregnancy. This renders the nipple tough but elastic.

Stomach-ache. Is common in dyspeptics. Carminatives are appropriate for it. One of the best of these is oil of cajuput, five drops at a dose on a lump of sugar; or take of spirits of chloroform, compound tincture of cardamoms, of each one ounce; mix, and take a teaspoonful three or four times a day.

Sweating of the Feet. Take of hydrate of chloral, twenty grains, alcohol, three ounces; mix, bathe the feet thoroughly in castile soapsuds. Apply the solution with the sponge, and put on socks while feet are wet.

Tape Worm. It is formed of flat segments, often several hundred in number, connected with the head by a slender neck. Each segment has male and female organs; as those at the tail mature, they are cast off. Some persons thus pass six or eight fragments from the bowels in a day.

The whole length of the parasite is from ten to thirty feet. The symptoms caused by tapeworm are uneasy sensations in the abdomen, and general nervous irritation, lowness of spirits, indigestion, irregularity of appetite, and of the action of the bowels; itching of the nose and sometimes of the anus. The remedies against tapeworm are many, as: Oil of turpentine in half ounce or ounce doses will generally purge and bring away the worm. The ethereal extract of male fern in the dose of a drachm and a half to two drachms, is esteemed highly. Powder Kooso in half ounce doses mixed with water, given on an empty stomach, is almost certain to destroy or remove the parasite. Pumpkin seeds plentifully taken on an empty stomach are also quite effectual. As immature tapeworms find residence in the bodies of animals used for food, and thus get opportunity to enter the human alimentary canal, the avoidance of raw or undercooked meat is the precept of prophylaxis suggested, and confirmed by experience. This applies not only to the prevention of tapeworm, but also to that of other parasites, especially trichina. Tapeworms are derivable from infected beef, even oftener than from pork.

To Abort a Felon. Apply the following with cloth until pain ceases: Take of tincture of iodine, three drachms, tincture of aconite, of arnica, of cantharides, of each two drachms; mix, and apply. Another method is the following: Take a teaspoonful of common salt, roasted in a hot stove until all the chlorine gas is thrown off, or is dry as can be made. Also a teaspoonful of powdered castile soap, add a teaspoonful of Venice turpentine; mix them into a poultice, and apply to the felon. Renew the poultice twice a day.

Tonsillitis. Commonly known as quinsy. The symptoms are soreness of the throat in swallowing, with pain of one or both tonsils, and fever. A dose of citrate of magnesia should be taken at once. Apply externally a poultice of flaxseed meal, to which lard and laudanum have been added, bathe, when the poultice is changed, with liniment of ammonia or soap liniment. Internally the following mixture will be found very useful: Take of chlorate of potash, sixty grains, sweet spirits of nitre, four drachms, tincture of guaiac, twelve drachms; mix. Dose for adults, a teaspoonful every three hours. Shake well before taking, and follow with water. The following gargles will be found excellent: Take of ammoniated tincture of guaiac, two drachms, compound tincture of Peruvian bark, two drachms, clarified honey, six drachms; mix well and add slowly while shaking, water, three ounces, chlorate of potash, one drachm; mix, and use as gargle. Or, take of hydrate of chloral, one drachm, glycerine, half an ounce, water, one and one-half ounces; mix, gargle when there is ulceration of fauces, with great swelling and redness and pain extending from throat to ear. Or, mix one ounce of bromo-chloralum in eleven ounces of water, and gargle. Alum and chlorate potash dissolved in water also make good gargles. In chronic cases, use gargles of tannin. If the tonsils will remain chronically enlarged, and thereby causing considerable inconvenience, have them removed by a surgeon.

In Low Nervous Affections, with languid circulation, debility of stomach, take of muriated tincture of iron, two drachms, tincture Peruvian bark, two ounces, tincture of orange, one and one-half ounces; mix, and take a teaspoonful three times a day.

Toothache. Is sometimes purely neuralgic. More often it results from exposure of the nerve by the decay of a tooth. Again, it may attend inflammation of the jaw, or abscess at the root of the tooth affected. For toothache from exposed nerve, creosote is a certain remedy. Insert carefully into the hollow a plug of cotton, wrapped over the end of a knitting needle, and dipped in pure creosote. If the rattle run out into the mouth (which should be avoided if possible) rinse it at once with cold water. Oil of cloves, oil of cajeput, and laudanum introduced into the hollow of the tooth will also generally give relief.

Waterbrash. Can be relieved by taking a tablespoonful of glycerine to half tumblerful of milk. Bicarbonate of sodium in scruple doses is also effective. Astringents have also been highly recommended. Take of Ammonio-ferric alum two scruples, cinnamon water, four ounces; dissolve, and take a tablespoonful every two or three hours.

DISEASES OF INFANCY AND CHILDHOOD

Chicken Pox. This is a contagious but harmless disease of childhood, unattended by any constitutional disturbance, as a rule, and after running its course for a few days ends incomplete recovery. Often several children of the same family have it, one after the other. It affects both sexes alike, and all classes indiscriminately. After a period of incubation, the length of which is doubtful, a number of little red points suddenly appear on the skin, and in the course of twenty-four hours each has become a small blister, or vesicle, raised above the surface and surrounded by a pink areola or zone. The next day more red spots appear, which also form blisters and so on for about three or four days fresh crops appear, the previous ones attaining a maturer stage. The eruption is most abundant on the back and front of the body. In about a week the vesicles begin to wither and dry up, and in a week or ten days longer the scabs fall off, leaving as a rule no scar.

The Nurse.

Treatment.—As a rule, the child need only be kept in the

nursery and not in bed all day long; occasionally the little patient is restless and feverish, but in most cases it will play about as cheerfully as usual and appear to have nothing the matter with it. For a few days the child may be kept indoors and the diet should be plain and simple.

Convulsions. Some children are much more liable to suffer from convulsions than others, owing to the more impressionable nature of the nervous system.

Causes.—Difficulty in teething is a very frequent cause, the irritation of the gums affecting the brain; and when that irritation is removed, the convulsions disappear. Indigestible articles of food are another very frequent cause; fright may cause convulsions, and anything profoundly affecting the mother, such as anger, terror, grief, may so act upon her milk as to give rise to convulsions in the infant.

Symptoms.—Sometimes the convulsions are *partial*, thus an arm may twitch or certain portions of the face. The writer recollects being called to a child suffering from partial convulsions, whose mother, recognizing, from the inflamed condition of the gums, that the teething was at fault, took out her penknife and scratched the surface, which was really just what was required. Again, the convulsion may be *general*, when the muscles of the face, eyes, eyelids and limbs are in a violent state of rapid contraction alternating with relaxation. Froth may appear at the mouth, and if the tongue has been bitten it will be tinged with blood. The head is generally thrown back, and the thumbs pressed in upon the palms of the hands.

Treatment.—If the teeth are plainly at fault, the gums must be scarified, and three grains of bromide of potassium may be given in a little water. If due to some indigestible article of diet, then the best thing to do is to get rid of it as soon as possible. The writer gave a child that took a very severe fit during or immediately after dinner an emetic of mustard and water, which answered very well. Perhaps a safer emetic would be a teaspoonful of ipecacuanha wine in tepid water; drinks of tepid water being afterward given. This, of course, is only to be given if it is thought that some indigestible article of food has given rise to the convulsions, and if too long a time has not elapsed since it was swallowed. If some hours have elapsed, it will be better to give a teaspoonful of castor oil. The following mixture will be found useful; it may be given to children from one to three years old: Bromide of potassium, two drachms; iodide of potassium, half a drachm; syrup of orange peel, an ounce; water to make four ounces. A teaspoonful every three hours, till all tendency to twitching of the muscles has passed away. Another very useful item of treatment is a warm bath or a pack. A sheet should be wrung out of hot water and wrapped round the child from the neck downward, and over this one or two blankets. The child should remain in this for an hour, after which it may be taken out and dried with warm towels. Or the child may be immersed in a warm bath up to the neck, or put in a tub or hip-bath with as much water as can be got into it, so as to cover as much of the body as possible. It should remain in this for about fifteen minutes, during which cold cloths may be applied to the head.

Croup. Croup is an inflammatory disease of the larynx, or upper part of the windpipe, and occurs in children, being very common between two and five years of age.

Symptoms.—It is attended by very noisy inspiration on account of the narrowed condition of the glottis preventing the free entrance of air into the lungs. The child feels as if it were going to be choked, and it makes violent efforts with the muscles of the chest, so as to increase the supply of air within. Croup is a disease in which no delay should take place in treatment, as imminent danger may ensue from suffocation.

Treatment.—Give the child a warm bath if possible, and wring sponges out of hot water, and apply them constantly to the throat. Give a teaspoonful of ipecacuanha wine every fifteen minutes, with drinks of tepid water in between till the child vomits. After it has been made sick, or if the symptoms appear so mild that an emetic is not given, the following mixture will be found of use: Ipecacuanha wine, one drachm; iodide of potassium, one drachm; syrup of orange peel, one ounce; water to make four ounces; a teaspoonful to be given every three hours to a child from two to five years old. It is not necessary to say that medical aid should be sought at once. After an attack, care should be taken not to expose the child to draughts; flannel should be worn next to the skin, and a comforter wrapped round the throat.

Diarrhœa. The causes of diarrhœa in children being very varied, it is necessary, as far as possible, to determine what it is in each case; thus, for instance, *teething* is a very frequent cause when it is difficult and accompanied by a good deal of irritation. When the tooth is cut, the irritation ceases, and the diarrhœa passes away. Again, *cold* may give rise to diarrhœa, from the impression made upon the nerves of the skin. This is frequently seen in children who toss the bedclothes off during sleep. *Fright* may also give rise to diarrhœa, and of course, the eating of *indigestible articles of food* will do the same. A frequent cause of diarrhœa in infants is an overloaded condition of the stomach, or the giving of unsuitable articles of diet.

Treatment.—Diarrhœa in children ought never to be neglected, as, if allowed to run on from day to day, it weakens the child and may pass into inflammation of the bowels, a much more serious disorder. If the diet appear to be at fault, it must be corrected. Suppose, for instance, that the child, previous to the cutting of the teeth, has been given solid food, the probability is that it will disagree, and set up irritation in the bowels, which will cause diarrhœa. In such a case nothing but milk should be given for food, and a little lime water may be added to it with advantage. If the diarrhœa has continued for any length of time it is necessary to check it at once. For this purpose the compound powder of chalk and opium may be given in two grain doses every three hours to an infant one year old, or a little chalk mixture may be given—half to one teaspoonful every four hours to a child two or three years old. This may be combined with a little opium as follows: Laudanum, four drops; tincture of catechu, two drachms; chalk mixture to make two ounces; a teaspoonful to be given every four hours.

Infant's Colic. Take of best magnesia, one drachm, aromatic spirit of ammonia, forty drops, tincture of assafœtida, a fluid-drachm, essence of peppermint, fifteen drops, syrup of gum arabic, a fluid ounce, water enough to make four fluid ounces. Dose, teaspoonful.

Measles. This is a contagious, febrile disorder. It is nearly always more or less prevalent in this country, but at times it spreads with great rapidity and causes many deaths. As a rule, children and young people are attacked, but the exemption of adults and older people is probably due to the fact that most of them have had the disease in childhood. Sometimes people have a second attack.

Symptoms.—Before the appearance of the rash there are some precursory symptoms; the patient feels languid and hot, there is shivering, followed by a rise of temperature, a quick pulse, thirst, loss of appetite and sickness. The eyes become red and watery, and give the patient the appearance of having cried; the membrane which lines the nose, throat, larynx and trachea is red and swollen, and pours forth a watery secretion; thus the affected person appears to have a severe cold, with running from the eyes and nose; hence there is generally much sneezing, with a slightly sore throat and a dry, harsh cough. Convulsions occasionally occur in children. After these symptoms have lasted three or four days the rash appears. It begins in very small papules or minute pimples which rapidly multiply, and these run together into patches which have a tendency to a horseshoe, or crescent shape, while the portions of skin between are of a natural color. Commencing on the face and neck, it spreads to the arms, then the trunk of the body and gradually reaches the lower extremities. When the eruption has disappeared the part of the skin affected becomes covered with a dry scurf.

Complications are liable to occur. Convulsions at the commencement are usually without danger; if they come on at the end of the disease they may lead to a fatal issue. Inflammation of the lungs is very common in measles, and bronchitis, which may prove fatal to young children, adds to the danger.

Treatment.—The child must be kept in bed. The room should be airy and well ventilated, but the patient must not be exposed to draughts. All offensive excreta and dirty linen should be removed and disinfected. A fire should be kept burning and the temperature should be about 60° or 65° Fahrenheit. The blinds should be kept down on account of the patient's eyes, and he should lie with his back to the light. In all cases it is advisable to give the patient a hot bath at the very onset of the disease; then dry the surface of the body and put the child to bed directly. All sources of annoyance and irritation and all noises should be avoided. Food of the simplest nature should be given. Milk, milk and water, chicken broth, beef tea and toast and water may be given. When the fever subsides a small piece of chicken or fried sole may be given, toast or bread and butter, with a fresh egg may also be given, and, as the tongue cleans and the appetite returns, the patient may be allowed to resume his ordinary diet. Although children generally recover rapidly, yet there are times when much debility ensues and the general health becomes impaired, although the fever has quite left. Such children as are in bad health are liable to lumps or glandular swellings of the neck and under the jaws, or they may remain weak for a long time. In these cases chemical food may be given with advantage; Parrish's Syrup is another name for this. It may be given in doses of five to ten drops three times a day in a little water to children two or three years old. Fellows' syrup of the hypophosphites is a very useful preparation in such cases, and may be given in doses of five drops largely diluted with water, three times a day, immediately after food. The following mixture is useful: Steel drops, one drachm; solution of chloride of calcium, three drachms; glycerine, half an ounce; water to make four ounces. A teaspoonful for a child from three to five years old in water three times a day. A visit to the seaside is very beneficial.

Prickly Heat.—*Treatment.* Take two teaspoonfuls of cream tartar, and pour on it one pint of boiling water, sweeten to taste, drink frequently unless it acts upon the bowels; in that case take less.

Ringworm. This disease is caused by the growth in the skin of a low form of vegetable life allied to ordinary mold. When some of the scales of a hair affected with ringworm are placed in liquid, and magnified about 300 times, we can then very readily see the *spores* or seeds, and the *mycelium* or thread of the fungus.

Ringworm of the scalp shows itself as a dry, scurfy or scaly condition of some portion of the scalp, generally in separate patches more or less circular, on which the hairs are broken off, and the surface presents a dirty appearance, with some redness beneath.

On the face, body or limbs the disease appears in the form of rings of various sizes, generally pretty round, and of a reddish color; they commence as minute points, and increase in size pretty rapidly, healing in the center as the disease progresses centrifugally. As this disease is contagious, children suffering from it should not go to school or play with others till they are cured.

Treatment.—Amongst the popular remedies used in the treatment of this disease are ink and vinegar. The strong acetic acid is a useful preparation. It should be used once and well rubbed in. The liniment of iodine is a most useful preparation. It should be applied by means of a camel's hair brush or feather, and may be repeated in a few days if necessary. Great cleanliness is necessary in this affection, and if the disease is situated on the scalp, the hair must be cut away for some little distance round the diseased patch before applying the remedy.

Scarlet Fever or Scarlatina. This is an acute febrile disease, producing a scarlet rash upon the skin, attended by a sore throat, and often swelling of various glands, and sometimes followed by dropsy. It is more common in childhood than in adult life, and one attack confers great, if not complete, immunity from another. This disease gives rise to a great deal of mortality, and chiefly in those under ten years of age. Contagion is the main, if not only cause of scarlet fever; measles and whooping cough are more contagious; typhoid fever and diphtheria less contagious. The poison may be retain in clothes for a year or more and then give rise to fever. Both sexes are equally liable to an attack; between eighteen months and five years is the most common time to have the fever; no season has much influence upon it, but in this country it is perhaps most common between November and February. Many people confuse the terms scarlet fever and scarlatina, and imagine the latter is a milder affection; this is a geat mistake, for scarlatina is only the Latin name for scarlet fever, and not a different form. Scarlet fever may be very mild, or malignant, or latent. The period of incubation is generally about a week, but may be only twenty-four hours.

The onset is sudden; there is sore throat with tenderness at the angles of the lower jaw, and stiffness at the back of the neck; vomiting is very common, and chiefly so in children; shivering and rigors come on and occasionally convulsions in young children. The temperature rapidly rises and will go up to 104° or 105°; the pulse is very quick, the tongue is covered with a thin, white fur; there is thirst and loss of appetite. This stage lasts from twelve to thirty hours, and then a rash comes out. Sometimes the earlier symptoms are so slight that the rash is the first thing noticed. The rash consists of small scarlet dots, almost running together so as to give a flush all over the skin; the color disappears on pressure, but rapidly re-appears when the pressure is removed. It generally appears at first on the sides of the neck and upper part of the chest and in the bends of the joints; it then spreads downward and is found to come out last on the legs; it begins to fade on the fourth or fifth day and is generally quite gone within a week.

Diarrhœa may be profuse, and exhaust the patient. Bleeding from the nose may occur, but is not often a bad symptom. Perforation of the bowel may occur from an error in diet, and is very fatal. Inflammation of the peritoneum adds greatly to the danger. Bronchitis and pneumonia may supervene and increase the danger.

Treatment.—Place the patient in a well-ventilated room. Remove all curtains, carpets and bed-hangings. Prevent exertion on the part of the patient. The greatest cleanliness must be observed, and all excreta removed at once, Pond's extract, carbolic acid, or chloride of lime being mixed with them. The diarrhœa need not be checked unless the motions are very frequent, and then a little starch injection may be given. The diet must be very light, and no solid food should be taken under six weeks or two months, because, in consequence of the ulceration of the bowels, the coats are very thin and liable to burst. Absolutely nothing should be given to the patient beyond what has been ordered by the medical attendant. Milk must form the main article of diet, and then an egg or two may be beaten up in it, or a custard may be given, and beef-tea. If there is much distension of the bowels, hot flannels sprinkled with turpentine will be useful.

Teething. The period of teething is one which is looked upon by many mothers with dread. Owing to the greater irritability of the system usually found to exist at this time, there are diseases which are more liable to attack the child; and in order that everything may be done on the mother's part to guard against these, it will be well that she should be made familiar with the usual time of appearance of the teeth, and with a few hints that may be of service in maintaining the health of the child during this period.

The first, or temporary, teeth, generally begin to make their appearance between the fifth and eighth month, in the following order: The two central front teeth of the lower jaw, called central incisors; the corresponding teeth in the upper jaw, the lateral incisors; the four anterior molars; the four canines, the two upper of which are popularly called *eye teeth;* and lastly, the four posterior molars.

During the cutting of the temporary teeth, the infant's head should be kept perfectly cool, and for this purpose all caps and wraps of every kind must be removed. The clothing should be light and warm. The apartments occupied by the child should be kept rather cool at this time. If the bowels are confined, the diet should be altered, and a little calcined magnesia may be given.

Thrush. This is a common affection in children. It may be seen in the mouth as small white specks on the lining membrane, but this may be so also in various parts of the

Diseases of Infancy and Childhood

intestinal canal. It is often due to malnutrition and bad feeding, and often when the milk is sour. The swallowing of food becomes difficult, there is thirst, and the water is scanty and high colored.

Treatment.—If the infant is bottle fed, have everything scrupulously clean. Give a little lime water in the milk, in the proportion of one part to four. Paint the mouth frequently with glycerine and borax, using a feather or small camel's hair brush; or dissolve some powdered borax in water and apply in the same way. Should this fail, thirty grains of cholrate of potassium may be mixed with one ounce of glycerine, and applied in the same manner as the glycerine and borax. Great attention must be paid to the diet, and any errors must at once be corrected. If the bowels are disordered and the motions offensive, benefit may be derived by giving the child one of the following powders twice a day: Gray powder, six grains; bicarbonate of soda, eighteen grains; powdered rhubarb, eight grains. Mix and divide into six powders. One twice a day to a child a year old.

Whooping Cough. This is a disease of great frequency in childhood, and a large proportion of infant mortality is due to this cause.

Symptoms.—The earliest is a common cold or catarrh, accompanied by a cough; there is also a slight amount of fever, restlessness, and sometimes running at the eyes and nose. The cough in a few days becomes most troublesome, and some glairy fluid may be brought up from the chest; in a week or ten days, but often later, the child will begin to have the characteristic whoop; the cough comes on in paroxysms and is more frequent by night than by day, each paroxysm begins with a deep and loud inspiration, followed by a succession of short and sharp expirations, again followed by a deep inspiration, and the repeated expirations; this may go on several times, and last one or two minutes, according to the severity of the case. Just before each attack comes on, the child clings to its nurse or mother; it sits in an erect position. During the paroxysm the face is flushed, the veins in the head and face prominent, the eyes suffused and watery, and generally there is some glairy fluid expelled from the mouth, or vomiting may come on. After the paroxysm the child will rest for a time, and appear pretty well until the next attack comes on. These symptoms last for three or four weeks, and then the cough abates in severity and frequency, and finally ceases altogether. In most cases there is some bronchitis attending this complaint, and this is shown by the hurried breathing, rise of temperature, and by hearing rattling noises over the chest. The more mischief there is in the lungs, the greater is the danger to the child. Convulsions are a sign of bad import, and are generally the immediate cause of death in such cases.

Treatment.—In all cases it is best for the child to be kept in the house as soon as the malady has declared itself; in a very mild case it need not be kept in bed, but it should be in a room of warm and even temperature, and protected from draught; it can then be allowed to play about as it likes. If there is any lung affection, it must be put to bed and treated according to the requirements of the case. Other children must not be allowed to come near it, unless they have had an attack previously, in order that its spreading may be prevented. The child must be fed in the usual way, but solid food should be given sparingly. Steel wine is very valuable in cases of whooping cough, and more especially when there is no fever and during convalescence: it may also stop the diarrhœa, which is now and then present. Numberless remedies have been tried for whooping cough, but as many of them are powerful and require careful watching, they ought only to be given under medical direction. Some sweet mucilaginous fluid may be given, such as the mucilage of gum acacia mixed with glycerine in the proportion of a teaspoonful of the latter to a tablespoonful of the former; a teaspoonful of this being given to a child three or four years old three or four times a day. The spine may be advantageously rubbed with a mixture of opodeldoc and belladonna liniment, two drachms of the latter to an ounce and a half of the former; it may be applied night and morning. Warm clothing ought to be worn, and during convalescence a nourishing diet, moderate exercise in the open air when fine, a tepid bath in the morning, and a tonic, as steel wine or cod liver oil, must be enjoined.

LINIMENTS, SYRUPS, TROCHES

The "Best Liniment." For sprains, bruises, pains, colic, etc. Take of chloroform, alcohol, ammonia water, spirits of camphor, tincture of aconite root, of each two ounces, sweet spirits of nitre, six ounces; mix, apply.

Stillingia Liniment. Take of oil of stillingia, one ounce, oil of cajuput, one-half ounce, oil of lobelia, two drachms, alcohol, two ounces; mix. To be used in croup, joint or glandular swellings, and in chronic rheumatism.

Stimulating Balsam. To stimulate ulcers and abscesses: Take of nitrate of mercury, twenty grains, iodoform, thirty grains, camphor, two drachms, balsam Peru, two ounces; mix. Apply or inject.

A Remedy for Burns. A celebrated German remedy for burns consists of fifteen ounces of the best white glue, broken in small pieces, into two pints of water, and allowed to become soft. Then dissolve, by means of a water-bath (an extemporaneous water-bath can be made by putting a tin pail into a kettle of boiling water), and two ounces of glycerine and six drachms of carbolic acid added, the heat being continued until all is thoroughly dissolved. On cooling, this hardens to an elastic mass, covered with a shining, parchment-like skin, and may be kept for any length of time.

When required for use it is placed for a few minutes in a water bath until sufficiently liquid, and applied to the burnt surface by means of a broad brush. It forms in about two minutes a shining, smooth, flexible, and nearly transparent skin, and will cause almost instantaneous relief to the sufferer.

An Excellent Cough Syrup. Take five cents' worth each of sweet spirits of nitre, paregoric, syrup of squills and sweet oil; put all in a pint of molasses, dose, a teaspoonful several times a day.

Cough Troches. One ounce of powdered licorice-root, one ounce of powdered gum-arabic, one ounce of powdered cubebs, mix all together with one pound of pulverized sugar, add enough water to make a stiff paste like bread dough; roll out thin and cut in shape with an open top thimble; arrange upon sheets of foolscap, and set away to dry. These troches will be found excellent.

The Invalid's Meal.

HOMŒOPATHIC MEDICINES AND THEIR USE IN THE FAMILY

Homœopathy Defined. In a work in which it is sought to give information on every branch of household management, and in which even the treatment of diseases and their prevention and cure, must of necessity be briefly discussed, it is manifest that the important mode and means of medical treatment known as Homœopathy ought not to be ignored. In order to arrive at a correct idea of what homœopathy is, it is necessary first of all to ascertain the meaning of the word itself, and to understand why it is used to designate that form of medical practice to which it was applied by the founder of this system of medicine, Dr. Samuel Hahnemann, who first announced his discovery to the medical world in 1796. Theory, generally speaking, forms the basis of practice in every art and science, and in no science is this more perceptible than in the science of medicine. Thus in medical practice it has arisen that there are two great and opposing schools of medicine, each of which is based on a widely different theory; that of the ordinary medical practitioner being *Contraria contrariis curantur*, a sentence in Latin which means, when rendered as simply and concisely as possible, "Opposites are cured by opposites;" and that of the homœopathic practitioner, *Similia similibus curantur*, another sentence in Latin, which means "Likes are cured by likes." Going a little deeper into the matter, the first of these sentences implies that in the treatment of any disease, be it what it may, drugs should be used which will produce in the body of the patient a condition *opposite* to that, induced by the disease to be cured, or in other words that it is needful to counteract the disease and arrest its progress by the administration of medicines that will produce effects different from those resulting from the disease itself. The second, on the contrary, implies that in the treatment of any disease, be it what it may, drugs should be used which would produce in a healthy person symptoms resembling, or *like* to, those occasioned by the disease by which the patient is affected. Hence Hahnemann was led to apply to the generally accepted mode of medical treatment the term ALLOPATHY from two Greek words, *allos*, another, and *pathos*, suffering; and to his own method the term HOMŒOPATHY, also from two Greek words, *homoios*, similar, or like, and *pathos*, suffering. Thus Allopathy, to be perfectly clear and plain even at the risk of repetition, implies that mode of medical practice which consists in using drugs to produce in the body a condition opposite to the disease to be cured, and which has been treated first in this department of TREASURES OLD AND NEW; and Homœopathy a mode of treating diseases by the administration of medicines capable of ecxiting in healthy persons symptoms closely similar to those of the disease for which they are given.

The Principle of Homœopathy. It is possible that some persons may entertain an idea that the medicines given by the homœopathist would produce in a healthy person precisely the same diseases as those which are given to counteract in any one suffering from disease. This is altogether erroneous for the symptoms produced by any particular drug or medicine in a healthy person are only *similar* or *like* those resulting from the disease itself, and not in any way the same as the symptoms excited by the disease or *identical* with them. It must be noted that the great principle of homœopathy is that *Likes cure likes*, not that *Identicals cure identicals*, and this must never be lost sight of. "Homœopathy," to quote the words of Dr. Richard Epps, "is the practical application of the law, *Likes are cured by likes*, to the cure of disease. This law, as an axiom, would read, *It is impossible for two similar diseases to exist in the same individual and at the same time.*" The morbific matter, state or condition, call it which you will, which has caused the disease, or generated the sickly state into which the patient has lapsed, is counteracted and neutralized by the action of the drug which, in a healthy person, would produce symptoms similar to, but not identical with, those which are excited by the disease.

The Principle Supported. The principle of homœopathy having been enunciated, it is now desirable to see if any results of general experience can be cited in its support. In the case, for example, of a severe burn is it the custom to apply cooling lotions or any substance that happens to be a good conductor of heat to the part affected? Certainly not, must be the reply; for although cooling applications of any kind may be soothing for a time and a source of comfort to the sufferer, it is well known that they tend to increase inflammation in the long run, and to render the pain of the burn more acutely felt. Then the theory that "Opposites are cured by opposites" does not hold good in this case. No; but the contrary theory that "Likes are cured by likes" does most assuredly, for such burns are most quickly cured by the application of oil of turpentine or heated spirits of wine, both of which, when applied to the skin, cause a burning or tingling sensation, and by wrapping the part affected with wadding or cotton wool which is a good non-conductor of heat, and maintains warmth in the part burnt, preventing the atmospheric air from obtaining free access to it. Again, in cases of frost-bite the best thing to be done is to rub the part that is frost-bitten with snow, which is frozen water, and not to hold it to the fire or bathe it with warm water, which would spoil any chance that might otherwise exist of restoring the injured part to its former condition. Now what are these but direct evidences in favor of the homœopathic theory, "Likes are cured by likes," and in opposition to the allopathic theory that "Opposites are cured by opposites."

The Practice of Homœopathy. At the introduction of homœopathy it was the general practice of medical men who favored and adopted the new theory to give medicines in the doses usually employed, but it was found that these acted too powerfully, and thus did injury, because patients who exhibited the morbid symptoms of the disease to counteract which the drugs were given, were all the more disposed to yield to the medicinal effects of the drugs themselves, which, as experience soon showed, were not required in such strong doses. Hence the quantities given were gradually reduced until a minimum was attained, which was possessed of power sufficient to counteract the morbid symptoms and effect a cure, without causing inconvenience, and often suffering, by excess of medicinal action. Thus it is that small doses have become the rule in homœopathic practice, not because large doses would fail to effect a cure, but because when it was discovered that small doses would do the work as well and even better, it was doing harm to the patient and really wasting power to persevere in a course which was found to be altogether unnecessary.

The Practice Supported. Following the course that has been adopted in the consideration of the principle of homœopathy, let us now see what reasons can be adduced in favor of small does *versus* large doses in addition to those which have just been given. It is a well known fact that children have sometimes got hold of a bottle of homœopathic globules or pilules and have swallowed the bottleful without inconvenience or any palpable effect, and because no harm has resulted from this wholesale consumption of medicine that is represented to be possessed of great power to cure certain ailments it has been argued that because it has done no harm in the cases to which reference has been made, it is equally impossible for it to do any good. But homœopathic medicine, be it remembered, will only act homœopathically, that is to say it will only produce the desired effect in persons who are suffering from any disorder, which may be counteracted by its use. The children in question were in no way predisposed by morbid symptoms to yield to the influence of the medicine, which, if taken even in single globules, was of sufficient strength to benefit any one who really needed it, but was not sufficiently strong, even collectively, to produce any effect on a healthy person, larger doses being required to produce medicinal effects than are required to counteract and cure morbid symptoms.

Preparation of Homœopathic Medicines. These are supplied in two forms, namely in globules or pilules and in tinctures, the latter form being considered preferable. Soluble drugs are prepared homœopathically by what is termed succussion or shaking, that is to say a mode of treatment which effects the dispersion of a drug through liquid, generally alcohol, until the drug is equally diffused through the whole of the liquid; and insoluble drugs by trituration, or rubbing up in some vehicle, generally sugar of milk, until the whole of the vehicle used is equally and thoroughly permeated by it. Thus it is that every individual globule or drop in medicine homœopathically prepared is of equal strength with its fellows. The potency of such minute subdivisions is ascribed to the extension of surface brought about by succussion or trituration, as the case may be. It is argued that the active power of any drug is enormously increased by this so called extension of surface, and as a piece of gold leaf one inch square may be hammered out into a thinner leaf ten inches square, its surface being thus increased a hundredfold, so mercury which may be taken in large quantities almost with impunity, because in too great bulk to be active in proportion to its bulk, has its active properties marvelously increased by rubbing it up with some vehicle so as to procure its equal subdivision, or, in other words, extension of surface. It is then from this extension of surface that homœopathic medicines derive their power and active properties. Evidence of this is obtained from the fact that the nutritive properties of the soil are brought into a better condition for their receptive assimilation as plant food by plants, by the action of the frost—God's plow--which breaks up the clods into minute pieces, setting free its various constituents by subdivision of matter. Now what is this but increasing the active properties of the soil by extension of surface?

Advantages of Homœopathy. Broadly stated, allopathists for the most part give copious doses of nauseous drugs which disgust the adult patient and terrify children, and by severity of action often tend to reduce bodily strength. Homœopathists, on the contrary, give medicines which, although they are sufficiently powerful to produce the effect that is desired are in no way calculated to induce weakness or interfere with any susceptibility peculiar to the patient, and have the merit of being perfectly tasteless. Surely these are good points, sufficient to induce every parent who has viewed with pain and sorrow the prolonged reluctance of children to swallow ordinary medicine, and every one who has any respect for his own palate and sense of taste, to give the system a fair trial.

Diet. In homœopathy strict attention to diet is required, and unquestionably this is most helpful in the treatment of all diseases, and in some ailments of a minor kind sufficient to effect a cure, although this is denied by homœopathic practitioners, who assert that attention to diet can never be effectual in effecting a cure, but is useful in allowing the full curative action of the medicine given. It is almost needless to add that close attention to diet is necessary only during treatment, though it is at all times desirable for every one, whether man, woman or child, to be temperate and prudent both in eating and drinking, if they desire to keep in good health.

Medicines used in Homœopathy. For home treatment medicine chests are supplied by all homœopathic chemists, and chemists and druggists in general, with the medicines that are most commonly used. The following list of such medicines is taken from Dr. Epps' "Epitome of the Homœopathic Family Instructor," a most useful manual for home use and home practice:

Aconitum napellus.	Drosera.
Antimonium tartaricum.	Dulcamara.
Arnica montana (*).	Hepar Sulphurus.
Arsenicum album.	Ignatia.
Belladonna.	Ipecacuanha.
Bryonia.	Mercurius.
Camomilla.	Nux Vomica.
China.	Opium.
Cina.	Pulsatilla.
Cocculus.	Rhus Toxicodendron (*).
Coffæa cruda.	Spongia.
Cuprum.	Sulphur.

The medicines marked above with an asterisk, with Calendula, Cantharides, Concentrated Tincture of Camphor and Ledum Palustre, are also used for external application.

HOMŒOPATHIC TREATMENT OF DISEASES

In so brief a notice of the principles and practice of homœopathy it is manifestly impossible to give even a list of the diseases to which human beings are unfortunately subject, and the special remedies that are used for their relief. The utmost that can be done under the circumstances, and the limited amount of space at command, is to enumerate in alphabetical order a few of the most common ailments that man is subject to, and briefly indicate the treatment that they require, and the medicines that are employed to counteract them.

Appetite, Failure of. For loss of appetite, accompanied by constipation of the bowels, pain in the stomach, especially a feeling of fulness at the pit of the stomach after eating, with broken and unrefreshing sleep, *Nux vomica* is needed, which may be taken in alternation with *Sulphur* in doses of one drop of the tinctures in a tablespoonful of water every three hours.

Biliousness. For an ordinary bilious attack, which frequently follows indulgence in what is called good eating and drinking, and is often the outcome of sedentary occupations, the usual remedies are *Mercurius* and *Nux vomica* in alternation, in doses of one drop of the tinctures in a tablespoonful of water every two hours until relief is obtained. *Pulsatilla* is prescribed for persons of fair complexion, especially women, instead of *Nux vomica*. The ordinary symptoms of such an attack are a foul tongue with nausea, and frequently actual vomiting.

Bruises. For simple bruises and contusions, make a lotion of one teaspoonful of *Arnica* tincture to four tablespoonfuls of water and apply to the part affected by lint doubled twice or thrice and soaked in the lotion. Cover with oiled silk, and change the lint or renew the dipping as soon as the lint is dry.

Catarrh, or Cold in the Head. The chief symptoms of this disorder are to be found in watering of the eyes, which feel hot and inflamed; a general feverishness, especially in the head, stoppage of and running from the nose, accompanied with sneezing, all these being sometimes followed by a troublesome cough. The principal remedies, in conjunction with general abstinence and the promotion of perspiration by a warm bath, are *Aconitum napellus* for symptoms as named above; *Belladonna* for sore throat and tickling in the throat, causing cough; *Mercurius* for running from the nose and frequent sneezing, and *Nux vomica* for stoppage in the nose accompanied by constipated bowels. The dose for either remedy is one drop of the tincture in one tablespoonful of water every two, three or four hours, according to the severity of the attack.

Camomilla in the same proportions and at the same intervals of time is a favorite and useful remedy for this complaint in women and children.

Colic, or Pain in the Bowels. This is occasioned by a variety of causes, which induce severe pain in the region of the bowels, accompanied by vomiting and cold perspiration all over the body. The sufferer should have a warm bath and be well covered up with clothes in bed, and have flannels plunged in warm water and wrung out as dry as possible, applied to the bowels. If the abdomen be very tender when touched and the patient be feverish, *Aconitum napellus* is indicated. For colic, accompanied by severe spasmodic pains, *Belladonna* is required; for colic arising from partaking of food too plentifully, accompanied by restlessness and grinding of the teeth in sleep, *Coffæa;* for intensification of pain at night, with nausea and loose greenish evacuations, *Mercurius;* for spasms and pain mainly caused by indigestion, *Mercurius;* for colic in children, *Camomilla.* Doses for adults, one drop of the tincture in one tablespoonful of water every three hours· for children, half the quantity; for infants, one-fourth the quantity.

Constipation. The symptoms of constipation are too well known to require mention here. Where the constipation is habitual and obstinate, an enema of warm water or of warm water gruel is of great assistance. For persons who have a bilious temperament and suffer from rheumatism, or when the constipation is accompanied by a chilly feeling, *Bryonia* is desirable; for constipation that is occasioned by sedentary occupation and accompanied by headache and a tendency to piles, *Nux vomica* is indicated, in alternation with *Sulphur* where constipation is habitual. *Pulsatilla* is better suited for women than *Nux vomica*, and *Opium* is useful when constipation is the result of lead poisoning, with great difficulty of evacuation, or utter inability in this direction. The doses in every case and of every remedy are one drop of the tincture in one tablespoonful of water, administered every four hours till relief is obtained.

Cough. For a hard, dry cough *Aconitum napellus* is required; for a cough with wheezing, difficulty of expectoration and need of keeping the head high in bed, *Antimonium tartaricum*; for a dry, spasmodic cough, with sore throat and thirst, or for a nervous cough, *Belladonna;* for cough with expectoration and pain, especially between the shoulders when coughing, *Bryonia;* for cough accompanied with constipation and fulness at the pit of the stomach, *Nux vomica;* for cough in children the most suitable remedy is *Ipecacuanha.* Dose, one drop of the tincture in one tablespoonful of water, given every two, three or four hours as needful.

Diarrhœa. For this disorder, when accompanied by great pain in the stomach and bowels, watery stools and exhaustion, *Arsenicum* is required; when caused by drinking cold water when heated, *Bryonia;* for griping pains and indications of dysentery, *Mercurius;* when caused by indigestion and indulgence in rich food and pastry, *Pulsatilla.* For diarrhœa in children *Camomilla* is a useful remedy. *Dose.*—One drop of the tincture in one tablespoonful of water to be given after each evacuation as it occurs.

Fever. For feverish attacks of a simple character *Aconitum napellus* is an effectual remedy, given every two, three or four hours, in doses of one drop of the tincture to one tablespoonful of water. For fever of a dangerous character, *Bryonia*, *Rhus toxicodendron* and *Arsenicum* are the remedies, with *Belladonna*, *Mercurius* and *Sulphur* in scarlet fever.

Headache. There are many kinds of headache, excited by various causes and presenting various symptoms, but the most common are headaches proceeding from indigestion, nervous headache and sick headache. For the first of these the remedy is *Nux vomica* or *Pulsatilla;* for the second, *Ignatia*, and for the third and last, *Belladonna* and *Ignatia*, with *Ipecacuanha* when the headache is accompanied by vomiting. *Dose.*—One drop of the tincture in one tablespoonful of water at intervals of six hours.

Indigestion. For this complaint in nervous and hypochondriacal patients, *Arnica montana* is usually prescribed; in bilious and rheumatic patients *Bryonia;* for chronic dyspepsia *Hepar Sulphuris;* and for indigestion produced by over eating or sedentary occupation, *Nux vomica.* *Dose.*— One drop of the tincture in one tablespoonful of water administered every two, three or four hours, according to circumstances.

THE END

RECIPES GATHERED BY THE WAY

...ter...... ...bread is velvety, tender and very nice.

SPANISH BUNS FOR TEA

A QUARTER of a pound of butter, one teacupful of cream, three-quarters of a pound of flour, three heaping teaspoonfuls of baking powder, half a pound of sugar, four eggs, and three teaspoonfuls of almond water. Sift the baking powder with the flour. Beat the eggs light, separately. Cream sugar and butter together; add the beaten egg yolk. Stir in the cream and flour and egg white alternately. Stir in well the three teaspoonfuls of almond water. Bake in a buttered pan and cut in squares.

THE FAVORITE N

Recipes Gathered by the Way

Recipes Gathered by the Way

Recipes Gathered by the Way

Recipes Gathered by the Way

Recipes Gathered by the Way

Recipes Gathered by the Way

Recipes Gathered by the Way

Recipes Gathered by the Way

Recipes Gathered by the Way

Recipes Gathered by the Way

Recipes Gathered by the Way

Recipes Gathered by the Way

Recipes Gathered by the Way

Recipes Gathered by the Way

Recipes Gathered by the Way

Recipes Gathered by the Way

www.ingramcontent.com/pod-product-compliance
Lightning Source LLC
Chambersburg PA
CBHW032010220426
43664CB00006B/204